# MS-DOS

GW00381210

*Up to and including version 6.2*

PRISMA Computer Courses are structured, practical guides to mastering the most popular computer programs. PRISMA books are course books, giving step-by-step instructions, which take the user through basic skills to advanced functions in easy to follow, manageable stages.

Now available:

dBase IV
Excel 4.0 for Windows
Lotus 1-2-3
MS-DOS
Novell Netware
UNIX
Windows
WordPerfect
WordPerfect for Windows

# Contents

# Foreword

The MS-DOS operating system has become the standard operating system for personal computers since the largest computer manufacturer, IBM, adopted this system for its products. Many other computer manufacturers have also adopted this system, which has led to even more rapid distribution.

For most computer users, the choice of a certain operating system depends upon whether good and inexpensive application programs can be run under the system in question. MS-DOS can certainly satisfy this criterion. Thousands of programs are based upon this system.

This book provides a clear introduction to working with personal computers which make use of the MS-DOS operating system. It is designed to be a supplement to the manuals supplied along with the computer.

These manuals do not make pleasant reading in general, due to the fact that they describe not only the important but also the unimportant details. In addition, the choice of language in a manual is often incomprehensible to the beginner. For these reasons, this book restricts itself to the information necessary to work with the computer in practice. This book deals with all DOS versions up to, and including, the most recent version, DOS 6.2.

- Chapters 1 to 8 make up the practical section of the book. This provides a description of the commands, along with appropriate examples. The screen is placed right in front of you, as it were.
- If you wish to increase your knowledge about the workings and construction of a PC, or wish to gain more information about topics outlined in the practical section, consult chapter 9.
- In the course of 1993, Microsoft issued version 6.0 and its update, 6.2. These provide considerable improvements to memory management, data protection

and the configuration. Chapters 6 and 13 discuss these facilities in particular.

- ■ The appendix contains a concise list of the most important DOS commands.
- ■ When dealing with elements which are only available from a certain version onwards, this is explicitly stated.
- ■ Sections which are accentuated by a vertical bar contain information to which you should pay special attention in order to prevent making serious errors.

# 1    First principles

The letters MS, in the name MS-DOS, are an abbreviation of the name of the manufacturer, MicroSoft. The letters DOS represent 'disk operating system'.

**The most important components and accessories** of the personal computer are:

- the system unit with one or two diskdrives and a harddisk
- the keyboard
- the monitor (the screen)
- the printer.

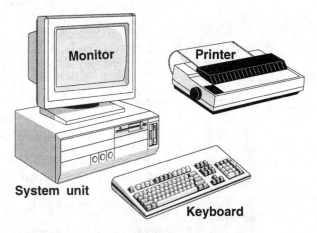

**Check before switching on the computer.**
Most components receive power via their own electricity cables. Sometimes the system unit has a plug for the monitor. Peripheral devices must be connected to the system unit by cables for the transmission of data.

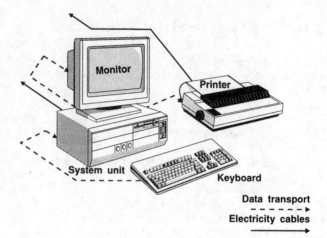

Data transport
Electricity cables

Check that all cables are correctly installed before switching on the computer. The interface cables (for data transport) often have small screws or clamps to prevent them becoming loose; ensure that these are finger-tight. The wiring is not identical for all types and sorts. Consult the manual if in doubt.

Most personal computer configurations contain the following cables and connections:

The system unit, the monitor (screen) and the printer have their own (detachable) *electricity cable*. (An earthed plug is preferable.)

The monitor, the printer and the keyboard are connected to the system unit by *interface cables* with many (internal) wires.

Most *printers* are connected to the parallel interface of the system unit. The following text often occurs next to the connector:

PRINTER
PARALLEL PORT

CENTRONICS (name of the standard parallel interface)
PRINTER PORT

The connection for the *monitor* depends on the way the display component of the system unit has been equipped. There are display adapters for monochrome monitors (green, amber, white) and for colour screens. Occasionally, the system unit has more than one connection. The most common names are:

MONITOR
MONOCHROME MONITOR
COLOUR MONITOR
VIDEO, TV
RGB (red, green, blue)

The *keyboard* connection seldom causes misunderstanding:

KEYBOARD, KEYB

Finally, check if there are still pieces of cardboard in the diskdrive slots. These pieces of cardboard are identical in size to the diskettes (floppies). They protect the moving parts of the drives against damage during transport.

## Switching on the computer and starting up the operating system

Nowadays most computers have at least one diskdrive (diskette station) and a harddisk. There are, however, computers with two diskdrives or even only one diskdrive without a harddisk. The start-up procedure depends on whether or not the computer has a harddisk.

### Starting up the computer from a harddisk

1    Ensure that the diskdrives are not locked.

**2**   Switch on the system unit power supply. In some
       cases the monitor may have its own power supply.

**3**   You only need to switch on the printer when you
       need it. We shall state this explicitly in the exer-
       cises.

**4**   If your computer has a harddisk upon which the
       operating system is already installed, the system
       will be started up automatically when you switch on
       the computer. Otherwise you will have to activate
       the computer using the system diskette (see point 9
       below). You may have to install the operating sys-
       tem first (see section 9.6).

**5**   If the computer displays an error message during
       the self-test, check if the connections have been
       properly made. Switch off the power supply, loosen
       the cable and reconnect it according to the instruc-
       tions in the manual. Start up the computer once
       more. If the same fault recurs, the hardware may
       be to blame. Consult the manual to find out what
       the error message means (the faults are often as-
       signed a number which you can look up) or ask
       your local dealer or another expert.

       You can rectify some disorders yourself:

       ■ Releasing hanging (stuck) keys.

       ■ Replacing blown fuses. Do not repeat this if the
         fuse blows again immediately. In this case, ex-
         pert assistance is necessary.

       ■ Defective cables and plugs - you can easily find
         these out if you have extra cables.

**6**   After testing itself, the computer will load the most
       important operating programs from the system
       disk. This is called *bootload* or *boot.*

If the system is being loaded from a diskette and the system disk is not yet in drive A:, or if the locks are still open, the computer will give an error message, for instance:

```
Non-System disk or disk error
Replace and strike any key when ready
```

In that case open the diskdrive and press any key. The starting-up process will be repeated automatically.

7   The rest of the procedure depends upon the commands in the start-up file AUTOEXEC.BAT and the configuration file CONFIG.SYS. We shall deal with the compilation of these files in chapter 6.

Generally, the manufacturer will have created these files so that you will not have to alter anything as yet. Some computers request you to enter the date and time. Type this as shown below, pressing Enter each time to confirm these.

```
Current date is Tue 01/01/1980
Enter new date (dd-mm-yy): 30-11-1993
Current time is 0:00:54.43
Enter new time: 11:37
```

*Possible mistakes:*   Incorrect registration of the date or time.
*Remedy:*   Repeat registration according to the example.

It is not absolutely necessary to specify the date and/or time. Pressing Enter can also suffice. The computer clock then assumes the system time. (Actually, the clock begins ticking a couple of seconds before the registration is shown on the screen.)

We advise you to enter the date and time, since the computer adds this information to the files which you save on disk. Otherwise it will appear that all files which you make originated on the 1st of January 1980.

It depends on the language of the MS-DOS version which method of date registration the computer expects. Use the English (dd-mm-yy) or the American (mm-dd-yy) methods where required, or adjust, if the MS-DOS version allows this, the language data using a command in the CONFIG.SYS file (see section 6.2).

In the example dealing with the time, we have only entered the hours and minutes. There are very few situations in which the clock has to be synchronized to the exact second, not to mention hundredth of a second. You may try it out if you wish. Type a nice round number and press Enter to coincide with the time signal from the radio or telephone. When dealing with time, you may use a period or a colon as a separation character.

Nowadays most computers have a clock powered by a small battery. In such cases, you do not need to specify the time, except when certain settings in the automatic start-up file request this (see chapter 6).

**8**   The computer continues with the start-up file and will finally make a statement concerning the DOS type and version. After this process, the computer is at the level of the operating system. This is indicated by the C> prompt (from version 6.0 onwards this is C:\>). The prompt indicates that the computer is ready to carry out the command which you type at the position of the flashing stripe, the cursor. The dialogue between you and the computer is displayed below.

```
Current date is Tue 01/01/1980
Enter new date (dd-mm-yy): 30-11-93
Current time is 0:00:54.43
Enter new time: 11:37

MS-DOS Version 6.20

C:\>_
```

*Note:* Depending on the settings in the AUTOEXEC.BAT start-up file, the data shown on the screen may differ slightly from those mentioned or displayed here. The prompt in particular may assume various forms. More information about this topic is given in sections 7.2 and 8.2.

**Loading the operating system from a system disk**
PCs which have only diskdrives, or which do not as yet have the operating system loaded on the harddisk, must be started up from a system diskette.

Only use the original disk the very first time you switch on the computer. Otherwise, use a copy of the disk to prevent the original disk being damaged by an accidental manoeuvre. (We shall discuss how to make a copy of the system disk in sections 4.1 and 4.3.)

**9**  Switch on the computer (see points 1 and 2 above) and insert the diskette in the default (standard) diskdrive, mostly drive A:. Lock the drive if necessary using the lever.

If the operating system is not yet installed on a harddisk or diskette, you will have to do this first (see section 9.6).

With many computers, it is possible to lock the diskdrive before switching on the computer. It is advisable not to do this: the electricity can cause temporary strong magnetic fields in the mains adapter which may damage the data on the diskette.

Generally, the manufacturer has made diskdrive A: the default station. This means that normally all procedures will take place via diskdrive A: unless you explicitly specify a different diskdrive. When the computer has been started up, you can activate one of the other drives. If the computer has a harddisk, this automatically becomes the active diskdrive during the start-up procedure, under the name C:.

*Possible fault:*
If you have not placed the system diskette in disk-drive A: prior to the computer performing the self-test, the error message mentioned in point 6 will be displayed. This message will also appear if the diskette is not a system diskette, if the diskette is not in order or if the diskette has not been inserted properly in the drive or in the wrong drive.

*Remedy:*
In that case, place the system diskette in drive A:, lock the station and press a key in order to continue the start-up procedure as described under points 7 and 8. The A:\> prompt will appear instead of C:\>.

*Note:* PCs which are installed in a network can load the operating system from the server harddisk if they possess a so-called *Boot PROM*. In that case, these computers do not require diskette stations or a harddisk. However, these are necessary to exchange data and programs outside the network.

**Starting the operating system without switching the equipment off and on again.** The procedures which we have mentioned above are referred to as the *cold start* or *cold boot*. The computer begins at zero and the electricity supply has to reach the proper levels.

In daily use, all kinds of situations can occur which require you to restart the computer while you are busy with something. Mostly it is a fault in the program which causes the computer to go haywire and to jam (freeze, hang, crash). It is not necessary to use the electricity switches to start up the system again.

If the system programs are located on the diskette in the default diskdrive or on the harddisk, you can start up the system again by means of a special key combination. This is called the *warm start* or *warm boot*.

## Scheme of personal computer starting-up procedure

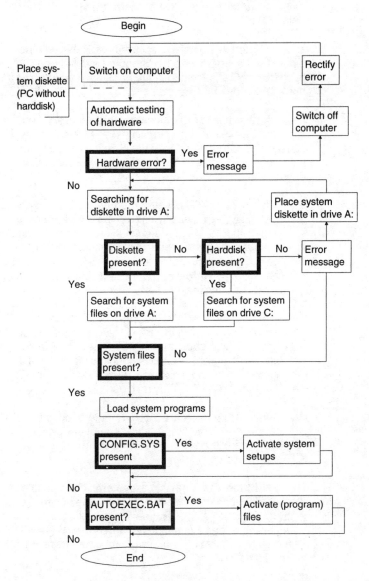

**To implement this warm boot, press the Ctrl and Alt keys simultaneously, hold them down and then press Del.**

The keyboard layout differs according to sort and type. On an MF keyboard with 101 or more keys, Alt and Ctrl occur twice. Del is located in the numeric keypad at the right-hand side of the keyboard.

If the system files are not located on the current disk, the computer will give the error message which we discussed above (point 6). Open the drive lock if your computer has a harddisk, or insert a system disk in the drive.

In the case of complicated program errors it is occasionally necessary to implement a cold boot. If your computer has a harddisk, you must wait until the harddisk has stopped completely before switching on again. If not, the start procedure will make a detour along an error treatment routine which will consume unnecessary time.

With both the cold and the warm boot, the information which was in memory at that moment will be lost. MS-DOS has no RESET instruction which brings a program back to the original state. For this reason, you should always save a new program on disk before you begin trying it out.

Many of the more recent computers do indeed have a reset button, but this does not perform anything more than implement the warm boot in an easy manner.

**Discontinuing the operating system.** Occasionally, the specified command does not lead to the desired result. In this case, there is no sense in waiting until the command has been completely carried out. With MS-DOS you are able to discontinue a procedure by using a key combination.

**Discontinue a procedure by simultaneously pressing Ctrl and C or Ctrl and Break.**

At the discontinue command, the system returns to DOS. You can then enter a new command behind the prompt.

> The Ctrl-C and Ctrl-Break key combinations normally only work during procedures dealing with the processing of input or output under DOS. If a program is jammed in a loop which does not involve these procedures, you will only be able to begin again with a warm boot, or even a cold boot in some rather persistent cases.

> In section 6.3, we shall discuss the possibility of extending the scope of the Break command, over and above the procedures concerning normal input and ouput.

**Discontinuing a computer session and stopping the operating system.** There is no instruction and no key combination to turn off the operating system.
If you wish to cease working with the computer, proceed as follows:

- ■ Open all the diskdrives.
- ■ Switch off the electricity supply to all devices.

> It is much more convenient if all equipment is connected to a junction box. In that case, you only need to remove the plug from the socket and no device will be left on unintentionally.

> The manufacturers recommend that some devices be switched on and off separately. Conform to the instructions in these cases.

# 2    MS-DOS basic skills

**Entering commands.** The MS-DOS operating system
is managed using keyboard instructions. The key combinations for a warm boot and for discontinuing a process have been discussed in the previous chapter. In
this chapter, we shall become familiar with more keys
which implement commands in MS-DOS.

Most DOS functions are activated by means of a command which you type on the keyboard. It makes no difference whether you type these commands using small
letters, capitals or a mixture of both. Internally, MS-DOS
works with capitals. The letters which you type appear
first on the screen. The text is only passed on to the
computer when you complete the input by pressing
Enter. Subsequently, the command, if valid, will be implemented.

**A command, step by step:**

■ Type the command using small letters, capitals or a
   mixture of these.
■ Conclude the command by pressing Enter.
■ The command will appear on the screen at the position of the cursor (insertion point).

Before an instruction or a file name is passed on to the
computer you can make alterations to it - this is called
*editing*. In this, the following keys may be used:

■ To delete a word or a whole line *one character at a
   time* from right to left: Backspace or cursor left.
■ To delete the entire input: press Esc.

The Esc key adds a backslash (\) to the command typed
up until now and the cursor jumps to the next line. Subsequently, type the required command and confirm it
using Enter. If you wish, you can first press Enter so that
the prompt A:\> or C:\> appears on the screen. This

method of using Esc works a great deal quicker than repeatedly pressing Backspace to delete the characters
one by one (you can hold the key down for automatic
repetition of the function).

*Example:* Changing input

```
A:\>DISKCOPY B: A:                              (1)
  ++++++++++++++
A:\>DISKCOPY B: A:\                             (2)
A:\>                                            (3)
```

(1) The entire text is deleted one character at a time
using the Backspace key.
(2) The Esc key invalidates the entire text (backslash).
(3) Confirm the backslash by pressing Enter. The text
is deleted from the input buffer and the prompt appears again on the screen.

While you type a command, it does not only appear on
the screen - it is also retained in a buffer (an interim or
help-memory). The command is implemented by the
system when you confirm it using Enter.

If you wish to give the same command again immediately, it is not necessary to type it again. You can copy
the complete command or parts of it back to the screen.
The edit keys which we mentioned above also have an
effect on the contents of the buffer.

**You can recall the contents of the buffer using F1
and F3:**

**F1**  Individual character    Copies the contents of the
                                buffer one character at a
                                time, from the beginning.

**F3**  Entire command          Copies the entire command
                                from the buffer.

**Entering an incorrect command**. As mentioned, it is
not a serious matter if you specify a command which
MS-DOS does not understand due to a typing error or a
non-existent file name. The operating system displays
an error message and returns to the prompt. You can
then correct the command as described above.

*Example:* Entering an incorrect command:

```
C:\> DISKKOPY A: B:        (1)
Bad command or file name   (2)

C:\>                       (3)
```

(1)  Bad command: the command is incorrectly typed.
(2)  Error message from the operating system.
(3)  Prompt.

If DOS 5, 6.0 or 6.2 is installed on your system, you can
use the specified commands anew. See section 14.2.

**Executing commands and program files.** Each command is linked to an MS-DOS program. A command activates a program of the same name.

Some programs are loaded automatically when the operating system is activated (they belong to the COMMAND.COM program). These so-called *internal commands* are placed in computer working memory and do not need to be loaded from the system diskette or harddisk first. If you type an internal command on the command line and press Enter to confirm it, this command is executed immediately.

In order to save memory capacity, the less-often used commands are not included in the internal part of the operating system. An *external command* activates a program which has to be loaded from the system diskette or harddisk before it can be implemented. The diskette must then be inserted in the active drive or a path to the directory containing the operating system commands must be specified (see section 3.1). We shall deal more extensively with the structure of MS-DOS in section 9.2. The external commands are explicitly indicated in the list of commands in the appendix.

You can, of course, load and activate executable applications in addition to system programs. You can recognize system and application programs in the directories by their extensions:

```
COM EXE BAT
```

In order to load and activate a program, you do not need to specify the extension, the name will suffice. For example, the WP.EXE program is activated by typing WP.

**A program, just like a DOS command, is only executed when you press Enter.**

**Activating a program from a diskette which is not located in the specified drive.** It will undoubtedly occur that you will attempt to activate a system or application program when the diskette is not located in the specified drive. MS-DOS then displays an error message. Discontinue the command by typing A (Abort) or insert the diskette in the proper drive and press R (Retry). The F (Fail) option is not useful in this case because the same error message appears once again.

*Example:* Activating a program from a diskette which is not located in the specified drive.

```
C:\> A:PRINT command.bat      (1)

Not ready reading drive A     (2)
Abort, Retry, Fail?a          (3)

C:\>                          (4)
```

(1) The command to activate the print program from the diskette in drive A:.
(2) The diskette is not in the drive. An error message appears.
(3) Press A (Abort) to cancel the command.
(4) The computer is ready for the next command.

# 3 The most important commands in MS-DOS

## 3.1 Files and directories

**File names.** Programs and data are saved in files. By assigning names to these files, you can easily retrieve them later from disk. You may choose the names freely, but they must conform to these rules:

■ A file name may consist of a maximum of *eight* alphanumeric or other permitted characters. For example:
TABLE
TEXT27
PROTOCOL

■ A file name may be supplemented by an extension consisting of a point and a maximum of *three* characters. For example:
FILENAME.EXT
TEXT.DOC
HOUSE.123
12345678.XYZ

■ Internally, MS-DOS fills up short names and short or absent extensions with spaces. You have already seen that the extension point is not shown in the file lists on the screen. For example (x represents a space):
LETTER.TXT becomes LETTERxx TXT
INTER93.3 becomes INTER93x 3xx
NEW.A becomes NEWxxxxx Axx

■ You may write file names using small or capital letters. Internally, MS-DOS uses only capitals. For example:
saving93.xyz becomes SAVING93 XYZ
OldFile.ABC becomes OLDFILE ABC

■ A file name may only occur once on the same diskette (unless in different directories). The same name

may, of course, occur on different diskettes. Files
may have the same name if the extension differs. For
example:
NOTES.001
NOTES.002
NOTES.003

■ A file name or extension may consist of the letters of
the alphabet, all numbers and certain special characters. Up until version 3.0 of DOS, it was not allowed
to include letters possessing tildes and accents in file
names. This is possible with more recent versions but
not really advisable since many programs which orig-
inate in the USA cannot easily handle these characters. In addition, there are certain restrictions on the
usage of special characters because MS-DOS requires certain characters for file processing.

**The following characters may not be used in file
names:**

. , ; : = + < > [ ] / | * ?

**A name may not include spaces, not even at the be-
ginning**

In order to prevent problems with the operating system
and with the exchange of data between the different
operating system versions, it is advisable not to use tildes and accents, and to only use the hyphen and the
underline character in file names.

**Using directories.** A harddisk is a relatively large storage area with a capacity of many megabytes. Thus, a
hundred files can easily be stored on a harddisk. However, keeping a clear overview of all these files is not
straightforward. The directory list is tediously lengthy
and it takes several seconds before all files have been
displayed on the screen. In addition, there is a great risk
of unintentionally removing or replacing files when using
wildcards (* and ?, see section 9.5).

From version 2.0 onwards, MS-DOS provides the possibility of organizing files on diskette and on the harddisk in groups with their own name: (sub)directories.

Directories provide the following advantages:

■ orderly layout,
■ quicker access,
■ the command only covers the specified or current directory.

The 'basic' directory on a disk is always the main directory, the *root* of the directory tree which has a branching structure. This directory is always designated by a backslash (\). You can create subdirectories of the root directory. Each subdirectory can be subdivided into more subsubdirectories, each divided from its parent directory by a backslash. In this way the inverted tree structure is created and one refers thus to the directory tree of a disk. In order to avoid having to refer to subsubsubdirectories etc., all subdivisions are simply called directories, regardless of their level.

The operating system manages a directory in the same way as a file. The same rules apply to the names: eight characters and an extension consisting of a point and three characters if required.

An example of a harddisk directory is shown on the following page.

(1) The root directory contains all system files, such as COMMAND.COM, CONFIG.SYS and AUTO-EXEC.BAT. The external system files are generally not stored in the root directory but in a separate subdirectory which is called DOS.

(2) There are five directories with names which help clarify their contents: for BASIC and Pascal the interpreter/compiler plus the programs, all kinds of text files and the word processor, and two standard

applications: a bookkeeping program with spread-sheets and a graphic program with images.

(3) The TEXT directory is subdivided into a directory for WordPerfect program files and two directories for various sorts of text: private (LETTERS) and business (MEMO).

(4) The MEMO directory contains directories for three different kinds of business texts: mailing, office bulletins and minutes from meetings.

(5) The names of the internal messages refer to the directory structure: TMO.TXT (\TEXT\MEMO\OFFICE).

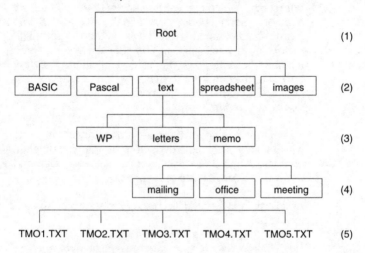

As mentioned, the root directory is only designated by a backslash. If a subdirectory is used in a command, in most cases the backslash is also specified along with the drive letter and the colon. The full name of the TEXT subdirectory on the C: harddisk is thus C:\TEXT, and for the TMO1 text file, this is C:\TEXT\MEMO\OFFICE\TMO1.TXT.

## 3.2    Switching to another drive

When the operating system has been loaded, the DOS prompt appears on the screen. Generally, the prompt is made up of the current drive letter and a 'greater than' sign. When the computer is started up, the current drive is A or C, the default drive which has been specified by the manufacturer.

Using a certain command, you can make another drive the current drive, assuming that this drive is available.

**Switch to another standard drive using a command consisting of the new drive letter plus a colon. Confirm the command by pressing Enter.**

Command: Switch to another drive

```
d:
```

d = drive letter of a chosen harddisk or diskdrive, assuming it is connected.

*Example:* Switching to other drives

```
C:\> A:                                              (1)

A:\>                                                 (2)
A:\> B:                                              (3)


Insert diskette for drive B: and press any key when ready

B:\>
B:\> C:                                              (4)

C:\>
```

(1)  Drive C: is the current drive. Type A and : (without a
     space between) to switch to drive A:. Confirm the
     command by pressing Enter.
(2)  The computer displays the prompt for drive A:.
(3)  Switching from diskdrive A: to B:. Insert a diskette
     in the appropriate drive (if the drive is still empty)
     and press a key.
(4)  Back to the harddisk from drive B:.

**Advantage of changing drives.** Occasionally, it is
necessary to execute a whole series of commands consecutively using programs and/or files from a disk in a
drive which is not the standard drive. In this case, you
have to explicitly specify the drive in question. Assuming that A: is the current drive, you can activate the
PROG program on a disk in drive B: by typing B:PROG.

You can place the disk in another drive or make drive B:
the current drive as shown above. The second method
is easier and quicker.

## 3.3    Displaying the directory

If files are stored on a diskette or harddisk, this will contain at least one directory whose contents you can display on the screen. Of course, this can only be done if
the diskette is located in the specified drive.

**The following command displays the directory from
the disk or harddisk specified in the prompt (current drive).**

```
DIR [/P] [/W]
from DOS 5.0 onwards also:
  [/A(+attributes)] [/O(+order)] [/S] [/B]
from DOS 6.0 onwards also: [/C]
```

DIR                 Display directory command.
/P (page)           Display directory (screen) page by
                    (screen) page.

| /W (wide) | Display directory wide (in 5 columns). |
| /A (attributes) | Show files with certain attributes: h = hidden files. Usage: Dir/Ah, or for example Dir/P/Ah s = system files a = archive files r = read only files |
| /O (order) | Display files in specified order: n = alphabetical order of names. Usage Dir/On, or for example Dir/P/On e = alphabetical order of extension d = date and time s = file size g = directory names first, then files |
| /S (subdirectories) | Lists every occurrence, in the specified directory and all subdirectories, of the specified file name. |
| /B (bare) | Display file names without extra information. |
| /C (compression) | Display the extent of compression of the files. |

*Note:* The parts of the command between the square brackets are optional - you can type them behind the command if required. Do not type the brackets, they are not part of the command.

*Example:* Drive A: is displayed in the prompt. You wish
to show the contents of the system disk in this drive on
the screen.

```
A:\> dir                                     (1)

  Volume in drive A has no label             (2)
  Directory of A:\

COMMAND  COM      54,619 30-09-93    6:20     (3)
CONFIG   SYS         495 15-11-93   10:42
AUTOEXEC BAT         303 15-11-93   10:42
ANSI     SYS       9,065 30-09-93    6:20
COUNTRY  SYS      19,546 30-09-93    6:20
DBLSPACE SYS      22,502 30-09-93    6:20
SMARTDRU SYS       8,335 09-04-91    5:00
XMA2EMS  SYS      29,252 01-09-89   12:00
DISPLAY  SYS      15,789 30-09-93    6:20
DRIVER   SYS       5,406 30-09-93    6:20
RAMDRIUE SYS       5,873 10-03-93    6:00
HIMEM    SYS      29,136 30-09-93    6:20
KEYBOARD SYS      34,598 30-09-93    6:20
PRINTER  SYS      18,804 09-04-91    5:00
CHKSTATE SYS      41,600 10-03-93    6:00
KEYBRD2  SYS      39,366 30-09-93    6:20
        16 file(s)       334,689 bytes       (4)
                       1,119,744 bytes free

      (5)           (6)    (7)      (8)
```

(1)  Command to show the directory of the disk in drive
     A:.
(2)  Statement from the operating system: the diskette
     has no name.
(3)  List of file names with corresponding information.
     The files in this example are all operating system
     programs. We shall return to this topic at various
     points in this book. Refer to the index if you now
     wish to find out more.
(4)  The number of files on the disk, the number of
     bytes they occupy and the amount of free space on
     disk.
(5)  File names.
(6)  Size of the file in bytes (characters).
(7)  Date of creation or when last saved.
(8)  Time of creation or when last saved.

(The size of the system files and the date and time differ
according to the MS-DOS version.)

If the directory contains more files than there are lines on the screen, the list will shift upwards. This is called *scrolling*. In order to prevent the screen from scrolling, you can have the directory shown page by page (using the /P option). The display halts at the penultimate line on the screen. The message states that the instruction will be further implemented when you press a random key.

*Example:* Displaying a directory page by page

```
A:\ dir/p                                  (1)

  Volume in drive A has no label
  Directory of A:\

COMMAND  COM      54,619 30-09-93    6:20    (2)
CONFIG   SYS         495 15-11-93   10:42
AUTOEXEC BAT         303 15-11-93   10:42
ANSI     SYS       9,065 30-09-93    6:20
COUNTRY  SYS      19,546 30-09-93    6:20
DBLSPACE SYS      22,502 30-09-93    6:20
SMARTDRV SYS       8,335 09-04-91    5:00
XMAZEMS  SYS      29,252 01-09-89   12:00
DISPLAY  SYS      15,789 30-09-93    6:20
DRIVER   SYS       5,406 30-09-93    6:20
EDIT     COM         413 10-03-93    6:00
RAMDRIVE SYS       5,873 10-03-93    6:00
HIMEM    SYS      29,136 30-09-93    6:20
KEYBOARD SYS      34,598 30-09-93    6:20
PRINTER  SYS      18,804 09-04-91    5:00
CHKSTATE SYS      41,600 10-03-93    6:00
KEYBRD2  SYS      39,366 30-09-93    6:20
UNFORMAT COM      12,738 10-03-93    6:00
Press any key to continue . . .             (3)
```

(1)  Command to display the directory pagewise.
(2)  Statement and information regarding the files.
(3)  The display stops here - continue by pressing any key.

It is also possible to display the directory without the size and the date and time of saving. In this case, five file names appear on one line. Then there is room on the screen for 80 files instead of 16. This is usually sufficient for a quick review of the contents of a disk.

*Example:* Display the directory wide

```
A:\> dir/w                                                          (1)

 Uolume in drive A has no label                                     (2)
 Directory of A:\

COMMAND.COM      CONFIG.SYS       AUTOEXEC.BAT     ANSI.SYS         COUNTRY.SYS  (3)
DBLSPACE.SYS     SMARTDRU.SYS     XMAZEMS.SYS      DISPLAY.SYS      DRIUER.SYS
EDIT.COM         RAMDRIUE.SYS     HIMEM.SYS        KEYBOARD.SYS     PRINTER.SYS
CHKSTATE.SYS     KEYBRD2.SYS      UNFORMAT.COM     MIRROR.COM       DISKCOMP.COM
DISKCOPY.COM     CHOICE.COM       DOSKEY.COM       MSHERC.COM       FORMAT.COM
GRAPHICS.COM     XDEL.COM         DOSSHELL.COM     KEYB.COM         HELP.COM
ASSIGN.COM       GRAFTABL.COM     MODE.COM         MORE.COM         LOADFIX.COM
SYS.COM          TREE.COM         USAFE.COM        MSD.COM
        39 file(s)          595,142 bytes
                            854,016 bytes free

A:\>
```

(1)  Command for wide display.
(2)  Statement as in the previous examples.
(3)  File names in five columns. Other information is not
     supplied.

It is not necessary to switch to another drive if the disk
containing the desired directory is not in the current
drive. Specify the corresponding drive letter with a colon
in the command.

*Example:* There are various possibilities to request the
directory of a diskette which is not in the current drive.

```
A:\>DIR B:                                                          (1)
A:\>DIR C:
A:\>DIR B:/W
A:\>DIR C:/P

B:\>DIR A:                                                          (2)
B:\>DIR A:/W

C:\>DIR A:                                                          (3)
C:\>DIR B:/P
```

(1) Drive A: is the current drive. You wish to see the directories of various drives and harddisks without having to switch. The /P and /W options have the functions already mentioned.

(2) As in (1), but in this case from drive B:.

(3) As in (1), from C:.

**Displaying part of a directory.** The method of specification of file names must conform to certain rules (see section 9.5). Instead of specifying the file names and typing in the full name you can replace parts of the name by the * and ? characters, the so-called 'wildcards'.

Imagine that, of all the files on a disk, you only wish to see the BASIC programs in the directory. Or perhaps you wish to find out if the same file name occurs with different extensions, or you wish to know which is the last file in a series of files with a number in the name. It is possible to display only a part of the directory instead of the entire directory.

*Example:* Displaying a selection from the directory by means of wildcards

```
A:\>dir *.bas              (1)

A:\>dir b:*.txt            (2)

A:\>dir try.*             (3)

A:\>dir c:table.*          (4)

C:\>dir b:letter??.*       (5)
```

These commands will produce the the following lists of files:

(1)  All file names with the extension .BAS (BASIC pro-
     gram).
(2)  All file names with the extension .TXT (text files) on
     the disk in drive B:.
(3)  All file names which begin with TRY with any exten-
     sion.
(4)  All file names which begin with TABLE with any ex-
     tension, which are on the harddisk.
(5)  All file names on drive B: which begin with LETTER
     plus any two other characters and which have any
     extension.

*Example:* MS-DOS 6.2 is installed on the computer. All
hidden files (with the h attribute) in the root directory of
the harddisk are to be displayed. In addition, all file
names with the name TEST in the root directory and its
subdirectories are to be displayed.

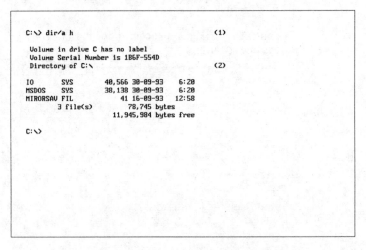

```
C:\> dir/a h                              (1)

  Volume in drive C has no label
  Volume Serial Number is 1B6F-554D
  Directory of C:\                        (2)

IO       SYS       40,566 30-09-93     6:20
MSDOS    SYS       38,138 30-09-93     6:20
MIRORSAV FIL           41 16-09-93    12:58
         3 file(s)        78,745 bytes
                      11,945,984 bytes free

C:\>
```

(1)  This command displays all file names in the current
     directory which are normally hidden. To do this, the
     h attribute is added to the /A parameter (see the
     ATTRIB command in section 7.3).

(2) Three hidden files in the root directory are found and displayed. You can acquire more information about the first two system files in section 9.2.

*Example:* All file names with the name TRIAL in the root directory and subdirectories are to be displayed.

```
C:\> dir trial.*/s                      (1)

  Volume in drive C has no label
  Volume Serial Number is 1B6F-554D

Directory of C:\                        (2)

TRIAL    TXT        21 18-11-93   17:28
TRIAL    LET       623 18-11-93   17:31
         2 file(s)         644 bytes

Directory of C:\WP51

TRIAL              609 18-11-93   17:27
         1 file(s)         609 bytes

Total files listed:
         3 file(s)        1,253 bytes
                     11,937,792 bytes free

C:\>
```

(1) The command to display all files called TRIAL, with any extension.
(2) Three files called TRIAL are found in two different directories. They have different extensions.

## 3.4 Interrupting or ending screen display

**Stopping rolling screen display.** Long directories do not fit into the screen. In addition to the /P option, there is also another method to interrupt the screen display in order to gain the opportunity to read the directory.

**The Pause key discontinues the display. Pressing any key resumes the display at the point of interruption.**

*Example:* Stopping the rolling screen

```
A:\>dir                                    (1)

  Volume in drive A has no label           (2)
  Directory of A:\

COMMAND  COM      54,619 30-09-93    6:20
CONFIG   SYS         495 15-11-93   10:42
AUTOEXEC BAT         303 15-11-93   10:42
ANSI     SYS       9,065 30-09-93    6:20
COUNTRY  SYS      19,546 30-09-93    6:20
DBLSPACE SYS      22,502 30-09-93    6:20
SMARTDRU SYS       8,335 09-04-91    5:00
XMAZEMS  SYS      29,252 01-09-89   12:00
DISPLAY  SYS      15,789 30-09-93    6:20
DRIVER   SYS       5,406 30-09-93    6:20
EDIT     COM         413 10-03-93    6:00
RAMDRIUE SYS       5,873 10-03-93    6:00
HIMEM    SYS      29,136 30-09-93    6:20
KEYBOARD SYS      34,598 30-09-93    6:20
PRINTER  SYS      18,804 09-04-91    5:00
CHKSTATE SYS      41,600 10-03-93    6:00
KEYBRD2  SYS      39,366 30-09-93    6:20
UN                                         (3)
```

(1) Command to display the directory.
(2) Statement and information as in previous examples.
(3) The moment the Pause key is pressed. The display continues from this point after pressing any key.

**Ending screen display.** If the information you require is located at the beginning of the screen display, you can cancel the rest.

**You can end the screen display by using the key combination Ctrl-C**

The operating system returns to the prompt. You can enter a new command immediately.

*Example:* Ending screen display (see following page)

(1) Command to display directory.
(2) Statement and information as in previous examples.
(3) The display position at the moment of key combination Ctrl-C.

```
A:\> dir                              (1)

  Volume in drive A has no label      (2)
  Directory of A:\

COMMAND   COM      54,619 30-09-93    6:20
CONFIG    SYS         495 15-11-93   10:42
AUTOEXEC  BAT         303 15-11-93   10:42
ANSI      SYS       9,065 30-09-93    6:20
COUNTRY   SYS      19,546 30-09-93    6:20
DBLSPACE  SYS      22,502 30-09-93    6:20
SMARTDRU  SYS       8,335 09-04-91    5:00
XMA2EMS   SYS      29,252 01-09-89   12:00
DISPLAY   SYS      15,789 30-09-93    6:20
DRIVER    SYS       5,406 30-09-93    6:20
EDIT      COM         413 10-03-93    6:00
RAMDRIVE  SYS       5,873 10-03-93    6:00
HIMEM     SYS      29,136 30-09-93    6:20
KEYBOARD  SYS      34,598 30-09-93    6:20
PRINTER   SYS      18,804 09-04-91    5:00
CHKSTATE  SYS      41,600 10-03-93    6:00
KEYBRD2   SYS      39,36^C                   (3)

A:\>
```

# 3.5    Clearing the screen display

The CLS command, confirmed with Enter, clears the current screen display. Subsequently, only the prompt is shown on the screen (upper left-hand corner).

**The CLS command clears the current screen display.**

CLS = clear screen

*Example:* Clearing the screen (see following page)

(1)   Command, statement, information and discontinuation as in previous examples.
(2)   Command to clear screen. Just as with other commands, CLS must also be confirmed by pressing Enter.

```
A:\> dir                                    (1)

Volume in drive A has no label
Directory of A:\

COMMAND  COM      54,619 30-09-93    6:20
CONFIG   SYS         495 15-11-93   10:42
AUTOEXEC BAT         303 15-11-93   10:42
ANSI     SYS       9,065 30-09-93    6:20
COUNTRY  SYS      19,546 30-09-93    6:20
DBLSPACE SYS      22,502 30-09-93    6:20
SMARTDRV SYS       8,335 09-04-91    5:00
XMAZEMS  SYS      29,252 01-09-89   12:00
DISPLAY  SYS      15,789 30-09-93    6:20
DRIVER   SYS       5,406 30-09-93    6:20
EDIT     COM         413 10-03-93    6:00
RAMDRIVE SYS       5,873 10-03-93    6:00
HIMEM    SYS      29,136 30-09-93    6:20
KEYBOARD SYS      34,598 30-09^C

A:\> cls                                    (2)
```

# 3.6    Printing the screen display

**Transporting the current screen contents to the printer.** If you have connected a printer to the computer, you can print the current contents of the screen (data shown on the monitor) using the printer. The printer copies the contents of the screen, in as much as the printer is able to reproduce the characters. This printed copy is called a *hardcopy*.

Check the following points before giving the print command:

> Is the printer connected?
> Is there paper in the printer?
> Is the printer switched on?
> Is the printer ON LINE (ready)?

**The Shift-PrintScreen key combination transports the current screen display to the printer.**
You may repeat this command as often as you like.

**Types of printers.** Not all printers are able to print all the characters shown on the screen.

A daisy wheel printer is only able to print characters which occur on the wheel, mostly only the alphanumeric characters which are also used on a typewriter.

Printers which construct the letters in another way using points (pin or matrix printer, laser printer, inkjet printer) can reproduce all the screen characters if they are connected to the computer by a suitable interface. This also applies to images on the screen. These kinds of printers are also called graphic printers. In addition, there are also printers for coloured images. These require a special interface.

**Printing the contents of a colour graphics screen.** If your computer has a graphic monitor, linked to the computer via a colour graphics adapter, a special *external system program* is needed to make a screendump (hardcopy).

**The GRAPHICS print program transports a graphic screen to the printer.**

```
GRAPHICS
from DOS 5.0 also: [printertype] [/R]
```

GRAPHICS            Images, pictures.
printertype       For instance, deskjet, LaserJet, graphics.
/R               White characters on a black background.

You only need to give the GRAPHICS command once. The program remains resident in memory as long as the computer is on. If you include this program in the automatic start-up file AUTOEXEC.BAT, you will not have to concern yourself further with starting up this program (see section 6.5).

## 3.7    Reproducing the screen contents on the printer

The flow of data from the computer to the screen can also be simultaneously reproduced on the printer. This is useful, for instance, for making a protocol if you are testing a program. You can also use this function to re-produce a long directory or text on paper as well as on the screen.

First check if the printer is ready (see section 3.6).

**The Ctrl-P or Ctrl-PrintScreen key combination en-sures that the data flow of a command is trans-ported not only to the screen but also to the printer. If you repeat this key combination, you disconnect the printer again**.

You can switch the protocol function on and off as often as you wish. It has no influence upon the data flow, apart from the fact that information is transported to the screen a little slower. This takes place at the pace of the printer.

If you activate this function when the printer is not ready, the computer will give an error message. You can only continue when you have adjusted the printer properly, or after a warm or cold restart.

## 3.8    Transporting the contents of a file to the screen or the printer

**Displaying the contents of a file on the screen.** You can not only request the names of the files on a disk, you can also request the contents of the file. This is use-ful if you no longer know the contents of the file, if you are searching for certain information in a file, or if you only wish to review the contents of the file.

Only files with alphanumeric contents are legible (ASCII format). This may be a normal text or a non-compiled program (source text with non-compiled commands). It is possible to transport the contents of a program in computer language to the screen, but you will then see a hotch-potch of strange characters with here and there a letter or a number.

**Specify behind the command and the space the complete name of the file you wish to examine.**

**If the file is located on a disk other than the current one or in a different directory, you must also specify the proper drive and directory.**

```
TYPE [d:][path]file.ext
```

TYPE      Type.
d:path    Letter of the drive with the disk and directory where the file is located.
file.ext  Name of the file (including extension).

With the TYPE command, the * and ? wildcards are not valid.

*Example:* The LETTER.TXT file which is located on the disk in drive B: is to be displayed on the screen (see following page).

(1)  The command to show the file. Do not forget to specify the drive and the extension.
(2)  The TYPE command does indeed show the text literally, but the original formatting characters (layout codes) are omitted. Only the characters for 'end paragraph' and the Tabs are retained.

If, using the TYPE command, you display a file which has been created using a word processing program such as WORD or WordPerfect, you will see all sorts of characters which are invisible in the word processor - break codes, italics, underlining etc.

Due to the fact that these codes are very specific, you will generally have to remove them if you wish to continue using the text in another way. Most word processors have an option enabling you to save text without the layout codes (excepting paragraphs and tabs) - in the so-called ASCII format.

```
A:\>type b:letter.txt                                    (1)

Dear Sir,                                                (2)
          As a loving and disquieted parent, I would like to
express my concern over the recent upsurge in joyriding. In
addition to general condemnation of this practice, perhaps
society can also take more preventative steps. Television
pictures show that joyriders seldom use the indicators and it
might be a good idea to give children at school a course in the
use of good old-fashioned hand signals. I would also recommend
that aeroplanes and submarines be wrapped in heavy chains at
night. I do not relish the thought of evil-smelling packages
being thrown down my chimney by irresponsible brats terrorising
the skies or the foundations of our beautiful beaches, which we
have defended so heroically against the Romans, Huns, Eskimos and
oilslicks, being battered by uneducated louts. My thirteen-year-
old son ensures me that it is quite easy to steal a car, thus I
would argue the case for compulsory tyre deflation at night and
each house being supplied with a compressed-air cylinder. After
all, where does our road tax go?
                              Yours faithfully,
                              Billy Binkerhill (Mrs.)

A:\>
```

**Displaying a file pagewise on the screen.** In the same way as with DIR/P, you can also display the contents of a file page by page on the screen. It would be rather tedious to have to press the Pause key after each page in order to get the chance to read the text.

If you extend the TYPE command with the pipe symbol ¦ and the MORE command, the data requested by the TYPE command are transported via a metaphorical pipe to the following command. In this case, that is the MORE instruction, which is a kind of line counter. The contents of the file no longer roll over the screen - they stop at the last screen line. The statement '--More--' is shown there. To display the following page, you only have to press a random key.

**The following command displays the contents of a file pagewise on the screen.**

```
TYPE [d:][path]file.ext¦MORE
```

d:path    The drive and directory containing the file to be displayed.

MORE    More.

¦    Vertical, broken stripe.

The pipe symbol is available on most keyboards. If this is not the case, you can create it using an Alt key combination - hold down the Alt key and press consecutively the numbers 1, 2 and 4 on the numeric keypad at the right-hand side of the keyboard (124 is the ASCII code for the pipe symbol).

*Example:* Displaying a file pagewise on the screen

```
A:\>type b:letter.txt¦more                              (1)

Dear Sir,
        As a loving and disquieted parent, I would like to
express my concern over the recent upsurge in joyriding. In
addition to general condemnation of this practice, perhaps
society can also take more preventative steps. Television
pictures show that joyriders seldom use the indicators and it
might be a good idea to give children at school a course in the
use of good old-fashioned hand signals. I would also recommend
that aeroplanes and submarines be wrapped in heavy chains at
night. I do not relish the thought of evil-smelling packages
being thrown down my chimney by irresponsible brats terrorising
the skies or the foundations of our beautiful beaches, which we
have defended so heroically against the Romans, Huns, Eskimos and
oilslicks, being battered by uneducated louts. My thirteen-year-
old son ensures me that it is quite easy to steal a car, thus I
would argue the case for compulsory tyre deflation at night and
each house being supplied with a compressed-air cylinder. After
all, where does our road tax go?
...
...
...
...
-- More --                                              (2)
```

(1)   Extended display command.

(2)   This statement appears at the bottom of the screen. Press a random key to show the following page.

**Reproducing the contents of a file using the printer.**
In this book, we shall discuss two possibilities.

■ Reproducing a file using the protocol mode.
■ Reproducing a file using a special DOS command.

**Possibility no.1**

We have already dealt with simultaneous reproduction
on screen and printer in section 3.7. We shall sum-
marize once more, paying attention to the current subject matter.

**The following three manoeuvres (also) reproduce a
file on the printer:**

1   Activate the protocol function for the printer using
    Ctrl-PrintScreen or Ctrl-P.

2   Display the contents of the file on the screen:

```
TYPE [d:][path]file.ext
```

The file is now not only shown on the screen, it is also
reproduced on the printer because the protocol function
is active.

3   Switch off the protocol function once more by
    pressing Ctrl-PrintScreen or Ctrl-P.

It is also possible to direct the output to the printer without activating the protocol function. To do this, extend
the command by adding the greater-than sign >, followed by the DOS name PRN for the printer:

```
type [d:][path]file.ext > PRN
```

**Possibility no.2**

The DOS program called PRINT provides the possibility
of printing without activating the protocol function.

**Transporting the contents of a file to the printer alone.**

```
PRINT [d:][path]file.ext
```

PRINT     Print.
d:path    Letter of the drive and path to the directory
          (if necessary) containing the file.
file.ext  Name of the file to be printed.

The * and ? wildcards are valid in the PRINT command.

The contents of the file are transported to the printer, *not* to the screen.

The first time you give a PRINT command when you have switched on the computer, the system will ask the name of the printer. Confirm the standard name PRN using Enter or type another name if you have installed another printer, LPT1 or LPT2, for example. In all subsequent instances, the PRINT command will be implemented (as long as you have not switched off the computer).

*Example:* Print the text files LETTER10 and INFO.TXT from the disk in drive B:

```
A:\>print b:\letter10.txt              (1)
Name of list device [PRN];             (2)
Resident part of PRINT installed       (3)

  B:\LETTER10.TXT is currently being printed  (4)

A:\>print b:\info.txt                   (5)

  B:\INFO.TXT is currently being printed   (6)
```

(1) PRINT command for the LETTER10 file on a disk in drive B:.

(2)  The PRINT command prompt for the name of the
     list device. If the printer is connected to the stan-
     dard interface for the printer, you only need to
     press Enter.
(3)  Part of the PRINT program remains available in
     memory. It becomes *resident*.
(4)  Statement: The command is executed.
(5)  The second PRINT command, now for the
     B:\INFO.TXT file.
(6)  The PRINT statement for the second file.

**More about the PRINT command**

The two methods of printing files have their own areas
of application.

The TYPE internal command with the protocol function
or the redirection of output is convenient for short files.

The PRINT external command provides benefits when
dealing with longer files, and is also advantageous if
you wish to print several files consecutively using one
command. While the PRINT command is being executed, you can use the computer for other tasks.

The PRINT command in MS-DOS has two exceptional
features:

■ The PRINT command can print a file *in the background* - in other words, you can use the computer for
  other jobs in the meantime (in the foreground). Due to
  the fact that the computer cannot really implement
  two jobs simultaneously, it switches rapidly between
  these two activities. A task in the foreground is executed noticeably slower - when displaying (another)
  file on the screen, for instance.
■ You may register several file names in one go behind
  the PRINT command. The names are recorded in a
  queue and the files are printed consecutively. As long
  as the computer is busy with printing, you can add
  files to, or remove them from, the queue.

When printing a queue, the following preconditions apply:

■ The printer must be ready.
■ The files named must be located on the specified disk.
■ The printer is not available for other commands while dealing with the queue.

**The PRINT queue.** You may register a *maximum of ten* files behind the PRINT command (from MS-DOS 5.0 this is thirteen):

```
PRINT file1.ext file2.ext ... filen.ext
```

The files are printed in the specified order of sequence.

A file can be added to the existing print queue:

```
PRINT file.ext[/P]
```

The FILE.EXT file is added to the existing queue and is printed when its turn comes around. The /P option is standard: you only need to state this option if you have already removed a file from the queue.

You remove files from the print queue as follows:

```
PRINT file1.ext/C file2.ext ...
```

The file with the /C option (cancel) disappears from the queue. This applies to all files specified before and behind this option. If one of these files is being printed at that moment, the command will break off the execution.

The printer gives an acoustic warning signal and the paper moves on to the next file if any.

Discontinuing the PRINT command:

```
PRINT /T
```

The /T option (terminate) removes the print queue and
breaks off the PRINT command with the statement:

```
Print queue is empty
```

The printer gives a warning signal and the paper moves
on to the next sheet.

Displaying the current contents of the queue:

```
PRINT
```

A list of the files in the queue appears on the screen
along with the file which is being printed at that moment.

*Example:* Using the queue to print several files

```
A:\>print letter.txt advert.123 request.dat          (1)

  A:\LETTER.TXT is currently being printed
  A:\ADVERT.123 is in queue
  A:\REQUEST.DAT is in queue

A:\>print order.opd                                  (2)

  A:\LETTER.TXT is currently being printed
  A:\ADVERT.123 is in queue
  A:\REQUEST.DAT is in queue
  A:\ORDER.OPD is in queue

A:\>print request.dat/c opder.opd action.305/p       (3)

  A:\LETTER.TXT is currently being printed
  A:\ADVERT.123 is in queue
  A:\ACTION.305 is in queue

A:\>print                                            (4)

  A:\ACTION.305 is currently being printed

A:\>print /t                                         (5)
PRINT queue is empty
```

(1) The LETTER.TXT, ADVERT.123 and RE-QUEST.DAT files are registered in the queue and subsequently printed.

(2) The ORDER.OPD file is added to the queue.

(3) The REQUEST.DAT and ORDER.OPD files are removed from the queue. ACTION.305 is added. No interrupt message is shown because neither of the removed files was being printed at that moment.

(4) Prints the files in the queue. It is obvious that only the file which is being printed at this moment is still in the list.

(5) This command concludes the printing of the only file still in the list. The queue has been processed and the command states that the queue is empty. The printer registers a break-off message for the last file, gives a warning signal and moves the paper on to the following sheet.

# 4    File management on floppies and harddisk

The operating system manages programs and information in the form of files. You can only retain files in the computer memory as long as the computer is switched on. In order to save them permanently, the files have to be saved in an external memory - on floppies or on a harddisk upon which information is stored magnetically. You must personally organize this management, assisted by the operating system. To do this, you must format diskettes, make backups, check the storage media and the files, (re)moving these where necessary, and undo errors.

We shall discuss the management functions for these procedures in this chapter. If you have very little experience of this, it is advisable to first read sections 9.4 and 9.5 which deal with diskettes and file names.
Some instructions only apply to floppies - we shall state this explicitly. The others also refer to the harddisk.

The instructions in this chapter should ensure few problems and if anything in a command is not quite correct, the system will give a clear error message. The only possible risk lurks in instructions which delete files, but we shall deal extensively with this in due course.

## 4.1    Copying an entire diskette

In the simplest method of making a copy of a diskette, the contents of the original diskette (*source diskette*) are copied in the same order of sequence, one character at a time, to the new diskette (*target diskette*).

Even if the target diskette has not been used previously, in most versions of MS-DOS it is generally not necessary to prepare this diskette for storage functions (formatting, see section 4.3). The DISKCOPY copying pro-

gram, which copies complete *diskettes*, does this automatically if required. In contrast, the COPY command
copies one or more separate *files* (see section 4.4) - this
command only works with a formatted target diskette.

Both programs can be run with either one or two diskdrives. This depends, of course, on the computer configuration. With two diskdrives, it is not necessary to repeatedly switch the source and target diskettes.

The DISKCOPY command will not copy the contents of a diskette to the harddisk nor to other types
of diskettes - thus not from a 5.25 inch diskette to a
3.5 inch diskette or vice versa.

If the target diskette still contains files, the copy program will overwrite these. Accordingly, the original
information is irretrievably lost.

Pay special attention to whether the target diskette
has already been used or has already been formatted. Do not place this diskette in the wrong
drive (read drive). This automatically entails that
the source diskette will be placed in the write drive.

You can protect the source diskette against unintentional overwriting by placing a sticker over the
write-protection slot (5.25 diskettes) or by opening
the sleeve (3.5 diskettes).

**The DISKCOPY command copies the contents of a
diskette to a new diskette, without any alteration.**

```
DISKCOPY [d1:] [d2:] [/1]
```

d1: Source drive.
d2: Target drive.
/1  Copy only one side.

When the copy program has been loaded, it asks you to
place the source diskette in the drive represented by *d1:*

and the target diskette in the drive represented by *d2:*.
In principle, it makes no difference if you specify the
order of sequence as being A-B or B-A, but in order to
avoid mistakes, it is advisable to employ always the
same order of sequence.

*Example:* Copy the contents of a diskette in drive A: to a
new diskette in drive B:. The diskettes are of the same
type, 5.25 inch, 360 Kb.

```
A:\>diskcopy a: b:                          (1)

Insert SOURCE diskette in drive A:          (2)

Press any key to continue . . .

Copying 40 tracks                           (3)
9 sectors per track, 2 side(s)

Insert TARGET diskette in drive B:          (4)

Press any key to continue . . .

Formatting while copying                    (5)

Volume Serial Number is 16F2-0A58

Copy another diskette (Y/N)? n              (6)

A:\>                                        (7)
```

(1)  The command loads the copy program into mem-
     ory and activates it.
(2)  The program gives a prompt to place the source
     diskette in the specified first drive. You may place
     the target diskette in drive B: to avoid mistakes.
     The program will begin copying as soon as you
     press a key.
(3)  The program states that it has loaded both sides of
     the diskette, each containing 40 tracks of 9 sectors,
     into the computer memory.
(4)  The program asks you to place the target diskette
     in drive B:, even if it is already located there. Press
     Enter to continue.
(5)  The program registers that the target diskette is un-
     formatted and states that the diskette will be pro-
     cessed during copying.

(6) The program asks if you wish to copy another diskette: an identical copy or a copy of another diskette. That is not our intention at the moment. Answer N (No).

(7) By answering N, the DISKCOPY program is ended and control is returned to MS-DOS. The prompt makes this evident.

If you omit both drives from the command, the program will only work with the current drive. This is the case, for instance, if your computer only has one diskdrive. In versions up to and including 6.0, the program uses the computer memory as a buffer for the data to be copied. The frequency of switching between source and target diskette depends upon the amount of memory in your computer and the type of diskettes. If this is less than 512 Kb, you will have to switch at least once since there is not sufficient capacity available to store all 360 Kb of the source diskette temporarily.

If you have MS-DOS version 6.2, the computer will carry out the task of copying the diskette in one go. The harddisk is used as an interim storage area. Thus, you will not need to switch the diskettes. Also, you will be able to make multiple copies of the same diskette quickly.

If your computer has two diskdrives, you can choose to work with either one or two drives when copying.

*Note:* You may also only use diskettes which have the same writing density (HD or DD) when applying this command.

*Example:* Various applications of the copy command (see following page)

(1) The command only uses A:, the current diskdrive. The source drive and the target drive are the same. The program states when the diskettes should be switched.

(2) As in (1), but now from B:.

(3) As in (1). The drive first specified is always inter-

preted as being the source drive. Because this is
the same as the current drive, this addition does
not change anything.
(4)  The source drive is B:, the target drive is A:. The
contents of the diskette in B: are copied to the diskette in A:.
(5)  The copy program is loaded and started up from
the harddisk. Just as in (1), A: is both source and
target drive.
(6)  The /1 option ensures that the copy program only
copies side 1 of the source diskette to side 1 of the
target diskette. This is an obsolete option, which
dates from the time that diskdrives had only one
write head.

```
A:\>diskcopy                        (1)

B:\>diskcopy                        (2)

A:\>diskcopy a:                     (3)

A:\>diskcopy b: a:                  (4)

C:\>diskcopy a: a:                  (5)

A:\>diskcopy a: b:/1                (6)
```

Advanced users make mistakes in giving commands
now and again, just as beginners do. This is generally
not serious, since the system will state in one way or another that the instruction is not correct. The following
example illustrates the effect of various mistakes.

*Example:* Error message in the DISKCOPY command

```
A:\>diskcopy a: b:
Bad command or file name              (1)

C:\>diskcopy a:

Invalid drive specification           (2)
Specified drive does not exist
or is non-removable

A:\>diskcopy a: b:

Insert SOURCE diskette in drive A:

Insert TARGET diskette in drive B:

Press any key to continue . . .
Not ready - A:                        (3)
Make sure a diskette is inserted into
the drive and the door is closed

Press CTRL+C to abort,
or correct this problem and press any other key to continue . . .

Write protect error                   (4)
```

(1) Error: The command is wrongly written.
    Remedy: Type again, or alter using the input buffer: F2, S, Ins, i, F3.

(2) Error: The command copies the contents of A: to the harddisk.
    Remedy: Switch to drive A:.

(3) Error: The diskette is not yet located in the specified drive or the drive is not yet locked.
    Remedy: Follow the instructions on the screen.

(4) Error: The write-protection slot has been taped over (in the case of a 3.5 inch diskette, the small sleeve is open).
    Remedy: Check if you still require the files. If not, remove the tape (or close the sleeve), otherwise use another diskette.

Files which you frequently use and modify remain an entity as regards administration, but they become more fragmented on the diskette with the passage of time. Loading and saving them becomes ever more time-consuming. The situation remains unchanged if you copy files using DISK-COPY. By using COPY (section 4.4), you can make the files an entity again on the target diskette.

# 4.2    Comparing diskettes

The DISKCOMP command enables you to:

■ compare copies of diskettes to each other and to the original,
■ trace faults in copies.

Use of this command is highly recommended if you wish to be sure that the copy of a diskette containing indispensable information is identical to the original. The DISKCOMP command is only usable in the case of diskettes which have been copied using DISKCOPY. To compare a single file or a group of files, the COMP command is available (see section 4.5).

 The DISKCOMP command can only be used for diskettes. If you attempt to compare the contents of a diskette to the contents of a harddisk, you will receive an error message.

The command activates a utility program which compares the copy, track by track, to the original. A message specifies each deviation. Possible causes of such messages are:

■ Something has gone wrong during the copying process. Perhaps the copy contains damaged tracks or sectors.
■ One of the files on the source diskette is protected against copying, leading to its absence on the copy.
■ One of the diskettes has been made using COPY. Then the files are written differently to the diskette.
■ You have altered something on the copy or on the original before the comparison.
■ The files on the diskettes are completely different.

You can attempt to correct copy errors by copying the original diskette to the target diskette once more. If, at the following comparison, the diskettes still differ, the conclusion is that the target diskette cannot be used with DISK-COPY. Do not immediately throw the diskette away - it can be useful, when formatted again, for storing odd files. If the format program states that the diskette contains unusable sectors, the diskette is not in order. If you format the diskette again, it may help, but if the trouble persists, you will not be able to use the diskette.

**The DISKCOMP instruction compares the contents of two diskettes.**

```
DISKCOMP d1: d2: [/1] [/8]
```

d1: Name of the first diskdrive.
d2: Name of the second diskdrive.

Special options (see also DISKCOPY).

/1   Compares only the first sides of the diskettes.
/8   Compares eight sectors of each track instead of nine.

It is possible to compare two diskettes using one diskdrive. The program then states when the diskettes have to be switched.

*Example:* Comparison of two identical diskettes in different diskdrives (see following page)

(1)  Command to compare the diskettes in drives A: and B:.
(2)  The prompt asks you to place the first diskette in drive A: and then to press any key.
(3)  The program registers the diskette features.
(4)  The prompt asks you to place the second diskette in B: and then to press any key.
(5)  The program states that the two diskettes are identical.

(6)  The program asks if you wish to compare more dis-
     kettes. Discontinue the program with N (Enter is not
     necessary).

```
A:\>diskcomp a: b:                      (1)

Insert FIRST diskette in drive A:       (2)

Press any key to continue . . .

Comparing 40 tracks                     (3)
9 sectors per track, 2 side(s)

Insert SECOND diskette in drive B:      (4)

Press any key to continue . . .

Compare OK                              (5)

Compare another diskette (Y/N) ?n       (6)

A:\>
```

*Example:* Comparison of two differing diskettes in one
diskdrive (A:)

```
A:\>diskcomp                            (1)

Insert FIRST diskette in drive A:       (2)

Press any key to continue . . .

Comparing 40 tracks                     (3)
9 sectors per track, 2 side(s)

Insert SECOND diskette in drive A:      (4)

Press any key to continue . . .

Compare error on                        (5)
side 0, track 10
      .
      .
      .
Compare error on
side 1, track 39

Compare another diskette (Y/N) ?n       (6)

A:\>
```

(1) Due to the fact that the comparison takes place in one diskdrive (the current drive), it is not really necessary to specify the diskdrives.

(2), (3) The statements and prompts are similar to those in the previous example.

(4) Replace the first diskette with the second one.

(5) The program registers a whole series of deviations along with the track and sectors in which these are located. Owing to shortage of space, we have omitted most of these.

(6) As in the previous example.

## 4.3 Formatting diskettes

A new diskette has to be prepared to be able to save files in an orderly way, so that they can easily be re-called. The format program writes concentric tracks on the diskette, each of these tracks being divided into a fixed number of sectors. In addition, on the first track, the program creates a book-keeping system for the file names and a table where the file blocks are located, the *file allocation table* (FAT). This process is called *formatting* (see section 9.4).

The DISKCOPY copy program is an exception, due to the fact that, in most MS-DOS versions, it formats the diskette itself if necessary. It has been specially constructed to facilitate making reserve copies of diskettes. The formatting program which we are discussing in this section is a part of DISKCOPY.

In DOS versions prior to 5.0, the formatting program deletes *all* data from the diskette or harddisk (!) specified in the command. Keep this in mind when you wish to format a used diskette or the harddisk.

Check if you have specified the correct (disk)drive before confirming the command. In chapter 12, you can discover how to undo an unintentional formatting of a disk.

*Caution:* Never give the format command without specifying the diskdrive.

Read section 7.1 before formatting the harddisk.

**The FORMAT command prepares a diskette or harddisk for storage of information.**

```
FORMAT [d:] [/S] [/V]
       [/1] [/8] [B] [/4] [/T:aa] [/N:bb]
       from MS-DOS 5.0 also:
       [/F:bytes] [/Q] [/U]
```

d:          Drive specified in the format command.
/S          Copy, in addition, the most important sys-
            tem programs.
/V          Ask, at completion, for a name for the dis-
            kette/harddisk (volume).

Structural deviations (for diskettes only)

/1          Format one side.
/8          Make 8 instead of 9 sectors per track.
/B          Format 8 sectors per track and reserve
            space in order to be able to add the system
            files later.
/4          Format a 5.25 inch DD-diskette in a HD-
            diskdrive (from MS-DOS version 3.0 on-
            wards; read section 9.4 first).
/T:aa       Make aa tracks (aa represents the required
            number of tracks).
            Example: for a 3.5 inch DD diskette (720
            Kb) in a HD drive (capacity 1.44 Mb), the
            number of tracks is 80.
            Note: /T:aa and /N:bb must always be used
            in combination.
/N:bb       Make bb sectors per track. In the example
            above bb=9.
/F:bytes    Specify the capacity of the diskette in Kb or
            or Mb, for instance 360, 720 (Kb), 1.2, 1.44
            or 2.88 (Mb).

/Q     Quick format of a previously formatted diskette. However, defective sectors will not be registered. The UNFORMAT command can undo the formatting.

/U     (From version 5 onwards only) unconditional format, which destroys all data on the target disk to prevent subsequent unformatting with the UNFORMAT command. Comparable to the FORMAT command of previous DOS versions. Chapter 12 contains more information concerning this option.

*Example:* Formatting a diskette and a harddisk

```
C:\> format A:                                    (1)
Insert new diskette for drive A:                  (2)
and press ENTER when ready...

Checking existing disk format.                    (3)
Saving UNFORMAT information.
Verifying 1.44M
Format complete.

    1,457,664 bytes total disk space              (4)
    1,457,664 bytes available on disk

Format another (Y/N)?                             (5)

A:\> format c:                                    (6)
WARNING: ALL DATA ON NON-REMOVABLE DISK           (7)
DRIVE C: WILL BE LOST!
Proceed with Format (Y/N)?

C:\> format a: /T:80 /N:9                         (8)

C:\> format b: /T:40 /N:9                         (9)

C:\> format b: /F:360                            (10)
```

(1) This command loads the format program. It is necessary to specify the target drive because this is not the current drive in this case.

(2) The program requests you to insert a diskette in the specified drive. Confirm this using Enter.

(3) The existing disk format is checked.

(4) The program registers the storage capacity which has been created and that which is available. Between these two lines, there may be a statement concerning the number of defective sectors if any

(these are automatically blocked) and the capacity
occupied by the system files.
(5) Finally, the program will ask if you wish to format
another disk. If you respond *N, Enter*, the program
will be closed and you will return to the prompt.
(6) The command to format the harddisk C:.
(7) The program asks, for security reasons, if you really wish to format the harddisk. If so, ensure that
all important data have been saved on diskette!
(8) This command formats a 3.5 inch diskette for normal density (DD) in a 3.5 inch drive for High Density
(HD). Normally, this diskdrive will format 80 tracks
containing 18 sectors which produces a capacity of
1.44 Mb. However, this can only be done using HD
diskettes. Using the options shown in the example,
the HD diskdrive will format a cheaper DD diskette
with 80 tracks of 9 sectors, producing a capacity of
720 Kb (see section 9.4)
(9) This command formats a 5.25 inch diskette for normal density (DD) in a diskdrive for High Density
(HD). Normally this type of diskdrive formats 80
tracks of 15 sectors, resulting in a capacity of 1.2
Mb. However, this can only be done with HD diskettes. Using options as shown in the example, the HD
diskdrive will format a cheaper DD diskette with 40
tracks of 9 sectors, producing a capacity of 360 Kb
(see section 9.4). You may also specify /4 instead
of the two options mentioned here.
(10) As under (9), but now from DOS version 5.0 onwards.

The two most important options of the format command
are outlined below.

**Making a start-up diskette.** Prior to being able to activate any program, the computer must have access to
the operating system files. If the computer has only
diskdrives, a start-up diskette will be required. But even
a computer with a harddisk may occasionally require a
start-up diskette, for instance if the harddisk is temporarily out of order.

A system diskette must be equipped with the most important system files: IO.SYS, MSDOS.SYS and COMMAND.COM. (In the case of original IBM PCs, the first two files are called IBMBIO.COM and IBMDOS.COM, respectively.) In the DOS 6.0 and 6.2 versions with a compressed diskette, DBLSPACE.BIN must also be on the diskette. The **/S** option in the FORMAT command automatically copies these system files during the formatting process.

If you display the directory of the formatted diskette, the list of files will contain only the COMMAND.COM file. The other files have been saved with the *hidden* attribute, making them not visible in the directory list. Nevertheless, by means of the DIR /Ah command and the CHKDSK command, you can check the existence of these files (see section 4.6). You can also use this command to transfer the system to the harddisk.

In some MS-DOS versions, the /S option must be specified last.

**The /V option, assigning a name to the diskette or harddisk**. You can only keep a clear overview of your diskettes if you attach labels to them with a title and/or concise summary. MS-DOS provides the facility of registering the name on the diskette itself. You can allocate a (functional) name using the /V option in the FORMAT command. (This can also be done later using the LABEL command - see below in this section.)
When using the /V option, after the tracks have been formatted, the command will ask for a name of maximum 11 letters. Confirm the name by pressing Enter.

**VOL, displaying the name of a diskette or harddisk**. The name of a diskette or harddisk is always stated during the implementation of the DIR instruction. You may also request the name separately.

**The VOL instruction requests the name of the specified drive.**

```
VOL d:
```

VOL        Volume (as in 'book').
d:         Drive letter.

*Example:* Format the diskette in drive B:. Copy the system files to this and assign a name to the diskette.

```
C:\> format b: /s/v                                    (1)
Insert new diskette for drive B:                       (2)
and press ENTER when ready...

Checking existing disk format.
Saving UNFORMAT information.
Verifying 1.44M
Format complete.
System transferred                                     (3)

Volume label (11 characters, ENTER for none)? TENNIS_CLUB   (4)

   1,457,664 bytes total disk space                    (5)
     198,656 bytes used by system
   1,259,008 bytes available on disk

       512 bytes in each allocation unit.
     2,459 allocation units available on disk.

Volume Serial Number is 0C29-11DC

Format another (Y/N)?                                  (6)
```

(1) A format command along with the system files copy option (/S) and name allocation (/V).

(2) Statement similar to that in the previous example.

(3) The program states that the system files have been copied.

(4) The prompt for a name of maximum 11 characters for the diskette/harddisk. In the example, the diskette is to be used for the tennis club records. It makes no difference whether you type small or capital letters - MS-DOS always saves the name in capitals. The name may also contain numbers. Confirm the name by pressing Enter. If, after all, you do not wish to assign a name, press only Enter.

(5) The format program registers the capacity occupied by the system files (in bytes).

(6) Dialogue as in the previous example.

*Example:* Displaying details of the formatted diskette

```
C:\> dir b:                              (1)

 Volume in drive B is TENNIS_CLUB        (2)
 Volume Serial Number is 0C29-11DC
 Directory of B:\

COMMAND  COM       54,619 30-09-93    6:20  (3)
        1 file(s)          54,619 bytes
                        1,259,008 bytes free

C:\> vol b:                              (4)

 Volume in drive B is TENNIS_CLUB        (5)
 Volume Serial Number is 0C29-11DC

C:\>
```

(1)  Displays the directory of the specified drive.
(2)  The name of the diskette.
(3)  The list of files only contains COMMAND.COM, which occupies 54,619 bytes. The previous example shows that the system files occupy a total of 198,656 bytes, which means that 198,656 - 54,619 = 144,037 bytes are required for the hidden files.
(4)  Requests the name of B:.
(5)  The name of the diskette and the return to the prompt.

**Copying the system files to a diskette or harddisk later.** If you forgot to copy the system files to a diskette using the /S option during formatting, this can nevertheless still be done by means of the SYS command, but only on condition that nothing has yet been saved on the diskette.

If you apply the SYS command to a used diskette, you will always receive an error message with DOS versions up to 4.0, even if you have deleted all files previously. During deletion, the file names are rendered in-

visible to the directory, but the information remains on
the diskette. The system files IO.SYS and MSDOS.SYS
must be located on the first track of a diskette.

The SYS instruction only copies the IO.SYS and
MSDOS.SYS files. COMMAND.COM and (if necessary) other system programs should be copied using
COPY (see section 4.4). From DOS version 5.0 onwards, you can place all three files on a written diskette.

**The SYS command copies hidden system files to a
blank formatted diskette.**

```
SYS [d1:] d2:
```

SYS        System.
d1:        Diskdrive containing the system files.
d2:        The diskdrive to which the system files are
           to be copied.

**Assigning a name to a diskette or harddisk later.**
From MS-DOS version 3.0 onwards, it is possible to assign a name to a diskette or harddisk later, or to alter an
existing name.

**The LABEL instruction assigns a name to the speci-
fied diskette or harddisk.**

```
LABEL d:
```

LABEL      Name.
d:         Drive letter.

*Example:* Copy the most important system files to an
empty, formatted diskette. The empty diskette is located
in drive B: (see following page).

```
C:\> sys b:                                              (1)
System transferred

C:\> copy command.com b:                                 (2)
Overwrite B:COMMAND.COM (Yes/No/All)?y
        1 file(s) copied

C:\> label b:                                            (3)
Volume in drive B has no label
Volume Serial Number is 8C29-11DC
Volume label (11 characters, ENTER for none)? TENNIS_CLUB  (4)

C:\> dir b:                                              (5)

 Volume in drive B is TENNIS_CLUB                        (6)
 Volume Serial Number is 8C29-11DC
 Directory of B:\

COMMAND  COM        54,619 30-09-93    6:20
        1 file(s)          54,619 bytes
                        1,259,008 bytes free

C:\>
```

(1) Copy the hidden system files from the harddisk to the empty, formatted diskette in B:. The program states that the command has been executed.

(2) Copy COMMAND.COM to the new diskette (see section 4.4). From version 5.0 onwards, the COMMAND.COM file is automatically transferred when the SYS command is given.

(3) Assign a name to the new diskette (if the diskette already has a name, this will be shown as in the case of VOL).

(4) Type the name, see the previous example.

(5) Display the directory of the new diskette.

(6) The data of the new diskette, analogous to the previous example.

*Example:* The most common error messages when using FORMAT (see following page)

(1) Error: Drive not ready
    Remedy: (Place diskette and) close drive.

(2) Error: The diskette to be formatted is write-protected.
    Remedy: Remove tape (5.25 inch) or close sleeve (3.5 inch).

(3) Error: An option has been used which is not valid for the specified drive.

Remedy: Repeat the command with other op-
tion(s).

```
A:\>format a:
Insert new diskette for drive A:
and press ENTER when ready...

Formatting 360K


Not ready                                       (1)
Format terminated.

Write protect error                             (2)

Parameters not compatible                       (3)

Invalid drive specification                     (4)

Invalid media or Track 0 bad - disk unusable    (5)

Invalid characters in volume label              (6)
```

(4)  Error: Wrong drive, formatting not possible.
     Remedy: Specify the proper drive, ensure that the
     parameters are valid for the specified drive. Per-
     haps the drive is defective.
(5)  Error: It is not possible to copy the system files to
     the diskette to be formatted.
     Remedy: Repeat the command. If the error occurs
     again, the system cannot be transferred. Perhaps
     the diskette can be used to store data.
(6)  Error: Invalid characters specified in the file name.
     Remedy: Assign a new file name.

On the diskettes of some applications with copy
protection, the manufacturer has left some space
free for the most important MS-DOS system programs. When you have copied the system files to
these diskettes, you can activate the application
without having to use the separate system diskette.
Consult the User Instructions or the application
manual.

# 4.4 Copying files

The copy command COPY enables you to:

- Copy individual files, groups of files or all files from one diskette to another. The diskettes need not be the same type.
- Copy files from a diskette to a harddisk or vice versa, or from one harddisk to another.
- Copy files from one directory to another on a harddisk (see section 4.12).
- Transport data between two peripheral devices or data from a diskette to a peripheral device or vice versa - for example, from the keyboard to a file on a diskette.
- Gather the dispersed blocks of a fragmented file into a compact file, in order to increase the working speed.
- Create backups of files by saving them once more under a different name.
- Gather odd files into a single file.

The target diskette must be formatted. The target diskette must have sufficient capacity for the files to be copied.

A file may only occur once on a diskette under a certain name (unless you make use of different directories).

*For versions up to and including 6.0:* If you copy a file of a certain name to a diskette containing a file of the same name, the file on the target disk will be overwritten without warning. Essential information may be lost!

If you are not sure, first display the directory on the screen in order to check if a certain name is already in use on the target diskette.

*For version 6.2:* The COPY command asks for confirmation before overwriting a file of the same name. This improvement helps protect your data.

Specify the names of the source file and the target file in
the command. If the copy is to have the same name as
the original, it is not necessary to specify the target file.
The way in which the names are specified influences
the target direction. The ? and * wildcards may be used
in the copy command.

**The COPY command copies files between diskettes, harddisks and other devices.**

```
COPY [d1:][path1]file1.ext [d2:][path2]
                                  [file2.ext]
     [/A] [/B] [/V]
```

d1:  Letter of the source drive.
d2:  Letter of the target drive.

Special options:

/A   (ASCII) - copy files in ASCII format: until the first
     end-of-file character (^Z, Ctrl-Z).
/B   (BINARY) - copy files in binary format: until the real
     end of the file.
/V   (VERIFY) - compare the copy to the source file.

*Example:* Copying individual files with A: as current
drive

```
A:\>copy a:comm1.dat b:comm1.dat          (1)

A:\>copy comm1.dat b:                      (2)

A:\>copy a:comm1.dat b:nota.123            (3)

A:\>copy b:inter.92 a:inter.92             (4)

A:\>copy b:inter.92                        (5)

A:\>copy calculat.a16 price.a16            (6)

A:\>copy statist.186 statist.186           (7)

A:\>copy import.dat b:/v                   (8)
```

(1) The COMM1.DAT file is copied from the source diskette in drive A: to the target diskette in drive B:, under the same name.
Keep in mind the space between the command and the two file names.

(2) As in (1), but written more simply. If you do not specify a source drive, the command automatically applies to the current drive. It is always necessary to specify the target drive if this differs from the current drive. You may omit the second file name if the name of the copy is the same as the name of the original.

(3) The COMM1.DAT file on the diskette in drive A: is to be copied to drive B: under the name NOTA.123

(4) The INTER.93 file on the diskette in drive B: is to be copied to the diskette in drive A: under the same name.

(5) As in (4), but without explicitly naming the target drive because that is the current drive. The name of the copy is superfluous because it is not new.

(6) The command creates a copy of the CALCU-LAT.A16 file under the new name of PRICE.A16 on the same diskette in drive A:. When the process is completed, the diskette will contain two identical files with different names. You can work with one file and retain the other as backup.

(7) This command results in an error message because a file may not occur twice in the same directory under the same name.

(8) A copy is created of the IMPORT.DAT file from the diskette in drive A: on a diskette in drive B:. The /V option ensures that the copy program copies a sector and then compares the copy to the original. This somewhat retards the execution of the command.

*Example:* Copying groups of files

```
A:\>copy a:*.txt b:                        (1)

A:\>copy practice.* b:                      (2)

A:\>copy letter*.* b:                       (3)

A:\>copy copy ???guide.dat b:???value.dat   (4)

A:\>copy b:*.* a:                           (5)

A:\>copy a:*.* b:                           (6)

A:\>copy *.* b:                             (7)

A:\>copy c:\*.com b:                        (8)

B:\>copy *.bas c:*.txt                      (9)
```

With the exception of the last example, A: is the current
drive.

(1)  A copy is made on the diskette in drive B: of all the
     files on the diskette in drive A: which have the ex-
     tension .TXT.
(2)  As in (1), but now all files of the name PRACTICE
     with any extension.
(3)  As in (1), but now all files whose names begin with
     LETTER.
(4)  As in (1), but now for all files whose names begin
     with any three characters and end with GUIDE plus
     the extension .DAT. The copies of these files are
     saved under names with the same three characters
     at the beginning and end with VALUE.XYZ.
(5)  Copies all files on the diskette in drive B: to the dis-
     kette in drive A:.
(6)  As in (5), but now from drive A: to B:.
(7)  As in (6), but written more shortly.
(8)  Copies all files with the extension .COM (programs
     which are executable) from the harddisk to the dis-
     kette in drive B:.
(9)  Copies all files with the extension .BAS (BASIC

programs) from the diskette in drive B: to the harddisk C: and gives them the new extension .TXT
(text file).

*Example:* Merging files

```
A:\>copy a:part1.txt+b:part2.txt c:total.txt  (1)

A:\>copy address.prg+adr.prg                   (2)

A:\>copy *.txt total.tex                       (3)

A:\>copy total.txt+*.txt                       (4)

A:\>copy *.tx1+*.tx2 total.tex                 (5)

A:\>copy value.com/b+calc.com answer.com       (6)
```

(1) Merges PART1.TXT on the diskette in drive A: with
    PART2.TXT on the diskette in drive B: to make the
    TOTAL.TXT file on the harddisk.
    If the /B option is not specified, the contents of the
    files are combined as characters (ASCII format).
    Accordingly, text files and source texts of non-com-
    piled files can be merged in a simple manner.
    The command is implemented if at least one of the
    specified files is present.
(2) The contents of the ADDRESS.PRG and
    ADR.PRG files on the diskette in drive A: are
    merged under the name of the file first mentioned in
    the current drive.
    If you do not specify a target file, the second and all
    subsequent files will be added to the file first men-
    tioned.
(3) Combines all files with the extension .TXT on the
    diskette in drive A: to form one single file under the
    name TOTAL.TEX on the same diskette.

(4)  The TOTAL.TXT file and all other files with the ex-
     tension .TXT are combined in a new version of
     TOTAL.TXT. The difference with examples (3) and
     (4) is that in the former, the combined file has a new
     name, while in the latter, the combined file acquires
     the name of the first original file which is then in fact
     lost. The command attempts to copy TOTAL.TXT
     onto itself, which produces the ('error') message:
     'Content of destination lost before copy'.

(5)  Combines two groups of files into one file.

(6)  The executable two files, VALUE.COM and
     CALC.COM are combined, using the binary option,
     into the file ANSWER.COM. The /B option also ap-
     plies to all subsequent files until other specifica-
     tions are made.

     The /B option ensures that the files are entirely co-
     pied - thus not only up to a random end-of-file char-
     acter (^Z) somewhere in the middle of a file.

*Example:* Copying text from the keyboard directly to a
file. Combining two files and showing the result on the
screen.

```
B:\>copy con part1.txt                                    (1)
This text has come directly from the keyboard.
It is only necessary to to press Enter if a sentence has to begin on a new line.
^Z
        1 file(s) copied

B:\>copy con part2.txt                                    (2)
The PART1.TXT text is concluded using Ctrl+Z or F6. After pressing Enter, the fi
le will be written to the current drive under the specified name.^Z
        1 file(s) copied

B:\>copy part1.txt+part2.txt total.txt                    (3)

PART1.TXT
PART2.TXT
        1 file(s) copied

B:\>type total.txt                                        (4)
This text has come directly from the keyboard.
It is only necessary to to press Enter if a sentence has to begin on a new line.


The PART1.TXT text is concluded using Ctrl+Z or F6. After pressing Enter, the fi
le will be written to the current drive under the specified name.
B:\>
```

(1) In this example, we shall copy characters directly from a device to a file. The CON: (console) device is made up of two components: the keyboard for the input and the screen for the output. A copy procedure using COPY CON is concluded by pressing Ctrl-Z (^Z). The specified text is copied from working memory to a file on disk.

(2) As in (1), but now without new lines, even in the case of ^Z. The entire text is saved as one long line.

(3) The PART1.TXT and PART2.TXT files are saved on the current diskette under the name TOTAL.TXT.

(4) Displays the contents of TOTAL.TXT on the screen. Lines of more than 80 characters continue on the following line.

*Example:* The most common error messages concerning COPY

```
A:\>copy a:binker.txt b:                (1)

Not ready reading drive A
Abort, Retry, Fail?a

A:\>copy a:binker.xtx alpha.txt         (2)
File not found - A:BINKER.XTX
        0 file(s) copied

A:\>copy a:binker.txt b:                (3)
Insufficient disk space
        0 file(s) copied

A:\>copy binker.txt binker.txt          (4)
File cannot be copied onto itself
        0 file(s) copied

A:\>
```

(1) Error: There is no diskette in drive A:, or the drive is not locked.
Remedy: Place diskette in the drive and/or lock the drive.

(2)  Error: The file specified is not on the diskette - per-
      haps this is a typing error.
      Remedy: Display the list of files using DIR to
      search for the proper name.
(3)  Error: There is not sufficient capacity on the dis-
      kette for the specified file.
      Remedy: Use another diskette or delete the files
      you no longer need.
(4)  Error: The command attempts to save a file to a file
      with the same name in the same directory.
      Remedy: Allocate another name to the copy.

# 4.5    Comparing copied files

The COMP instruction (up to and including version 5.0)
enables you to:

■ Compare a copy of a file with the original on the same
   or another diskette or on harddisk.
■ Compare groups of files or all files as in the previous
   point.
■ Display the position of the differing data and display
   the differences themselves.

It is advisable to use the COMP instruction if you wish to
be absolutely sure that the copies of files are identical to
the originals. The DISKCOMP instruction does exactly
the same with copies of complete diskettes which are
made using DISKCOPY (see section 4.2).

The program which activates the COMP instruction
compares the original file to the copy, character by
character (bytes). If deviation is found, the program displays the following information:

■ The position, counted from 0, where the differing
   characters are located in the files (OFFSET).
■ The character in the file first specified and the character in the second file.

The comparison program continues registering differences to a maximum of 10 positions. If there are more differences, the progam gives a message to this effect and interrupts the comparison. It is then not worth the effort of correcting the differences - making a new copy can be done much more quickly.

**The COMP instruction compares files and registers the deviations.**

```
COMP [d1:][path1]file1.ext [d2:][path2]
                                    file2.ext
from version 5.0 onwards also:
[/D] [/A] [/L] [/N=line] [/C]
```

COMP          Compare.
d1:path1      Drive letter and directory of the original file.
d2:           Drive letter and directory of the file to be compared.
file1.ext     The original file.
file2.ext     The file to be compared.
/D            Display the differing characters in decimal code.
/A            Display the differing characters alphanumerically.
/L            Display the number of the line containing the differing characters.
/N=line       Compare the file contents up to the specified line number.
/C            Do not discriminate between capitals and small letters when comparing.

You only need to specify drives and directories when comparing files in different drives or directories. You may use the * and ? wildcards. In this way, you can compare groups of files.

*Example:* Comparison of two files which have been saved on different diskettes. Each diskette is located in its own drive.

```
A:\> comp a:testfle1.txt b:testfle3.txt                    (1)

Insert diskette for drive B: and press any key when ready


Insert diskette for drive A: and press any key when ready

Comparing A:TESTFLE1.TXT and B:TESTFLE3.TXT...            (2)

Insert diskette for drive B: and press any key when ready

Files are different sizes                                 (3)

Compare more files (Y/N) ? y                              (4)
Name of first file to compare: a:testfle1.txt             (5)
Name of second file to compare: a:testfle2.txt

Insert diskette for drive A: and press any key when ready

Option :                                                  (6)
Comparing A:TESTFLE1.TXT and A:TESTFLE2.TXT...
Files compare OK                                          (7)

Compare more files (Y/N) ? n                              (8)
```

(1) Compare TESTFLE1.TXT to TESTFLE3.TXT on the diskettes in the specified drives.
(2) The program states that the files are being compared.
(3) One file is longer than the other - the comparison is discontinued.
(4) The program asks if you wish to compare other files. In the example we have answered Y (Yes).
(5) Specify the new file names: TESTFLE1.TXT and TESTFLE2.TXT.
(6) You can specify options here: /d displays any differences in decimal format; /a displays differences as characters; /l displays the line on which any differences occur; /c performs a comparison which is not case-sensitive; /n=*number* - if the files are of different length, you should specify a number of lines for comparison, otherwise COMP will not begin the comparison. Press Enter to continue.
(7) The files are identical.
(8) As in (4), this time answer N.

*Example:* Compare two files which are located on the harddisk under different names. The only difference lies in the last letters, 'k' and 'l', respectively.

```
C:\>type t1.txt                          (1)
billy binkerhill

C:\>type t2.txt                          (2)
billy binkerhilk

C:\>comp t1.txt t2.txt                   (3)
Comparing T1.TXT and T2.TXT...
Compare error at OFFSET F                (4)
file1 = 6C                               (5)
file2 = 6B                               (6)

Compare more files (Y/N) ? n             (7)

C:\>
```

(1) & (2) Display the contents of the T1.TXT and T2.TXT files.

(3)      The comparison instruction, analogous to the previous example.

(4)      Registration of a difference at hexadecimal position F, which is decimal position 15 (see information below). The program begins counting at zero - the *sixteenth* character differs.

(5)      The deviating character 'l' in the first file has the ASCII code 6C hexadecimal, which is 108 in the decimal system.

(6)      The deviating character 'k' in the second file has the ASCII code 6B hexadecimal, which is 107 decimally.

(7)      Question, analogous to the previous example.

In some MS-DOS versions, COMP is called FILE-COMP or FC. The last two system programs are more extensive than COMP - they are more geared to computer programmers than to consumers.

Hexadecimal numbers are closer to the internal processing of data (computer language) than decimal numbers. Computer programmers can, for instance, represent the contents of the computer memory in the form of hexadecimal numbers.

In the hexadecimal (base 16) numeric system, sixteen different characters 01..89ABCDEF can be placed at each position of a number. The first position represents values from 0 to 15, the second position multiples of 16, the third position multiples of 256 (16x16) etc.

Examples:

| hexadecimal | calculation | decimal |
|---|---|---|
| 12 | 1x16+2x1 | 18 |
| 66 | 6x16+6x1 | 102 |
| A7F | 10x256+7x16+15x1 | 2687 |

The A is the eleventh and F is the sixteenth number in the hexadecimal numeric system (0 is the first number).

# 4.6    Checking the diskette or harddisk

The contents of a diskette may be damaged as a result of various circumstances: careless treatment, wear and tear, the effects of a program etc. We wish to emphasize once again that it is extremely important to make at least one backup of each essential diskette.

If you suspect that a diskette contains errors, or even if you just wish to know how the contents of a diskette are divided, you can allow the diskette to be inspected by an MS-DOS utility program. The CHKDSK (Check Disk) program also contains an option which traces the faults and corrects them to a certain extent. (The information here concerning diskettes also refers to the harddisk.) In version 6.2, CHKDSK has been replaced by an improved version, SCANDISK. Below, we shall first discuss CHKDSK and then SCANDISK.

## CHKDSK

The CHKDSK program can implement the following procedures:

- Check a diskette for errors in the directory and in the FAT (file allocation table).
- Display statements concerning errors on the screen.
- Correct simple errors.
- Display the non-coherent sections of files on the diskette.
- Give a summary of the names and the size of all files (including hidden files) on the diskette.
- Calculate the available capacity on the diskette.
- Calculate the total and the available capacities of the computer memory.

The program does not examine the state of the files on the data section of the diskette (MS-DOS cannot be expected to know what should be there). If it appears that information has been damaged, you can try to restore it by using the RECOVER command (see section 4.7).

The system program checks if the indications in the directory conform to the (fragmented) chains of file clusters in the data section of the diskette. All information which is found during this check is displayed on the screen along with information concerning the computer.

You can determine the intensity of this inspection by using various command options, which have a bearing upon the length of the report. The options deal with:

- The names of some or all files and the directory levels over which these are divided (see section 7.2).
- A list of information concerning incorrect indications in the directory or the FAT with reference to data clusters - for instance, lost clusters which are no longer part of a cluster chain in a file.
- The total storage capacity (bytes) of the diskette and the part of this in use for files and the part still available.

- The total capacity of the computer memory and the part of this still available.
- The amount of clusters on the diskette where (parts of) files are stored.

**The CHKDSK instruction inspects a diskette or harddisk for errors and corrects these if possible. The program produces a report which includes a list of all files and information concerning the total and available computer capacity.**

```
CHKDSK [d:][path][file name] [/F] [/V]
```

CHKDSK      Check disk.
d:path      Drive letter and directory of the dis-
            kette/harddisk to be inspected.
file name   Name of one or more files to be inspected
            for fragmentation.
/F          (FIX) Automatic correction of errors, as
            much as possible.
/V          (VERIFY) Displays the name of each file
            and directory checked.

*Example:* Check the diskette in drive B: and then display the directory

```
C:\> chkdsk b:                                          (1)

Volume TENNIS_CLUB created 19-11-1993 11:12             (2)
Volume Serial Number is 0C29-11DC

    1,457,664 bytes total disk space                    (3)
      143,872 bytes in 3 hidden files
       54,784 bytes in 1 user files
    1,259,008 bytes available on disk

          512 bytes in each allocation unit
        2,847 total allocation units on disk
        2,459 available allocation units on disk

      655,360 total bytes memory                        (4)
      559,280 bytes free

C:\> dir b:                                             (5)

 Volume in drive B is TENNIS_CLUB
 Volume Serial Number is 0C29-11DC
 Directory of B:\

COMMAND  COM      54,619 30-09-93   6:20
```

(1) The checking program is activated.

(2) The report displays information concerning the dis- kette: the name (if any), the date and time of for- matting.

(3) The report contains further information concerning the division of the storage capacity. The three hidden files are: IO.SYS (IBMBIO.COM) and MSDOS.SYS (IBMDOS.COM) and the file containing the data con- cerning the diskette (only the name consisting of a maximum of eleven characters, contents 0 bytes). In our case, these files occupy 143,872 characters (bytes). The user file occupies 54,784 bytes. These data do not seem to correspond to the data produced by the DIR command: one file and the different num- ber of bytes in use.

The differences can be explained as follows:

■ The COMMAND.COM system program counts as a user file because it is accessible to modifi- cation. Some people replace it by another pro- gram.

■ The DIR command produces the real size of the file.

■ The CHKDSK command registers the capacity occupied by a file on the diskette. This is always expressed in blocks of 1024 bytes (1 Kb). There may not be data from different files in one block.

(4) The working memory capacity is 655,360 bytes (640 Kb). 559,200 bytes of this is still available.

(5) Display the directory list of the diskette. Note that the available capacity conforms to that indicated by the CHKDSK command. Thus this value is not equal to the capacity of the diskette minus the size of the files.

*Example:* Check the harddisk C:, without automatic cor- rection of faults (see following page)

(1) The command activates the check program from the harddisk: if no letter is specified, the command refers to C: (the harddisk).

(2) The program states that errors have been de- tected, but these will not be written to the disk,

since you have not specified the /F option (see the example below).

```
C:\>chkdsk                                        (1)
Volume Serial Number is 184A-546C
Errors found, F parameter not specified           (2)
Corrections will not be written to disk


    1 lost allocation units found in 1 chains.    (3)
       2048 bytes disk space would be freed

  33,449,984 bytes total disk space               (4)
     129,024 bytes in 4 hidden files
      92,160 bytes in 29 directories
  24,872,960 bytes in 1082 user files
   8,353,792 bytes available on disk

       2,048 bytes in each allocation unit
      16,333 total allocation units on disk
       4,079 available allocation units on disk

     655,360 total bytes memory                   (5)
     487,200 bytes free

C:\>
```

(3)  The program registers that there is information on the disk which does not belong to any file. It then asks whether these data should be converted to files. If you reply N, the program will register the capacity which then becomes available. If you respond Y, each cluster will be converted into a separate file and the program will register the number of files created, along with their sizes.

(4)  The statements are analogous to those in the previous example, only now there are more hidden files. That may be a result of the fact that the system files are located in different directories at several places on the harddisk or that an application has created hidden files.

The remaining storage capacity of the harddisk is a little more than 8 Mb (1 Mb = 1024 Kb = 1024*1024 bytes = 1,048,576 bytes.

(5)  The computer memory, analogous to the previous example.

*Example:* Check the harddisk, just as in the previous example, but now using the automatic correction function.

```
C:\>chkdsk /f                                    (1)
Volume Serial Number is 184A-546C

   1 lost allocation units found in 1 chains.    (2)
Convert lost chains to files (Y/N)?y

  33,449,984 bytes total disk space
     129,024 bytes in 4 hidden files
      92,160 bytes in 29 directories
  24,872,960 bytes in 1082 user files
       2,048 bytes in 1 recovered files          (3)
   8,353,792 bytes available on disk

     655,360 total bytes memory
     487,200 bytes free

C:\>dir file*.*                                  (4)

 Volume in drive C has no label
 Volume Serial Number is 184A-546C
 Directory of C:\

FILE0000 CHK      2,048 11/11/93   11:24          (5)
        1 file(s)      2,048 bytes
                    8353792 bytes free
```

(1) The /F option makes corrections and saves these as files on the harddisk.

(2) The program asks if the lost clusters should be saved as files on the disk.

(3) Until now, the statements are identical to those in the previous example. The program now registers the number of bytes taken up by (temporary) files.

(4) The files created for the lost clusters which have been discovered receive the name FILExxxx.CHK automatically. In this, xxxx represents an increasing number, beginning at 0000. In the example, the harddisk contains only one lost cluster - thus, the program creates only one file (FILE0000.CHK). This command also produces a list of files with the recalled clusters.

(5) If you wish to know what these files contain, display them using the TYPE command. You can give a functional name to important information by using the REN(AME) option. Unimportant files can be deleted using DEL.

*Example:* Examine the diskette in drive A:, give a list of all files which have been examined and check if the files are stored in a contiguous (unified) manner on the diskette.

```
C:\>CHKDSK a:*.*/U                              (1)

Volume TENNIS_CLUB created 19-11-1993 11:12
Volume Serial Number is 0C29-11DC
Directory A:\                                   (2)
A:\IO.SYS                                       (3)
A:\MSDOS.SYS
A:\COMMAND.COM
A:\DBLSPACE.BIN
A:\SYS.COM
A:\TESTDAT1.TXT
A:\TESTDAT2.TXT

   1,457,664 bytes total disk space
     143,872 bytes in 3 hidden files            (4)
      65,536 bytes in 4 user files
   1,248,256 bytes available on disk

     655,360 total bytes memory
     559,200 bytes free

A:\TESTDAT1.TXT                                 (5)
   contains 2 non-contiguous blocks
A:\TESTDAT2.TXT
   contains 2 non-contiguous blocks
```

(1) Activates the program from the harddisk. The *.* file pattern ensures that the program checks all files. The /V option results in the program registering all files which have been checked, including the directories in which they are located.

(2) The program begins in the root directory. The standard name for this directory is \ (backslash). This character is placed in front of all files which have been checked.
    In the example, the contents of the diskette are not divided into (sub)directories: there are no other prefixes (paths) with the files.

(3) The CHKDSK instruction also checks the hidden files. Among other things, the diskette includes the system files IO.SYS and MSDOS.SYS.

(4) From the fact that the program finds three hidden files, we can conclude that the diskette has a name.

(5) This statement indicates that the data blocks of the TESTDAT1.TXT and TESTDAT2.TXT files are not contiguous on the diskette. These files have prob-

ably been saved again after modification. The greater the extent of fragmentation of a file, the more time-consuming all subsequent processes will be. If necessary, use COPY to make a copy of the file on another diskette or on the same diskette under a different name. This command reads an existing file block by block and writes them contiguously to the target file.

If the specified files are all coherent, the program states 'All specified file(s) are contiguous'.

For those who have MS-DOS version 6.0 or 6.20, there is the utility program *DeFrag* for regrouping files on the harddisk. This leads to more efficient usage of disk capacity and reduces waiting time. See section 13.4 for more information about this.

## SCANDISK

The SCANDISK program in MS-DOS version 6.2 is the successor to CHKDSK. It is able to trace and rectify more errors and causes of problems. It is menu-driven, making it more user-oriented.

SCANDISK is able to execute the following tasks:

- It can trace file fragmentation, which can subsequently be rectified using the DEFRAG program (see section 13.4).
- It can trace and rectify errors in the FAT (File Allocation Table).
- Faults in the disk structure, such as lost or crosslinked clusters can be tracked down and rectified.
- Errors in the directory structure can be traced and rectified.
- Damaged clusters can be located and file data can be moved to healthy clusters if possible.
- Faults in the boot sector can be traced and rectified.
- Faults in the structure of DBLSPACE disks can be traced and rectified (see section 13.5).

**The command SCANDISK examines a diskette or harddisk for faults and rectifies these if possible. The program produces a report which can be stored in a file if required.**

```
SCANDISK [drive: [drive: ...] | /ALL]
[/AUTOFIX] [/CHECKONLY] [/CUSTOM]
[/SURFACE] [/MONO]
SCANDISK /UNDO drive:
SCANDISK /FRAGMENT [d:][path]file_name
```

SCANDISK        Examine the disk.

drive           This is the drive containing the disk to be examined. If you do not specify anything here, SCANDISK will examine the current drive. You may also specify several drives in succession.

/ALL            SCANDISK examines all available drives.

/AUTOFIX        If you specify this option, SCANDISK will rectify any faults automatically. The program normally requests confirmation.

/CHECKONLY      If you specify this option, faults and problems are indicated but not rectified.

/CUSTOM         SCANDISK uses the default settings from the SCANDISK.INI file.

/SURFACE        SCANDISK also performs an automatic test of the disk surface. If you do not specify this option, SCANDISK will ask whether or not you wish to have this test done.

/MONO           SCANDISK uses a monochrome colour screen, even if a colour card is available.

/UNDO           SCANDISK undoes the last alterations on the specified drive.

/FRAGMENT       SCANDISK examines one or more files for fragmentation. File specification must be given behind /FRAGMENT.

| | |
|---|---|
| d:path | The drive and, if required, the directory containing the files to be examined. |
| file_name | The name of one or more files to be examined for fragmentation. |

You may shorten all of the options as long as the abbreviation is unique. For instance, you can shorten /FRAGMENT to /F.

*Example:* Check the harddisk

Start SCANDISK using the command:

```
scandisk
```

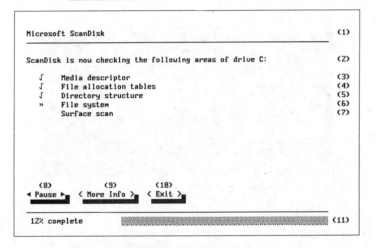

(1) The program copyright message.
(2) The message that SCANDISK is checking the harddisk C:.
(3), (4), (5)
    The mediacode, the FATs and the directory structure have been checked and have been found to be in order.
(6) SCANDISK is now checking the file system.

(7)  Lastly, a surface test will be carried out if required.
(8)  You can interrupt the disk check by pressing the Pause key.
(9)  By pressing the More Info button, you can obtain more extensive information about the item which is currently being checked by SCANDISK.
(10) SCANDISK is terminated by activating the Exit button.
(11) The progression bar at the bottom of the screen indicates the current control situation.

*Example:* Rectifying a fault

Imagine that the following screen appears during the check:

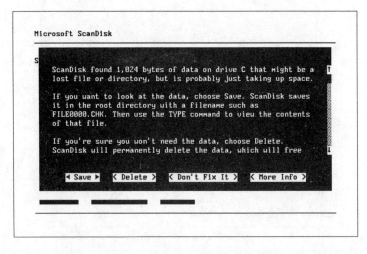

The Problem Found window provides a description of the nature of the fault. In this case, this concerns lost clusters.

(1)  By activating Save, you can can store the contents of the clusters in a file in the root directory of the disk under the name FILExxxx.CHK, where xxxx represents a number consisting of four digits (this is the same system as used by CHKDSK).

(2) If you activate the Delete button, you will make the clusters available for use once more. You should only do this if you are sure that you have not lost any files or directories recently.

(3) If you activate the Don't Fix It button, everything will remain just as it was. The problem is not solved, but SCANDISK continues with further checks. At completion, SCANDISK will state 'There are still errors on drive C'.

(4) If you activate More Info, you will receive more technical information concerning the fault.

At the end of the session, you can examine the check report by selecting View Log. This provides a description of the error:

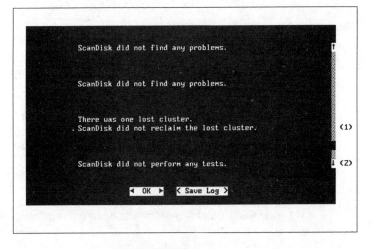

(1) Reference to lost clusters. The user chose the Don't Fix It option.

(2) No surface check has been carried out.

(3) Confirm that you have read the report by pressing OK. You do not need to save the report.

(4) If you do select Save Log, the report is stored in the disk root directory under the name SCANDISK.LOG.

*Example:* Check whether the files in the current directory are contiguous on the disk

```
C:\>scandisk /f *.*                                    (1)
C:\IO.SYS contains 2 non-contiguous blocks             (2)
C:\COMMAND.COM contains 2 non-contiguous blocks

C:\>cd dos                                             (3)

C:\DOS>scandisk /f *.*                                 (4)
All specified file(s) are contiguous.                  (5)

C:\DOS>
```

(1) The command to check if there is file fragmentation
    in the root directory of C:. The /FRAGMENT option
    is abbreviated to /F.
(2) SCANDISK states that two files contain non-con-
    tiguous blocks. You can rectify this fragmentation
    by applying the DEFRAG program (see section
    13.4).
(3) Switch to the C:\DOS directory to check for frag-
    mentation there.
(4) The SCANDISK command to check this directory.
(5) SCANDISK states that there is no fragmentation in
    this directory.

*Example:* Checking a DBLSPACEd disk

If you wish to check a disk which has been compressed
using DBLSPACE (see section 13.5), SCANDISK will
ask you to check the host drive first.

If you have implemented this check on a previous occasion, you can now select No. If this is the first time you
are checking a DBLSPACEd drive, it is advisable to

check the host drive. You should also have a surface
scan executed when SCANDISK asks, even if this is
rather time-consuming.

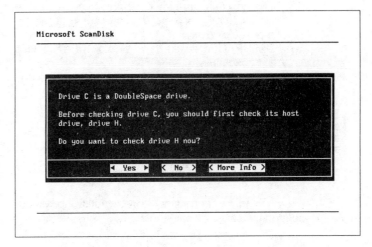

If no problems have been found on the host drive, you
can begin checking the DBLSPACEd drive.

The check takes place in the following stages:

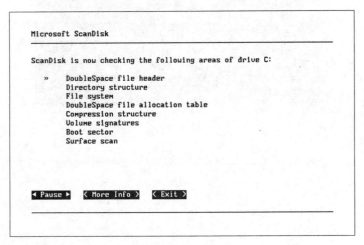

(1)    The check begins with the DBLSPACE initial record. Without this, no access to the DBLSPACE drive can be gained.

(2,3)  The next items are the directory structure and the file system. These are also present in non-compressed drives.

(4)    DBLSPACEd drives have their own FAT. These are checked next.

(5)    The compression structure of the compressed drive is tested.

(6)    Then comes the volume code.

(7)    The boot sector.

(8)    The surface scan is performed as the last test. This only takes place if the user requests it.

(9-11)  The Pause, More Info and Exit buttons, just as with the normal SCANDISK check.

If everything has gone smoothly, the following will appear on the screen:

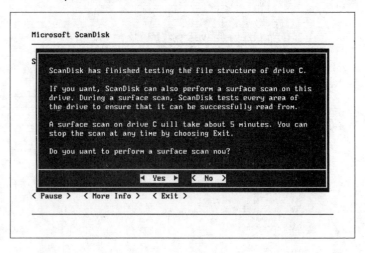

```
Microsoft ScanDisk
_____

ScanDisk did not find any problems on drive C.




◄ View Log ►   ❮ Exit ❯
_____
```

## 4.7 Correcting defective files (up to MS-DOS 5.0)

Imagine that the computer is loading a program from a diskette or that is is reading a data file. The following message is shown:

```
Data error reading drive A:
Abort, Retry, Fail?
```

Perhaps the reading problem will be solved if you press R (Retry). If the same message reappears, press A (Abort). This means that the current program will be discontinued. Start up the program again and see if reading is now possible.

In this section we shall discuss what you can do if the error message concerning the reading problem persists.

Reading errors occur due to, among other things, information being incorrectly stored in the directory or in the data section of a disk, or due to damage to the data. If

the FAT (file allocation table) on the diskette is still intact, it is usually possible to reconstruct the directions
between the file blocks. The success of the recovery
program depends on the extent of the damage.

**Prevent problems, make frequent backups!**

The MS-DOS RECOVER utility program (up to version
5.0) deals with errors on a diskette or harddisk in the following way:

- Traces damaged sectors of a file and marks them.
- Makes undamaged sectors accessible and combines
  them into a usable file.
- Reconstructs a damaged directory and, accordingly,
  makes all files legible again.

The RECOVER program reads a file, sector by sector.
Damaged sectors are marked and set aside (outside
the sector chain of the file). At the end of the operation,
the reconstructed file will probably have a different
layout than the original file - not only have some sectors
been cut away, the file will be stored in complete clusters of 1024 bytes again. The result may be that, at the
end of the file, some unidentifiable characters, which did
not appear in the original file, remain over. If the file contains text, you can then, using a word-processor, insert
the lost passages, and delete the nonsense at the end.

It is almost always possible to make a disk legible again
when the directory has been damaged. The pre-condi-
tion of this is that the *file allocation table* is still in order.
The RECOVER correction program scrutinizes this
table and assigns new names to all file registrations.
These default file names have the FILExxxx.REC pattern. In this, xxxx represents an increasing number, beginning at 0001. Lost clusters which remain over after
applying RECOVER can be made accessible using the
CHKDSK command (see section 4.6).

**The RECOVER instruction (up to and including version 5.0) reconstructs a file or makes all files on a diskette accessible again.**

```
RECOVER [d:][path]file_name
RECOVER d:
```

RECOVER          Recover, reconstruct
d:path           Letter of the drive and the directory
                 containing the illegible files
file name        A specific file with an error

In the first version of the command, the program reconstructs only one (specified) file. The * and ? wildcards are allowed, but they have no effect. Only one file is dealt with.

The second syntax applies to a diskette in which all files have become inaccessible, owing to a damaged directory.

For most users, it is advisable to apply the first version of RECOVER only to files in ASCII format. In the case of programs which have been compiled in computer language (with the extensions EXE and COM), there is a greater chance of irreversible damage since indispensible components of the program have disappeared.

Use the second syntax only if all other attempts to make the diskette legible again have failed (COPY to another disk and CHKDSK).

If the directory of a harddisk is damaged, it is generally no longer possible to copy files. If you have backups of all files, the quickest method is to format the harddisk once more, create the directory structure again and copy the programs back again.

When the RECOVER program has been used, all files and directories have new names. Delete what you no longer need, allocate the original names to the files and correct the contents of the files.

**Reconstructing one file**

(1) Make a copy of the file or of the whole diskette on another diskette.
(2) Activate the RECOVER program (see the previous two examples).
(3) Display the contents of the reconstructed file using TYPE.
(4) In the case of a text file or of another ASCII file, replace the missing parts and delete the superfluous characters.
(5) If the reconstructed file is located on a diskette, copy all files to another diskette. Try to make the old diskette serviceable again by using the FORMAT instruction. Discard the diskette if the command states that the diskette contains defective sectors.

**Making a diskette or harddisk accessible when the directory has been damaged.**

(1) See if it is possible to display the directory using DIR. If this works, you can copy the files to another diskette using the COPY command. In order to copy an entire diskette, you can use the DISK-COPY command.
(2) If the errors are located in one directory of the root directory, the files in the other directories will still be usable. First try CHKDSK on the directory containing the errors.
(3) Activate the RECOVER program (see the second example following). If the error is located in the directory of the harddisk, you cannot load RECOVER from the harddisk - use the system diskette.
(4) Use CHKDSK to make lost blocks on the diskette accessible.

(5) Examine the new files using TYPE and check the contents.

(6) Using COPY, copy the usable files under functional names to another diskette.

(7) Format the harddisk when you have gathered all the files safely. The FORMAT command prevents the damaged sectors from being written upon. It is advisable to discard defective diskettes.

(8) Restore text files using an editor (word-processor) and copy them back to the harddisk, if required.

*Example:* Reconstruct the MSDOS04.TXT file on the diskette in drive A:.

```
C:\> recover a:msdos04.txt                      (1)

Press any key to begin recovery of the         (2)
file(s) on drive A:

10.360 0f 10.360 bytes recovered               (3)

C:\> dir a:                                     (4)

 Volume in drive A is TENNIS_CLUB
 Volume Serial Number is 0C29-11DC
 Directory of A:\

COMMAND  COM      54,619 30-09-93    6:20
SYS      COM       9,432 30-09-93    6:20
TESTDAT1 TXT          42 19-11-93   14:15
TESTDAT2 TXT          81 19-11-93   14:15
MSDOS04  TXT      10,360 16-10-92   11:50       (5)
        5 file(s)         74,534 bytes
                       1,237,504 bytes free

C:\>
```

(1) Load the RECOVER program from the harddisk and specify that the file is located on the diskette in drive A:.

(2) The program pauses to allow you the chance to load the diskette containing the damaged file - it will proceed when you press a random key.

(3) This statement means that the file has been reconstructed successfully.

(4) Display the directory of the diskette in drive A:.

(5) The file name is unchanged and the length of the file is unaltered since there are no defective sectors.

*Example*: Reconstruct all files on the diskette in drive A:.

```
C:\> recover a:                                 (1)

Press any key to begin recovery of the         (2)
file(s) on drive A:

6 file(s) recovered                             (3)

C:\> dir a:                                     (4)

 Volume in drive A has no label
 Volume Serial Number is 0C29-11DC
 Directory of A:\

FILE0001 REC        40,960 22-11-93    10:30    (5)
FILE0002 REC        38,400 22-11-93    10:30
FILE0003 REC        64,512 22-11-93    10:30
FILE0004 REC        10,752 22-11-93    10:30
FILE0005 REC        54,784 22-11-93    10:30
FILE0006 REC         9,728 22-11-93    10:30
        6 file(s)        219,136 bytes
                       1,238,528 bytes free

C:\>
```

(1) Activate the program from the harddisk. Do not specify any files because the instruction is aimed at making the entire diskette in the specified drive accessible again.
(2) The same prompt as in the previous example.
(3) The program registers the number of files it has reconstructed.
(4) Display the directory to view the names of the new files.
(5) The date and time of the command to reconstruct the files is shown adjacent to the files. The files can now be processed as described above.

The root directory of a disk cannot contain an unlimited amount of files. Due to the fact that all reconstructed files are placed in the root directory, this may become overfull. The RECOVER program is then discontinued and displays the message:

```
WARNING - directory full
```

Create space in the directory by using COPY to copy to another diskette those files which have already been reconstructed and files which are still intact. Then delete them from the damaged diskette using DEL. Start up the RECOVER program once more.

The recovered versions of files from branch directories are all saved in the root directory. The names of the directories are treated in the same way as files: the directories are also stored under the FILExxxx.REC name.

When you have recovered some or all of the files on a diskette, it is advisable not to use this diskette again. If the errors are a consequence of mechanical damage to the magnetic layer, reading errors can always recur. In the case of a harddisk, the defective sectors are rendered harmless by the FORMAT command, which blocks these sectors.

The RECOVER command will not help in the case of badly damaged files or diskettes. If the files are indispensable, you can try to recover them using one of the special utility programs which are available in computer shops - for instance, PC Tools or Norton Utilities.

In the case of MS-DOS 5.0, a RECOVER process can be undone in certain circumstances (see chapter 12).

# 4.8 Changing the name of a file

All kinds of circumstances occur which make it advisable to alter the name of a file:

- the contents of the file have been altered
- a new application of an unchanged file
- changing a default name, such as FILExxxx given by CHKDSK or RECOVER, to a functional name.

We already know that it is possible to save a file under a
new name on the same or on another diskette when
using COPY. But if you use this method for a large
amount of files, the original files still occupy disk capacity, and this makes the whole process rather inefficient if
the diskette is too full to accommodate a copy of the file.
This entails copying to another diskette, deleting the
original file and copying the file back to the first diskette
under a new name. If there is enough room on the diskette, an extra diskette will, of course, not be required,
but the renaming process still requires two stages. In
addition, the COPY command rewrites the file completely on the diskette and this is quite time-consuming.

MS-DOS has a special command which enables you to
change the name of a file or a group of files directly.

**The RENAME command changes the name of a file.**

```
RENAME [d:][path]oldfile.ext newfile.ext
[REN]
```

RENAME         Rename.
REN            Abbreviated version of the com-
               mand.
d:path         Drive and directory containing file to
               be renamed.
oldfile.ext    Old file name with extension.
newfile.ext    New file name with (new) exten-
               sion.

The REN instruction does not make a copy - a drive letter in front of the new file name results in an error message and the command will not be implemented. Even if
the original file is not located in the specified drive, the
program will give an error message.

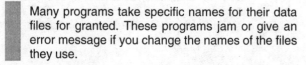

Many programs take specific names for their data
files for granted. These programs jam or give an
error message if you change the names of the files
they use.

*Example:* Changing the name of the TESTFILE.TXT in
drive A: to WORKFLE1.TXT

```
A:\> dir                                              (1)

...
TESTFLE1 TXT              10 19-11-93   12:01
TESTFLE3 TXT              11 19-11-93   11:46
TESTFLE2 TXT              10 19-11-93   12:01
...

A:\> rename a:testfle1.txt a:workfle1.txt             (2)
Invalid parameter

A:\> rename a:testfle1.txt workfle1.txt               (3)

A:\> dir                                              (4)

...
WORKFLE1 TXT             10 19-11-93   12:01
TESTFLE3 TXT             11 19-11-93   11:46
TESTFLE2 TXT             10 19-11-93   12:01
...

A:\>
```

(1)  Displays the directory of the diskette in drive A:.
(2)  The command to change the name to A:WORK-
     FLE1.TXT is invalid due to the drive specification.
     The program gives an error message.
(3)  The correct way of writing the command. Because
     A: is the current drive, it is not necessary to specify
     this in front of the original file name.
(4)  The new list of files shows that the name change
     has taken place correctly.

*Example:* An attempt to rename a non-existent file, and
renaming groups of files (see following page)

(1)  The T1.TXT file is not located on the current dis-
     kette - the program gives an error message (....not
     found). The program also gives an error message if
     the new name already exists on the current disk
     (...duplicate file).
(2)  The list of files on the diskette we are using in this
     example.
(3)  All files retain their names - only those files with the
     extension .TXT have their extension altered to
     .DAT.

```
A:\>rename t1.txt values.123                    (1)
Duplicate file name or file not found

DATA      TXT        56 19/11/93    13:55       (2)
T2        TXT        11 19/11/93    14:02
          2 file(s)          67 bytes
                        360.448 bytes free

A:\>rename *.txt *.dat                          (3)

DATA      DAT        56 19/11/93    13:55       (4)
T2        DAT        11 19/11/93    14:02
          2 file(s)          67 bytes
                        360.448 bytes free

A:\>rename *.* *.txt                            (5)

DATA      TXT        56 19/11/93    13:55       (6)
T2        TXT        11 19/11/93    14:02
          2 file(s)          67 bytes
                        360.448 bytes free
```

(4)  The alteration of the extensions has taken place correctly.

(5)  The names of the files remain unchanged, but all extensions are altered to .TXT.

(6)  The file list after the extension changes.

# 4.9    Deleting a file

To save room on the disk, it is better to delete files which are no longer in use and files which are full of nonsense. Even if you are not planning to replace these with new files, a short file list has the advantage of being easy to refer to.

The instruction which we shall deal with in this section can be used to delete both individual files and groups of files and also all files in one go. The instruction is not valid for hidden system files.

Consider carefully before you delete one or more files. Up until version 4.01 of MS-DOS, it is not possible to recover deleted files. The deletion program makes the file name untraceable by changing the first character of the name.

From MS-DOS 5.0 onwards, you can undo the
deletion under certain conditions.

MS-DOS contains two instructions to delete files; both
have the same effect.

**The DEL and ERASE instructions remove one or
more files.**

```
DEL [d:][path]file.ext
ERASE [d:][path]file.ext
```

DEL       Delete.
ERASE     Erase.
d:path    Drive and directory containing the file to be
          deleted.
file.ext  Name of the file to be deleted.

The ? and * wildcards may be used in file names in
deletion commands.

Due to the fact that wildcards generally make a command valid for various files, there is a reasonable
chance that a delete command containing wildcards
will delete files which should be retained. Accordingly, when applying the delete command, check
whether you really wish to delete the specified files.

The most drastic delete command is DEL *.*. MS-
DOS will automatically respond with the question
as to whether you are really sure. Reconsider before confirming.

The delete commands cannot delete a (sub)direc-
tory from the directory structure. To do this, the
RMDIR instruction is necessary (see section 4.14).

From MS-DOS version 3.0 onwards, you can write-
protect a file using the ATTRIB instruction. This
concerns the Read Only attribute. Files with this attribute cannot be overwritten or deleted.

*Example:* Delete the LETTER0.TXT file on the diskette
in drive A:.

```
A:\>dir                                    (1)

 Volume in drive A has no label
 Volume Serial Number is 1348-17E2
 Directory of A:\

LETTER0   TXT     2,048 16/09/93   14:07
LETTER1   TXT     2,064 16/09/93   14:07
LETTER2   TXT       932 16/09/93   14:07
        3 file(s)        5,044 bytes
                       356,352 bytes free

A:\>del letter0.txt                        (2)

A:\>dir                                    (3)

 Volume in drive A has no label
 Volume Serial Number is 1348-17E2
 Directory of A:\

LETTER1   TXT     2,064 16/09/93   14:07    (4)
LETTER2   TXT       932 16/09/93   14:07
        2 file(s)        2,996 bytes
                       358,400 bytes free
A:\>
```

(1)  The list of files on the diskette in drive A:.
(2)  In this case, the drive does not have to be specified
     in the command because drive A: is the current
     drive. If the file has an extension, it may not be
     omitted from the command (use the * wildcard if
     necessary).
(3)  The list of files on the diskette in drive A: again.
(4)  The LETTER0.TXT is deleted. The 2048 bytes oc-
     cupied by the file are available for use again - the
     number of bytes available on the diskette has risen
     from 356,352 to 358,400.

*Example:* Delete all files with the .SCR extension from
the harddisk C: (see following page)

(1)  Drive A: is the current drive. The command dis-
     plays the list of all files on the harddisk C: which
     have the .SCR extension.
(2)  The drive letter of the harddisk must be specified
     because A: is the current drive.
(3)  Inspect the result of the delete command.

```
A:\>dir c:*.scr                        (1)

  Volume in drive C has no label
  Volume Serial Number is 184A-546C
  Directory of C:\

BILLY    SCR          8 16/09/93   14:13
BINKER   SCR          6 16/09/93   14:13
HILL     SCR         30 16/09/93   14:13
        3 file(s)           44 bytes
                  8,347,648 bytes free

A:\>del c:*.scr                        (2)

A:\>dir c:*.scr                        (3)

  Volume in drive C has no label
  Volume Serial Number is 184A-546C
  Directory of C:\

File not found                         (4)

A:\>
```

(4) The program registers that there is no (further) file
conforming to the specified file pattern.

*Example:* Delete all files on the diskette in drive A:

```
A:\> dir                               (1)
  Volume in drive A has no label
  Volume Serial Number is 0C29-11DC
  Directory of A:\

LETTER1  TXT      9,728 22-11-93   10:30
LETTER2  TXT        512 22-11-93   10:30
LETTER3  TXT        512 22-11-93   10:30
        3 file(s)       10,752 bytes
                  1,446,912 bytes free

A:\> erase *.*                         (2)
All files in directory will be deleted!
Are you sure (Y/N)?n                   (3)
A:\> del *.*                           (4)
All files in directory will be deleted!
Are you sure (Y/N)?y

A:\> dir                               (5)
  Volume in drive A has no label
  Volume Serial Number is 0C29-11DC
  Directory of A:\

File not found                         (6)
```

(1) The instruction displays the list of all files on the
diskette in drive A:.

(2) For a change, we shall use the ERASE command.

The *.* file pattern represents all files except the hidden system files which are write-protected.

(3) Only affirm if you are certain that all files should be deleted. Answering N results in the program being discontinued and the system returning to the prompt A:\>.

(4) Repeat the command using DEL this time. The answer Y results in the specified files being deleted. When the command has been executed, the program returns to the system prompt.

(5) Checking the list of files once more.

(6) Because all files have been deleted, no file can be found.

# 4.10   Moving files and changing directory names

Up to and including version 5.0 of MS-DOS, it was not possible to directly move files from directory to directory or to change directory names. They first had to be copied to the new directory using the COPY or XCOPY command and then the old file name had to be deleted using the DEL command. The directory name was also rather laborious: first a new directory had to be created, the files from the old directory were then transferred and then the old directory was deleted using RD.

The MOVE command in MS-DOS 6.0 and 6.2 provides the following possibilities:

■ Individual files, groups of files or all files can be moved from one directory to another directory or drive.

■ The names of the directories can be altered.

*Caution:* When using this command, it is possible to overwrite files of the same name in the target directory. In MS-DOS versions up to and including 6.0, the command will overwrite files or a directory of the same name without warning. In version 6.2 an extra safeguard against unintentional overwriting has been incorporated. You will be asked for confirmation.

**Using the MOVE command, it is possible to directly move files to another directory and to change directory names.**

```
MOVE [d1:][source_directory]file1
                              [,file2,...]
     [d2:][target_directory][file]
MOVE [d:]old_directory_name
                    new_directory_name
```

| | |
|---|---|
| d1:source directory | Specify, if necessary, the drive and directory of the file to be moved. |
| file1 | The name of the file to be moved. |
| file2 | It is possible to specify several files at once, separated by a comma. |
| d2:target directory | The drive and directory in which the file is to be located. |
| file | The name of one file to be moved can also be immediately altered. |
| d:old directory name | The name of the directory you wish to alter, supplemented by the drive and complete path if that is not active. |
| new directory name | New directory name. |

*Example:* The T1.TXT file is to be moved from the root directory on the diskette in drive A: to the TEXT\LETTERS subdirectory. Then the name of the TABLES directory is to be altered to PLANDAT (see following page).

```
A:\dir

TABLES   <DIR>       05-07-93  17:18               (1)
TEXT     <DIR>       05-07-93  17:18
T1   TXT        111  05-07-93  17:19
T2   TXT        356  05-07-93  17:19

A:\>move t1.txt \text\letters                      (2)
a:\t1.txt => a:\text\letters\t1.txt   [ok]

A:\>dir                                             (3)

TABLES   <DIR>       05-07-93  17:18
TEXT     <DIR>       05-07-93  17:18
T2   TXT        356  05_07_93  17:19

A:\>cd \text\letters                               (4)

A:\TEXT\LETTERS>dir

 Volume in drive A has no label
 Directory of A:\TEXT\LETTERS

.        <DIR>       05_07_93  17:20
..       <DIR>       05-07-93  17:20
T1   TXT        111  05-07-93   17:19
     3 file(s)       111 bytes
               1025024 bytes free

A:\TEXT\LETTERS>cd\                                 (5)

A:\>move tables plandat                            (6)
a:\tables => a:\plandat  [ok]

A:\>dir                                             (7)

PLANDAT  <DIR>       05-07-93  17:18
TEXT     <DIR>       05-07-93  17:18
T2   TXT        356  05-07-93  17:19
     4 file(s)       55163 bytes
               1025024 bytes free
```

(1) The directory list of the diskette in drive A:. Information which does not directly refer to the present topic will not be shown here.

(2) In the command, the name of the file to be moved, T1.TXT, and the full name of the target directory, \TEXT\LETTERS are given. MS-DOS states that the relocation has been properly carried out.

(3) True enough: the file no longer exists in the directory list.

(4) The LETTERS subdirectory is activated, followed by a directory list. The file has been correctly relocated.

(5) The root directory is activated once more.

(6) This command changes the name of the TABLES directory to PLANDAT. Since this directory is a subdirectory of the root directory, no path need be specified. The program indicates that the name change has been carried out properly.

(7) The new name is shown in the directory list.

# 4.11 Creating directories

The significance of directories in the organization of disks was dealt with in section 3.1. In order to be able to work efficiently with programs and data, a number of directories need to be created first.

**The MKDIR (or MD) command creates a subdirectory of the current directory or of the root directory if you specify the full path, beginning with the \ root backslash.**

```
MKDIR [d:][\]directory[\directory...]
MD [d:][\]directory[\directory...]
```

MKDIR     Make directory.
MD        Abbreviated version of MKDIR.
d:        The drive where the directory is to be created.
\         (Backslash) The beginning of the path to

the new directory: without \ at the beginning,
the command applies from the current directory.

directory    The name of a directory (analogous to a file
name); each subsequent name (preceded
by \) refers to a lower level.

*Example:* Creating directories on the harddisk C:, as in
the scheme shown in section 3.1.

```
C:\> mkdir \basic                    (1)

C:\> md pascal                       (2)

C:\> md text                         (3)

C:\> cd text                         (4)

C:\TEXT> md memo

C:\TEXT> cd memo                     (5)

C:\TEXT\MEMO> md office

C:\TEXT\MEMO> md \text\memo\office   (6)
Directory already exists

C:\TEXT\MEMO>
```

(1)  Creates the BASIC directory in the root directory. If
you specify the backslash at the beginning of the
command, it makes no difference from which directory you give the command. Refer to the CD command (section 4.12) for how to display the name of
the current directory. See section 8.2 for information about the inclusion of the current directory in
the prompt (for versions prior to MS-DOS 6).
(2)  Create the PASCAL directory from the currently active root directory.
(3)  As in (2), but now for the TEXT directory.
(4)  The first command activates the TEXT directory
(see the following section). The second command
creates a directory called MEMO in the TEXT directory.

(5) Switch to MEMO and create the OFFICE directory there.

(6) You can also create the OFFICE directory without switching. (The TEXT and MEMO directories must already exist.) In this case, the directory has already been created.

# 4.12   Access to files in subdirectories

A directory structure is constructed in such a way that it is impossible to remove or write to files in more than one directory at one time. Thus, the DEL*.* command is only valid for the current directory. It is possible to copy files from one directory to another.

When the computer is started up, the root directory is normally the active directory. In order to be able to read or to write to files in a directory, the directory must, in principle, be active.

**The CHDIR (or CD) command switches to the specified directory. The command without further specification produces the current directory.**

```
CHDIR [d:][\]directory[\directory...]
CD [d:][\]directory[\directory...]
```

CHDIR       Change directory.

CD          Abbreviated version of CHDIR. CD without further specification produces the currently active directory.

d:          The drive where the directory switch is to take place.

\           (Backslash) The beginning of the path to the new directory. Without \ at the beginning, the command applies from the current directory.

directory   The name of the directory to be activated. A backslash alone will switch to the root directory.

*Example:* Activate various directories and display the active directory

```
C:\> chdir basic          (1)

C:\BASIC> cd\             (2)

C:\> cd \text\memo\office  (3)

C:\TEXT\MEMO\OFFICE> cd\   (4)

C:\> cd text              (5)

C:\TEXT> cd memo

C:\TEXT\MEMO> cd office

C:\TEXT\MEMO\OFFICE> cd    (6)
C:\TEXT\MEMO\OFFICE

C:\TEXT\MEMO\OFFICE> cd\   (7)

C:\> cd                   (8)
C:\

C:\>
```

(1)  The root directory is active. The command switches to the BASIC directory.
(2)  Switches back to the root directory.
(3)  This is one way of activating the OFFICE directory.
(4)  Switches back to the root directory.
(5)  These three commands in conjunction have the same effect as the command in point (3).
(6)  CD without any further specifications produces the currently active directory.
(7)  Switches back to the root directory.
(8)  Shows the name of the active directory.

**Displaying subdirectories.** The operating system does not automatically state that the switch to a different directory has been carried out successfully. By means of the PROMPT command, you can change the appearance of the prompt so that the currently active directory is always indicated (see sections 6.5 and 8.2). The command PROMPT $p$g generates a prompt showing the current directory. From version 6.0 of MS-DOS, this prompt is automatically displayed.

**Displaying the contents of a directory.** If you display the contents of a directory by typing DIR without further specification, you can see whether or not the current directory is the root directory by examining the first two lines of the list.

In a random directory, the first two lines contain the standard registration for the current directory itself (.), and for the directory (..) at one level higher, the parent directory. (See the example below). By typing the two dots, you can switch to the parent directory, without having to specify the name. You may also repeat the two dots: for instance, you can switch back to C:\ from C:\TEXT\MEMO\OFFICE by giving the CD..\.. command. The <DIR> code in the column for the file size means that the file on that line is actually a directory.

**Activating a program which is located in a directory.** In the next example, we shall attempt to activate the BASIC interpreter GWBASIC from the root directory. This is not successful because the program is not located in the currently active directory. In the example, we shall remedy that after the error message. The directory list then indicates that the appropriate directory has been activated. The activation of GWBASIC is then successful. (This is an example for versions preceding MS-DOS 6.)

*Example:* Displaying a directory list and activating a program.

(1) Switches to the root directory.
(2) Attempt to activate the GWBASIC interpreter. This produces an error message because the program is not located in the currently active directory.
(3) Switch to the BASIC directory.
(4) Display the directory list of the current directory.
(5) The dot indicates that the currently active directory is not the root directory.
(6) The two dots is the registration for the parent directory.
(7) The current directory contains the WINFORM directory.

```
C:\BOOKS> cd\                                         (1)

C:\> gwbasic                                          (2)
Bad command or file name

C:\> cd basic                                         (3)

C:\BASIC> dir                                         (4)

 Volume in drive C has no label
 Volume Serial Number is 1B6F-554D
 Directory of C:\BASIC

.            <DIR>        22-11-93   10:59            (5)
..           <DIR>        22-11-93   10:59            (6)
WINFORM      <DIR>        22-11-93   11:41            (7)
GWBASIC  COM    65,262 22-11-93   11:38              (8)
INTEREST BAS     1,936 22-11-93   11:39
DISCOUNT BAS     2,237 22-11-93   11:40
        6 file(s)         69,435 bytes               (9)
                      61,630,208 bytes free

C:\BASIC> gwbasic                                     (10)
```

(8) The BASIC interpreter is in the currently active directory.

(9) The operating system treats all directories as files: accordingly, this makes a total of six in the BASIC directory.

(10) It is now possible to activate the GWBASIC interpreter from the BASIC directory.

**Summary.** Programs and data files can be copied and activated (loaded and started up) from a random directory, if you specify the appropriate search path when activating them.

If you start up a program outside the currently active directory, it has no automatic link with the data files which belong to it: in that case, you should always specify the search path. The example below makes this clear.

*Example:* Addressing program and data files in the various directories of the harddisk. The point of departure here is the directory structure scheme shown in section 3.1.

```
C:\>CD text                                   (1)

C:\TEXT>wp                                    (2)

memo\office\tmo.txt                           (3)


C:\>\text\wp                                  (4)

\text\memo\office\tmo.txt                     (5)


C:\>COPY \text\memo\office\tmo.txt \          (6)

C:\>COPY \basic\prog.bas \text                (7)


C:\>\basic\gwbasic                            (8)

SAVE"\basic\prog.bas"                         (9)
```

(1) Activate the TEXT directory.
(2) Start up the WordPerfect word processor from the TEXT directory.
(3) We wish to alter the TMO.TXT file in the OFFICE directory. Open this file in WordPerfect from the directory from which you activated WordPerfect (TEXT), by means of the Shift-F10 key combination. Type the path (3). It is not necessary to specify the entire path from the root directory (\TEXT\MEMO\OFFICE\TMO.TXT); do this from the currently active TEXT directory - MEMO and OFFICE are subdirectories. (The figure does not show the WordPerfect screen.)
(4) The word processor is activated from the root directory by means of this command. The word processor now has no direct access to the files in the TEXT directory.
(5) Load the same file as in (3). In this case, it is necessary to specify the path from the root directory.
(6) Copy the TMO.TXT file to the root directory. The first backslash need not be typed if the root direc-

tory is active. In the form displayed here, the command is independent of the currently active directory.

(7) The PROG.BAS program which is stored in ASCII
form in the BASIC directory is to be copied to the
\TEXT directory (pay attention to the necessary
backslash here).

(8) Start GWBASIC, the BASIC interpreter, which is located in the BASIC directory, from the root directory. (The figure does not show the GWBASIC
screen.)

(9) From GWBASIC, the PROG.BAS program is saved
in the BASIC directory by means of the BASIC co-
mand SAVE (the root directory is currently active!).

**Switching more simply using a batch file.** If you have
structured the harddisk to create a practical directory
structure, you will either have to repeatedly switch directories or type (lengthy) directory paths.

Using a batch file, you can quickly activate a different directory and start up a program directly if required. Save
this type of batch file under a conspicuous name in the
root directory, so that the operating system can always
find them.

*Example:* Create a batch file, TX.BAT, in the root directory to activate the TEXT directory and to subsequently
activate the WordPerfect word processor

```
C:\BOOKS> cd\                    (1)

C:\> copy con tx.bat             (2)
cd \text                         (3)
up                               (4)
^Z
          1 file(s) copied

C:\>                             (5)
C:\> tx                          (6)

C:\> cd \text                    (7)
C:\TEXT> up                      (8)
```

(1) Activate the root directory.
(2) Write the TX.BAT file using the COPY CON command.
(3) Activate the TEXT directory.
(4) Activate the WordPerfect word processor from TEXT.
(5) Conclude the batch file and write it to the root directory.
(6) Start up the batch file.
(7) & (8) The ECHOES of the batch file along with the commands specified in steps (3) and (4).

**Activating executable files from a random directory.**
The operating system can only directly execute files with the extensions COM, EXE and BAT. These are executable programs or batch files. When this type of program is activated, the operating system searches in the current directory or in the directory specified in the search path of the command. However, it is rather laborious to have to specify a path if this occurs often.

MS-DOS has a command which spares you the effort of having to type the paths to executable files. The command stores one or more paths to the directories containing the executable files in a separate part of working memory, the *environment*. These paths remain active as long as the computer is switched on, or until you remove the paths.

Even when a permanent search path is installed, the operating system first looks in the active directory and then successively in the directories which are specified in the search paths.

**The PATH command installs a permanent search path to the specified directories. PATH on its own displays the search path.**

```
PATH [[d:]path[;[d:]path]...]
```

PATH    Path. The command on its own displays the
        currently active search path.
d:      The drive to which the path is applicable.
path    The path specification with \ and directory
        names.

*Example:* Installing a search path

```
C:\> cd basic\basicpro                  (1)

C:\BASIC\BASICPRO> path \basic;\dos     (2)

C:\BASIC\BASICPRO> path                 (3)
PATH=\BASIC;\DOS

C:\BASIC\BASICPRO> diskcopy a: b:       (4)

Insert SOURCE diskette in drive A:

Press any key to continue . . .
^C

C:\BASIC\BASICPRO> cd\                   (5)

C:\> path \text                         (6)
```

(1) In the harddisk root directory, there is a directory
    called BASIC with a subdirectory BASICPRO for
    the programs. This command activates the latter di-
    rectory.
(2) The command creates two paths from the root di-
    rectory (they begin with a backslash) which are al-
    ways accessible: one is to the BASIC directory and
    the other, separated by a semi-colon, is to the
    \DOS directory where the utility programs are
    stored.
(3) The command without further specification displays
    the currently active search path. This is shown on
    the next screen line.
(4) As a test, from the BASICPRO directory we shall
    activate the DISKCOPY.COM program which is lo-
    cated in the DOS directory. The command works;
    we discontinue it immediately by pressing Ctrl-C.

(5)   Switch back to the root directory.

(6)   Installs a path to the \TEXT directory containing the WordPerfect word processor.

**Activating non-executable files from a random directory.** From MS-DOS version 3.3 onwards, it is possible to define not only search paths to executable files (programs) but also to (passive) data files and text files. Many programs cannot load corresponding data files from a directory other than their own. The PATH command does not provide a solution in this case.

If you activate the word processor from the WordPerfect directory and then wish to edit a chosen text in another directory, that can only be done if you specify the path to the text file in front of the file name (beginning at the WordPerfect directory). From version 3.3 onwards you can install a path which also applies to non-executable files.

**From MS-DOS version 3.3 onwards, you can apply the APPEND command to install, display and remove search paths to files.**

```
APPEND [/e][/x][;][d:][path];[d:][path]
                                    ;...]
```

APPEND   Append. The command on its own displays the currently active search path.

/e       (Environment) Saves the path in an environment variable. You can display the variable using the SET command.

/x       (Executable) Makes the path valid for executable files.
         Note:
         The /e and /x options may not be defined simultaneously along with a path. Two commands are required.
         APPEND /E /X plus 'APPEND path' is equivalent to 'PATH path'. Both types of path may be installed simultaneously.

;           Removes the active search path.
d:          The drive for which the path is valid.
path        \ plus the directory name. The total length of
            the paths (separated by ;) has a maximum
            of 128 characters.

*Example:* Installing, activating, testing and removing
two paths to common files

```
C:\> append/e/x                    (1)

C:\> append \up\letters:\up\ccc    (2)

C:\> append                        (3)
APPEND=\WP\LETTERS:\WP\CCC

C:\> cd\                            (4)

C:\> type test.txt                 (5)
This is just a test

C:\> append ;                      (6)

C:\> append
No Append                          (7)

C:\>
```

(1) The command should first be given with these two
    options. The /E option stores the path in a DOS
    variable which you can display using the SET com-
    mand. The /X option makes the paths also valid for
    executable files (COM, EXE, BAT).
(2) This command installs two permanent paths to the
    (text) files in the \WP\LETTERS and \WP\CCC di-
    rectories. Keep in mind the separator, the semi-
    colon.
(3) The command without any other specifications dis-
    plays the current search path. The operating sys-
    tem changes small letters to capitals automatically
    and places the equals sign between the variable
    and the currently active value.
(4) Switch to the root directory for the following text, re-
    gardless of the previous position.

(5) The TEST.TXT file is located in the \WP\LETTERS directory. By means of the search path it is possible to display this file using a command from the root directory.
(6) Removes the entire search path which was installed using APPEND.
(7) The statement indicates that there is no longer a search path.

# 4.13 Displaying the directory structure of a disk

You can display the directory structure of a disk on the screen by means of the TREE command.

**The TREE command produces an overview on the screen of all directories and file names on the harddisk or diskette. Using the key combination Ctrl-P(rtScreen), the output is also directed to the printer.**

```
TREE [d:][/F][/A]
```

TREE  Produces the entire directory structure of the disk. Stop the display by pressing the Pause key. Continue by pressing a random key.
d:    The drive to which the command applies.
/F    The program also displays the file names.
/A    The lines between the subdirectories are displayed using text characters instead of graphic signs.

*Example:* Display the directory structure of the harddisk, both with and without files (see following page)

(1) Displays the directory structure.
(2) Shows the first directory. This directory contains subdirectories.
(3) The display is discontinued using Ctrl-C.

```
C:\> tree                              (1)
Directory PATH listing
Volume Serial Number is 1B6F-554D
C:.
├───123R23                             (2)
│       ├───WYSIWYG
│       ├───TUTOR
│       └───WYSYGO
^C                                     (3)

C:\> tree /f                           (4)
Directory PATH listing
Volume Serial Number is 1B6F-554D
C:.
│   COREL.KID                          (5)
│   FLAPENG1.KID
│   FLAPENG2.KID
│   WINDOSE.KID
│   FLAPENG.KID
│   CONF^C

C:\>
```

(4) Displays the directory structure including the files.
(5) The /F option ensures that the program produces a list for each directory. The display is discontinued using Ctrl-C.

# 4.14 Deleting directories

A directory can only be removed if it is empty (in versions previous to MS-DOS 6). When using the RMDIR or RD commands, the following should be taken into account:

■ First use DEL *.* to remove all files after activating the directory. (For safety reasons, display the contents of the directory first!)
■ An (empty) directory can only be removed from the parent directory.
■ The root directory cannot be removed.

**The RMDIR (or RD) command removes an empty directory from the parent directory.**

```
RMDIR [d:]path
RD [d:]path
```

RMDIR      Remove Directory.
RD          Abbreviated version of RMDIR.
d:           The drive to which the command applies.
path       \ plus the directory names. The last name is
             the name of the directory to be deleted.

*Example:* Deleting a directory

```
C:\> cd basic\basicpro                         (1)

C:\BASIC\BASICPRO> dir                         (2)

 Volume in drive C has no label
 Volume Serial Number is 1B6F-554D
 Directory of C:\BASIC\BASICPRO

 .            <DIR>        22-11-93   12:16
 ..           <DIR>        22-11-93   12:16
 INTEREST BAS          194 22-11-93   13:03
         3 file(s)          194 bytes
                      11,634,688 bytes free

C:\BASIC\BASICPRO> del *.*                      (3)
All files in directory will be deleted!
Are you sure (Y/N)?y

C:\BASIC\BASICPRO> cd..                         (4)

C:\BASIC> rmdir basicpro                        (5)

C:\BASIC> cd basicpro                           (6)
Invalid directory
```

(1) Switch to the BASICPRO directory which we created in a previous example.
(2) Displays the directory list of the currrent directory.
In addition to the standard registrations, there is
only the INTEREST.BAS program file.
(3) Deletes all files. In this case, that is only INTER-
EST.BAS.
(4) Switches to the parent directory (BASIC).
(5) Deletes the BASICPRO directory.
(6) Attempt to switch to the directory which has just
been deleted. This is unsuccessful, causing an
error message.

**Deleting a subdirectory with contents (from MS-
DOS version 6.0 onwards).**
Using the following command, you can delete a direc-
tory along with all its files and subdirectories in one go.

You can save a great deal of time, especially if you wish to remove complete directory structures. It is, in MS-DOS 6.0, no longer necessary to delete all files and subdirectories first.

*Caution:* Take particular care that you have made back-ups of all important files from these directories.

**You can delete a directory including all files and subdirectories in one go using the DELTREE command.**

```
DELTREE [d1:]directory1
                         [[d2:]directory2...]
```

DELTREE             Delete tree.
d1:directory1       Specify the directory to be deleted;
                    enter the name of the drive if the di-
                    rectory is located in a different
                    drive.
d2:directory2...    It is possible to specify several di-
                    rectories (and drives), separated by
                    a space.

*Example:* The \TEXT directory containing the \MEMO subdirectory is located on the harddisk. The OFFICE subdirectory is located in MEMO subdirectory. This entire structure is to be removed (see following page).

(1) Displays the structure of the \TEXT directory on the harddisk. The directory contains one subdirectory which also has a subdirectory.
(2) The \MEMO subdirectory contains the OFFICE subdirectory.
(3) The \TEXT directory including the subdirectories are deleted.
(4) The directory no longer exists and thus is not shown in the directory list.

```
C:\> tree text                                                    (1)
Directory PATH listing
Volume Serial Number is 1B6F-554D
C:TEXT
L——MEMO
    L——OFFICE

C:\> dir text\memo                                                (2)

.              <DIR>        22-11-93    11:02
..             <DIR>        22-11-93    11:02
OFFICE         <DIR>        22-11-93    11:03

C:\> deltree text                                                 (3)
Delete directory "text" and all its subdirectories? [yn] y
Deleting text...

C:\> dir text                                                     (4)

 Volume in drive C has no label
 Volume Serial Number is 1B6F-554D
 Directory of C:\

File not found
```

# 5    Batch files

## 5.1    Operation and application of batch files

In many procedures involving the operating system, you
have to specify different commands in succession. If, for
instance, you make a copy of a diskette and then wish
to view the contents of the copy, the following two instructions are necessary:

Copy command              DISKCOPY A: B:
Display list of files     DIR B:

MS-DOS provides the possibility of combining one or
more instructions into a package which can be activated
and then implemented successively by the operating
system. A package like this is called a *batch*. The instructions are stored in a text file with the extension
'BAT'. If you activate this file, the operating system
reads the separate commands and executes these in
the given order of sequence.

Batch files make working with your computer much easier. For example, they enable you to:

■  reduce the amount of typing work
■  limit errors in input
■  use own names for instructions without changing the
    file names
■  allow system setups to be done automatically when
    the computer is started up
■  save new data automatically when a program is ter-
    minated.

The instructions for the computer are written to a file in
the same order of sequence as you type them. The
computer implements the batch file as follows:

- The operating system reads the first command in the batch file.
- The computer executes the instruction.
- The operating system returns to the batch file and continues with the next instruction, until all commands have been implemented.

The .BAT extension is reserved for batch files (see section 9.5). The same rules apply to the names of batch files as to other files.

## 5.2 Starting up a batch file

**Start up a batch file by specifying the name.**

```
[d:][path]file[.BAT]
```

d:path    Drive letter of the diskette and the directory (if required) containing the batch file.
If you do not specify a drive letter, the operating system will search for the batch file in the current drive.
file    The name of the batch file
.BAT    The standard extension, which you do not need to enter.

*Example:* The DUPLIC.BAT file contains the following instructions:

```
DISKCOPY A: B:
DIR B:
```

Activate the batch file by typing 'DUPLIC' and pressing Enter. The operating system will automatically execute both commands in the specified order of sequence.

## 5.3    Creating a batch file

A batch file can be created using practically any word processor. The only condition is that the text file may not contain any formatting codes from the word processor, but that is not a problem for most word processors.

If you are working with MS-DOS 5.0, 6.0 or 6.20 you can make use of the DOS editor, EDIT (see chapter 11).

Because most batch files are quite short, the COPY CON command is an efficient alternative (see section 4.4).

The COPY CON instruction enables you to write a text from the keyboard directly to a file (text file, ASCII format). The disadvantage of this method is that you can only alter a line as long as you have not yet pressed Enter in order to move on to the next line (the next command) instruction. If you subsequently discover an error, you have to type the whole file again, which is not disastrous since the size of the file is never very large. Nevertheless, it is advisable to work out the commands on paper first. (Of course, you can always load the batch file into your word-processor and rectify the error there.) The example below illustrates the COPY CON process.

*Example:* Write the DUPLIC.BAT batch file (see sections 5.1 and 5.2) and implement it (see illustration on the following page)

(1)    The harddisk is the current drive. The COPY CON instruction copies the keyboard input to the DU-PLIC.BAT file. Place each instruction on a separate line and complete each line by pressing Enter. The batch file consists of only two commands.

(2)    The F6 function key places an end-of-file mark. Instead of F6, you can also press the Ctrl-Z key combination. As soon as you indicate the end of the file by pressing Enter, it is written to the DUPLIC.BAT file on the diskette in the current drive (to the hard-disk C: in our example).

```
C:\> copy con duplic.bat          (1)
diskcopy a: b:
dir b:
^Z
        1 file(s) copied          (2)

C:\> duplic                       (3)

C:\> diskcopy a: b:               (4)

Insert SOURCE diskette in drive A: (5)

Press any key to continue . . .   (6)
^C

C:\> dir b:                       (7)

  Volume in drive B has no label
  Volume Serial Number is 0C29-11DC
  Directory of B:\

File not found                    (8)

C:\>
```

(3) To implement the DUPLIC.BAT file, type DUPLIC and press Enter.

(4) The file is started up: the DISKCOPY instruction is activated automatically.

(5) The two statements from the DISKCOPY instruction are displayed successively, followed immediately by the prompt for any random key.

(6) It is not really our intention to make a copy of a diskette during this test. Discontinue the command by pressing the Ctrl-C key combination.

(7) The operating system continues with the next instruction in the batch file: displaying the list of files on the diskette in drive B:.

(8) Because nothing has been copied, the directory is empty and DIR displays a statement to this effect.

# 5.4    Commands in batch files

You can not only use the normal DOS commands in batch files, you can also use instructions which are valid only for batch files. There are special instructions for the following objectives:

■ Including commentary (information) in the file and displaying it on the screen.

■ Displaying or suppressing statements from the operating system.
■ Interrupting the execution of the batch file, displaying
  a statement, and resuming the execution by pressing
  a random key.
■ By-passing the execution of a part of batch file or
  stopping the implementation completely.
■ Specifying variable pieces of information which can
  be slotted into the commands in the batch file at a
  chosen place when the batch file is started up.
■ The operation of small programs.

We shall first deal with the batch instructions individually. We shall apply them in a logical combination in
two subsequent examples. A further example is given in
section 7.2.

The operating commands for batch programs, such as
CALL, FOR, GOTO, IF and CHOICE (from MS-DOS
6.0 onwards) lie outside the scope of this book. They
are mentioned in the appendix.

**The REM batch command places a remark in a batch
file. The remark also appears on the screen, unless
the system statements have been switched off.**

```
REM [text]
```

REM     Remark.
text    Chosen text (without apostrophes), max. 123
        characters. In the case of no text, REM places
        an empty line in the batch file.

*Example:*

```
REM*** Start up the GWBASIC interpreter
                               automatically ***
```

This line will be automatically displayed by a batch file, if
the system statements are switched on (see ECHO).

**The ECHO batch instruction switches the display of
the instructions and the commentary on and off,
along with any subsequent text.**

```
ECHO [ON/OFF/text]
```

ECHO   The instruction runs the current mode if no pa-
       rameters are specified.

ON     Display instructions.

OFF    No display, only execution of instructions.

*text*   The instruction will display the *'text'*, even if
       ECHO is set to the OFF mode.

*Example:* If the ECHO command itself is not to be displayed, place the at sign (@) in front of ECHO OFF.

*Example:*

```
ECHO OFF
ECHO Insert a diskette in B: and lock the
                                    diskdrive
```

A batch file with these lines displays the following on the
screen:

```
A:\>ECHO OFF
Insert a diskette in B: and lock the
                                    diskdrive
```

The first line switches off the display of the instructions:
the text display appears *without* the word ECHO. If the
@ sign had been placed in front of the first command,
the entire first line would not have been shown:

```
@ECHO OFF
Insert a diskette in drive B: and lock the
                                    diskdrive
```

This produces the result:

```
Insert a diskette in drive B: and lock the
                                    diskdrive
```

**The PAUSE batch instruction interrupts the execution of a batch file, shows a statement if required, and continues the execution when you press a random key.**

```
PAUSE [text]
```

PAUSE      Pause.
text       Chosen text (without apostrophes), max.
           121 characters. The text will not appear on
           the screen if ECHO is set to OFF.

*Example:*

```
PAUSE Now insert a diskette in drive B:
```

If this line is located in a batch file, the following will appear on the screen:

```
A:\>PAUSE Insert a diskette in drive B:
Press any key to continue ...
```

**You can always stop the execution of a batch file by using the Ctrl-C or Ctrl-Break key combinations.**

The operating system will ask whether you wish to terminate the batch file (Terminate batch program (Y/N)?). If you respond N, only the current instruction (or the activation of a program) will be discontinued.

*Example:* Create a batch file illustrating the REM, ECHO and PAUSE instructions and the discontinue function (see illustration on the following page)

(1)  The harddisk is the current drive. Assign the name TEST3.BAT to the batch file.
(2)  End of file - press Enter to write the file to the harddisk.
(3)  Activate the batch file.
(4)  Do not display the commands.
(5)  The test is displayed via the ECHO instruction. The

same text behind the REM instruction would not, in this case (ECHO OFF), be displayed.

(6) This text is shown on the screen by the *first* PAUSE instruction. These system statements have high priority - they are implemented despite the ECHO OFF mode. Accordingly, the text behind the first PAUSE instruction is not displayed.

The Ctrl-C key combination has been pressed here. This interrupts the current operating system process - 'Press any key....'.

```
C:\>copy con test3.bat                           (1)
echo off
echo Test the PAUSE instruction
pause This text does not appear on the screen
echo on
pause This text DOES appear on the screen
rem ****** End of the test ******
^Z
        1 file(s) copied                         (2)

C:\>test3                                         (3)

C:\>echo off                                      (4)
Test the PAUSE instruction                        (5)
Press any key to continue . . .                   (6)
^C

Terminate batch job (Y/N)?n                        (7)

C:\>pause This text DOES appear on the screen     (8)
Press any key to continue . . .

C:\>rem ****** End of the test ******             (9)

C:\>
```

(7) The operating system continues with the following command, which is also a system statement with high priority. Owing to the N response, the current command in the batch file is discontinued, but the operating system continues with the following command in the batch file.

(8) Because the ECHO mode is ON, the text behind the second PAUSE instruction is displayed on the screen. The operating system continues with the following command in the batch file when you press any key.

(9) Owing to ECHO ON, not only the instruction but also the text appears on the screen.

Behind the command to activate a batch file, you can also register parameters which can be specified in the commands in the batch file. You can register a maximum of *nine parameters* in each instruction. (We shall not discuss, at this stage, the possibility of extending this amount using the SHIFT instruction; see the appendix.) The variables have the codes %1 to %9 in the batch file. They may appear anywhere in the instruction. The tenth variable, %0, contains the name of the file itself. The name must be saved in order to be able to return to the file after another batch file has been activated.

**The following syntax enables you supply information to the instructions in a batch file.**

```
batch name value1 value2 ...value9
```

batch name         Name of the batch file.
value1             Value of a variable in the batch file;
                   use the space as separation character.

*Example:* Create a batch file, TEST, in order to simplify the creation of a backup of the diskette in drive A:

```
A:\>copy con test.bat             (1)
copy a:%1 a:%2                    (2)
dir a:%2                          (3)
type a:%0.bat                     (4)
^Z
        1 file(s) copied          (5)

A:\>test data.txt values.123      (6)
A:\>copy a:data.txt a:values.123  (7)
        1 file(s) copied

A:\>dir a:values.123              (8)

 Volume in drive A has no label
 Volume Serial Number is 1348-17E2
 Directory of A:\

VALUES   123         8 16/11/93   16:16
        1 file(s)           8 bytes
                    359,424 bytes free

A:\>type a:test.bat               (9)
copy a:%1 a:%2
dir a:%2
type a:%0.bat
```

(1) Create the TEST.BAT batch file.
(2) Copy command. The file represented by the name in %1 is to be copied to a file represented by %2 on the diskette in drive A:. The variables receive values when activated as shown in point (6). The name of the batch file is located in %0, the first parameter in %1, the second in %2 and so forth. An instruction can consist of a maximum of ten elements including the name of the batch file. These elements are separated by spaces. Specification of the drives is not necessary in this command because A: is the current drive.
(3) Display only the information of those files whose name corresponds to %2 in the file list. Accordingly, you can check if the command has been properly implemented - after copying, the copy is located on the diskette under the name which occurs in the %2 variable.
(4) Display the contents of the file whose name corresponds to the %0 variable - this is the batch file itself.
(5) Save the completed batch file on the diskette.
(6) Activate the TEST.BAT batch file (see point (2)). Here, the extension does not need to be specified. The name of the batch file is saved in %0, DATA.TXT in %1 and VALUES.123 in %2.
(7) The operating system executes the first command. The system statements show that the parameters have taken the place of the variables.
(8) Shows the registration of the copy in the directory (under the name VALUES.123).
(9) Displays the contents of the batch file.

# 6 Adjusting the operating system

## 6.1 The configuration file CONFIG.SYS

It is desirable to adjust the operating system as precisely as possible to the specific combination of devices in and around your computer. Perhaps you have extended memory or a diskdrive, a printer or a keyboard which are not compatible with MS-DOS norms. It may also occur that a program with which you are working requires a special memory setup (buffers, extensions).

In these cases, *drivers* are necessary for the proper link between device and operating system. Normally, there are several drivers on the system diskette - you only need to activate them. If you acquire a new peripheral device, a corresponding driver is generally supplied along with it. The required adjustments and settings should preferably be integrated into the system in such a way that future processes cost a minimum of effort.

MS-DOS has a special file where the instructions for the drivers and their parameters are located. This has the advantage that the configuration is automatically set up in the correct manner when the computer is started up. (A configuration is the combination of linked components in the computer.) This file has the compulsory name CONFIG.SYS.

You are not obliged to use a configuration file. In its absence, the operating system works using defaults. When a new version of MS-DOS is installed, a simple configuration file is created on the startup diskette.

*Note:* Ensure that programs which are summoned using CONFIG.SYS are available at the specified place on the system disk. Otherwise, the operating system will not be able to locate them when starting up and you will receive an error statement.

# 6.2 Compiling or altering CONFIG.SYS

The configuration file is a text file (ASCII format). With respect to the operating system, it fulfils the function of a permanent external memory for commands and program names.

A configuration file is generally not very long, so that, just as in the case of the starting-up file, it can be written using the COPY CON command or, from MS-DOS version 5.0 onwards, using the DOS editor EDIT. You may also use a word processor, such as WordPerfect. In this case, you must save the text as DOS text.

Examine whether a CONFIG.SYS file is present on the system diskette or harddisk, and, if so, inspect the contents. Protect this file by assigning it another name or by making a copy on another diskette. Assign a neutral name to the new file in the meantime, and rename it CONFIG.SYS when you have corrected any erroneous elements in the content.

*Example:* Check if there is a file called CONFIG.SYS in the root directory of the harddisk. If so, display the contents on the screen and write a new configuration file under the name CONFIG.NEW.

```
A:\>dir config.sys                         (1)

 Volume in drive A has no label
 Volume Serial Number is 1348-17E2
 Directory of A:\

CONFIG   SYS        8 16/11/93   16:32      (2)
        1 file(s)           8 bytes
                      358,400 bytes free

A:\>type config.sys                        (3)
break on                                   (4)
A:\>copy con contest.bat                   (5)
break on                                   (6)
buffers=15
files=20
^Z                                         (7)
        1 file(s) copied

A:\>type contest.bat                       (8)

A:\>del config.sys                         (9)

A:\>ren contest.bat config.sys             (10)
```

(1) Search for the CONFIG.SYS file.
(2) The system has located the file.
(3) Show the contents on the screen.
(4) The file contains only one instruction (see section 6.3).
(5) Create a new file with the name CONTEST.BAT.
(6) For more information concerning these commands we refer you to section 6.3.
(7) Save the completed file.
(8) Show the contents of the file on the screen (not shown in the diagram).
(9) Delete the original configuration file.
(10) Assign the standard name CONFIG.SYS to the file.

# 6.3 The most important commands in CONFIG.SYS

Most computer users appear to deploy only a few of the instructions which are available to a configuration file. The commands which are important in all MS-DOS versions are DEVICE, BUFFERS, FILES, BREAK and REM.

From version 3 onwards, there are the additional commands COUNTRY, SHELL, LASTDRIVE and INSTALL. From version 5.0 onwards, additional important commands to optimize memory management are DEVICE-HIGH and DOS.

From MS-DOS 6.0 onwards, you can allow DOS to regulate the maximizing of memory management by means of the MEMMAKER program (see chapter 15). In addition, you can include in CONFIG.SYS the commands DBLSPACE.SYS for compressed files and IN-TERLNK for connecting two computers (see chapter 13). Moreover, it is possible to work with different configuration files on one computer (see section 6.4).

**Adjustment to non-standard devices.** The IO.SYS (IBMBIO.COM) and MSDOS.SYS (IBMDOS.COM) sys-

tem programs contain routines which regulate the exchange of data between the computer and the standard
peripheral devices: diskdrives, harddisks, monitors and
keyboards. If you connect a device which is not compatible with the standard software, you will require a
special driver.

**The DEVICE command installs a driver for a device
via the CONFIG.SYS file.**

```
DEVICE[HIGH]=driver [parameter]
```

DEVICE          Device.
DEVICEHIGH      From MS-DOS 5.0 onwards, the
                driver can be loaded in the high
                memory area using this command
                (see chapter 15 and the example in
                section 6.4).
driver          Driver from the manufacturer, or
                your own.
parameter       Driver options.

*Example:* With computers possessing a processor of
the type 80286, 80386 or 80486 and at least 1 Mb memory, it is possible to load parts of the resident operating
system in the high memory area (HMA). To do this, the
DOS HIMEM.SYS driver, for instance, must be installed. The command line in CONFIG.SYS is as follows:

```
DEVICE=C:\DOS\HIMEM.SYS
```

Check first whther the HIMEM.SYS program is located
in the DOS directory of the harddisk.

**Using extended memory.** When you have installed the
HIMEM.SYS and EMM386.SYS programs, you must in-
form the operating system that it can use parts of the
extended memory as high memory area and as upper
memory blocks for its own tasks (see chapter 15).

**Parts of the extended memory are reserved for the operating system by means of the DOS command.**

```
DOS=[HIGH|LOW] [,[UMB|NOUMB]]
```

*Example:* The HMA and the UMBs are to be used in a computer with a 80386 processor. The command for CONFIG.SYS is as follows:

```
DOS=HIGH,UMB
```

**Reserving blocks in working memory.** The exchange of data between the computer and the storage media takes place via buffers in working memory. Under MS-DOS, you can select the amount of buffers, ranging from 1 to 99. If you are working with a cache program such as SMARTDRIVE, you do not need to use the BUFFERS command. Normally MS-DOS works with 15 buffers when the computer has a working memory of 640 Kb. From version 5.0 onwards, the buffers are installed in the HMA (see chapter 15) if no more than 48 buffers are specified.

**The BUFFERS command installs a number of disk buffers for the operating system.**

```
BUFFERS=x[,y]
```

BUFFERS  Interim memory.
x        The number of buffers required, between 1 and 99.
y        The number of secondary buffers, between 1 and 8.

*Example:* The number of buffers must be set to 25 to accommodate a database program. Specify the following line in CONFIG.SYS:

```
BUFFERS=25
```

**Specifying the maximum number of simultaneously open files.** Data can only be written to, or read from, a file if that file is open. The operating system manages a data structure in which the status of each file is registered (open/closed). Normally, MS-DOS works with eight file control blocks (FCBs). A program can then read and write in a maximum of eight files. A larger number is required in the case of some applications. In older DOS versions, each FCB contains 39 bytes, from version 3.0 onwards, this is 48 bytes.

**The FILES command defines the maximum number of files which can be open simultaneously.**

```
FILES=x
```

FILES    Files.
x        The maximum number of simultaneously open files - between 8 and 255 (prior to version 3.0, between 5 and 99).

*Example:* Increase the maximum number of open files to 30 as required by a database program. The command line in CONFIG.SYS is as follows:

```
FILES=30
```

**Changing the program break mode.** In chapter 1, we mentioned that you can discontinue the running of the operating system by using the key combinations Ctrl-C or Ctrl-Break. The operating system will only accept this command in the standard mode if it is reading or writing data at that moment.

Thus, in the standard mode, it is not possible to break off a program if it is not engaged in exchanging data with the screen, the keyboard, the printer or via a communication port.

**The BREAK instruction switches the break-off mode of the operating system on and off**

```
BREAK [ON/OFF]
```

BREAK    Break, discontinue. This instruction on its own produces the current mode.
ON    Extended break-off mode.
OFF    Limited break-off mode (default value).

*Example:* Set the computer to the extended break-off mode in the startup process. Then examine the currently active break-off mode. The command in CONFIG.SYS is as follows:

```
BREAK=ON
```

Type the BREAK command behind the prompt when the computer has been started up. The operating system registers 'BREAK is on'.

**Setting the command interpreter**. If the COMMAND.COM command interpreter is not located in the root directory of the harddisk, or if you wish to use your own interpreter, specify a separate command in CONFIG.SYS.

**The SHELL command installs a command interpreter other than COMMAND.COM (or an additional command interpreter).**

```
SHELL=[d:][path]file[.ext] [d:][path][/P]
```

SHELL  Shell, casing.
d:path  Drive and directory in which the (new) interpreter is located.
file.ext  The name of the command interpreter.
d:path  The drive and directory are assigned to the COMSPEC system variable. In this way, COMMAND.COM can again be found when the resident part of the program has to be loaded.
/P    The command interpreter is permanently available for the system and the AUTOEXEC.BAT

file is activated immediately after the execution of CONFIG.SYS.

*Example:* The command interpreter is to be permanently available and the DOS directory must be included in the COMSPEC system variable. The command line in CONFIG.SYS is as follows:

```
SHELL=C:\DOS\COMMAND.COM C:\DOS /P
```

**Determining the number of diskdrives.** For the maximum number of drives, MS-DOS normally reserves one drive more than the number of drives physically present. For instance, if a computer has three drives, A,B and C, the letters A to D are reserved for drives. Some applications require more drives, such as the communication program INTERLNK (see chapter 13).

**The LASTDRIVE command defines the maximum number of drives to be used by the operating system.**

```
LASTDRIVE=D
```

LASTDRIVE      The last diskdrive.
D      This is a letter between A and Z, representing the number of drives assigned to the system. The minimum number is always at least the number of drives physically present.

*Example:* The system is to have eight letters representing drives. The command in CONFIG.SYS is as follows:

```
LASTDRIVE=H
```

### The COUNTRY command determines the date and time format.

```
COUNTRY=code[,[codetable][,[d:][path]
                                    file]]
```

COUNTRY          Land.
code             The international access number is
                 the country code. This is 044 for the
                 United Kingdom. Specifying this acti-
                 vates the customary way of register-
                 ing the date and time, and also the
                 unit of currency and the decimal point.
code table       For instance, the code table contain-
                 ing the international code 437. If you
                 wish to find out more about the
                 country codes, type the HELP
                 COUNTRY command behind the
                 prompt in order to activate the MS-
                 DOS help function.
d:path           The drive and directory containing the
                 file with the code numbers.
file             The file containing the code numbers,
                 normally COUNTRY.SYS.

*Example:* Install the country code for the UK. The command line in CONFIG.SYS is as follows:

```
COUNTRY=044,437,C:\DOS\COUNTRY.SYS
```

**Installing resident programs.** Resident programs can
be installed in the CONFIG.SYS configuration file.
These programs remain resident in the computer memory during the entire session.

**By means of the INSTALL command, it is possible
to install resident programs in the CONFIG.SYS file.
This command must be placed under the device
commands.**

```
INSTALL=[d:][path]file.ext [options]
```

INSTALL    Install.
d:path      The drive and directory containing the resident program file.
file.ext     The name of the program to be installed. The extension is obligatory.
options    The program parameters.

*Example:* Installing the FASTOPEN program in CONFIG.SYS instead of AUTOEXEC.BAT and regulating a maximum of 95 simultaneously open files on drive C:

```
INSTALL=C:\DOS\FASTOPEN.EXE C:=95
```

# 6.4    Using different configurations (from MS-DOS 6.0 onwards)

When using certain applications it may be convenient, or even necessary, to specify a separate configuration. If, for instance, you occasionally work with Windows while generally using DOS programs, it may be necessary to configure the extended memory differently. Windows demands a great deal of extended memory in order to be able to work effectively. But if you also require much extended memory for a certain DOS application, a different configuration will have to be specified.

Up until recently, this configuration switch could only be implemented in a rather roundabout way and with a considerable amount of difficulty. However, from MS-DOS version 6.0 onwards it is possible to compile nine different configurations. When the computer is started up, a menu appears on the screen, enabling you to select the required configuration.

**Compiling CONFIG.SYS for different configurations.** The options menu must be placed at the beginning of the CONFIG.SYS file. A menu always begins with the word MENU between square brackets: [MENU]. Each menu line must be defined using the MENUITEM command and the name of the command block to be executed. If you do not make any further specifications, the name of the command block will be displayed as menu text. Each block of commands begins with the defined name between square brackets. If required, it is possible to reserve certain commands, which recur in each block, as a separate block and to make them available under the name [COMMON] to all other blocks. This results in the following structure in the CONFIG.SYS file:

```
[MENU]
MENUITEM=command_block1
MENUITEM=command_block2

[COMMON]
...common commands...

[COMMAND_BLOCK1]
...commands...

[COMMAND_BLOCK2]
...commands...
```

Using the INCLUDE command, it is possible to adopt a defined command block into another block. If you prefer to use a certain configuration, you can have this started automatically within a period of between 0 and 90 seconds. Create the CONFIG.SYS file using a text editor, EDIT from MS-DOS for instance.

Here is an outline of the individual commands:

```
MENUITEM=command_block[,menu text]
```

command block       Reference to the command block
                    which is to be executed.
menutext            A text consisting of a maximum of
                    70 characters. If no text is entered,
                    the name of the command block is
                    displayed.

```
INCLUDE=command_block
```

command block     The reference to the command block which is to be included.

```
MENUDEFAULT=command_block[,time]
```

command block     The reference to the command block which is to be automatically executed (the default configuration).

time              The time in seconds (between 0 and 90) for the display of the menu before automatic execution takes place. If the time is set to 0 seconds the default configuration will be chosen without the menu being shown.

The following command can be used for the other different configurations:

*SUBMENU=submenu_block[,menu text]* enables you to include a submenu in the main menu. The command is shown as a menu option in the main menu. By selecting this option, the submenu is activated.

*MENULOCK=[ON|OFF]* enables you to determine in a menu block whether the NumLock key in the numeric keypad should be activated when the computer is started up.

*MENUCOLOR=colour_menu text[,background_colour]* determines the colour of the menu text and the background colour by means of a number between 1 and 15. Display the colour specifications using the help function (HELP MENUCOLOR).

*Example:* A computer is to be set to the following applications: 1. Standard, 2. Using RAM diskdrive and 3. Exchanging data with another computer. The shared commands should be included in a COMMON block. The menu is to be displayed for 15 seconds before activating the default configuration.

The listing below shows the menu when the computer has been started up:

```
MS-DOS 6 Startup menu                                    (1)

   1. Standard
   2. RAM drive
   3. Data exchange

Make a selection: 1                                      (2)











F5=Skip startup files   F8=Confirm each CONFIG.SYS line [N]   (3)
```

(1)  The user determines only the menu texts and the menu options. The rest of the texts and the numbers is determined by the system itself.
(2)  Option 1 is automatically proposed since Standard option represents the default configuration.
(3)  By pressing F5, you can skip the configuration which you have defined. A basic configuration is then started up instead.
     *Note:* If the COMMAND.COM command interpreter is not located in the root directory of the startup diskette, you will have to activate this separately, by typing C:\DOS\COMMAND.COM for instance.
     If you press F8, the commands in CONFIG.SYS are displayed on the screen one by one. You can then determine whether or not each individual command should be executed.

The configuration file with the menu looks something like this:

```
[menu]                                                    (1)
menuitem=Standard
menuitem=RAM drive
menuitem=Data exchange
menudefault=Standard,15


[common]                                                  (2)
DEVICE=C:\DOS\HIMEM.SYS
DEVICE=C:\DOS\EMM386.EXE NOEMS HIGHSCAN
BUFFERS=30,0
FILES=30
DOS=HIGH,UMB
LASTDRIVE=H
FCBS=4,0
DEVICEHIGH /L:1,12160 =C:\DOS\SETVER.EXE
DEVICEHIGH /L:1,37520 =C:\DOS\VGA\UTILS\FASTBIOS.SYS
DEVICEHIGH /L:1,2000 =C:\DOS\VGA\UTILS\EANSI.SYS
STACKS=9,256
COUNTRY=044,850 C:\DOS\COUNTRY.SYS
SHELL=C:\DOS\COMMAND.COM C:\DOS\ /p
DEVICEHIGH /L:1,44496 =C:\DOS\DBLSPACE.SYS /MOVE

[standard]                                                (3)

[RAM drive]                                               (4)
DEVICEHIGH=C:\DOS\RAMDRIVE.SYS 8192 512 1024 /e

[Data exchange]                                           (5)
LASTDRIVE=N
DEVICE=C:\DOS\INTERLNK.EXE
DEVICEHIGH=C:\DOS\POWER.EXE

[common]                                                  (6)
```

(1)  Define the three menu options. The Standard com-
     mand block must be automatically executed after
     15 seconds if no other selection is made before this
     time has elapsed.
(2)  The following commands are to be executed in all
     three configurations.
(3)  The commands which belong to the Standard
     block. The commands from the Common block are
     executed first. Since no additional commands are
     necessary for the standard configuration, the block
     is empty.
(4)  If option 2 is selected, the Common commands are
     also executed first. Subsequently, a RAM drive with
     a capacity of 8 Mb is created in the extended mem-
     ory.
(5)  If menu option 3 is selected, the maximum number
     of diskdrives which can be used is increased to N.
     In addition, the INTERLNK program for data ex-
     change with another computer and the energy-sav-
     ing program POWER are installed.
(6)  It is possible to define more Common blocks. Here
     an empty block has been defined to receive any
     commands from newly-installed programs. Includ-
     ing this line at the end of the CONFIG.SYS file en-
     sures that these programs will always be installed.

Based on the structure of CONFIG.SYS, additional configuration settings can be made in the AUTOEXEC.BAT
file. To do this, the reference to the block selected from
the menu in CONFIG.SYS is registered in a system
variable called %config%. The variable can then be processed in AUTOEXEC.BAT. To do this, place the same
headings as in CONFIG.SYS above the corresponding
command blocks in AUTOEXEC.BAT. Place the commands which are to be commonly executed at the beginning and then move, using the GOTO %config%
command, to the block with the name of the variable. At
the end of each command block, you will jump to the
end of the file. The structure is as follows:

```
common commands...
GOTO %config%

:block1
commands...
GOTO end

:block2
commands...
GOTO end

etc...

:end
```

## 6.5 The automatic startup file: AUTOEXEC.BAT

We have already seen, in chapter 1, that the starting up process under MS-DOS consists of three stages:

■ A computer self-test, independent of the operating system.
■ Executing the CONFIG.SYS configuration file if any.
■ Loading and executing the AUTOEXEC.BAT file if any.

The automatic startup file may be located in the root directory of the startup diskette as an external system file, but this need not be the case.

The startup file helps alleviate your workload when the computer is activated: specifying date and time, switching to the directory containing the word processor, activating the word processor etc. Since these tasks differ according to one's personal requirements, there are no standard contents for this file. A startup file may already be located on your system diskette. This can easily be checked because the name is always AUTOEXEC.BAT.

*Example:* Searching for AUTOEXEC.BAT on the hard-disk and displaying its contents

```
C:\> dir autoexec.bat                          (1)

 Volume in drive C has no label               (2)
 Volume Serial Number is 1B6F-554D
 Directory of C:\

AUTOEXEC BAT          28 22-11-93   13:39
        1 file(s)               28 bytes
                     11,583,488 bytes free

C:\> type autoexec.bat                         (3)
@ECHO OFF                                      (4)
DATE                                           (5)
TIME                                           (6)
VER                                            (7)

C:\>
```

(1) The harddisk is the active diskdrive. This is the command to display the data stored in AUTOEX-EC.BAT.
(2) The startup file is present. The file data are shown.
(3) Display the contents of the startup file on the screen.
(4) Switch off the system messages, including this command.
(5) Activate the internal system program to enter the date.
(6) Activate the internal system program to set the clock. The batch file stops to allow you the oppor-tunity to specify the date and time. Confirm these values by pressing Enter. These commands are superfluous if your computer has a battery-powered clock (see chapter 1).
(7) Shows the currently active version of MS-DOS on the screen.

You now have sufficient know-how to write a startup file on your own. Just to be completely sure, assign another name to the original startup file or make a backup on a diskette. You can always re-employ it if your own new file does not work properly. Another security measure would be to give your new startup file a preliminary name, such as AUTO.BAT.

Using AUTOEXEC.BAT, you can automatically activate the program with which you normally work: the word processor, spreadsheet, database program etc.

*Example:* The startup file is to be used to automatically load and activate the word processor, WordPerfect 5.1. The batch file is to receive the preliminary name AUTO.BAT and, if tested successfully, the definite name AUTOEXEC.BAT.

```
C:\>COPY CON auto.bat                      (1)
@echo off                                  (2)
path c:\;c:\dos;c:\wp51                     (3)
wp                                         (4)
^Z                                         (5)


C:\>TYPE auto.bat                          (6)

C:\>DEL autoexec.bat                       (7)

C:\>RENAME auto.bat autoexec.bat           (8)
```

(1) Command to create the AUTO.BAT batch file.
(2) Suppress the display of system messages, also including this command.
(3) Specify the search path: the root directory, the DOS directory and the directory containing the WordPerfect 5.1 word processor.
(4) This command activates the WordPerfect program.
(5) Close the batch file and write it to disk.
(6) Command to display the contents of the batch file on the screen.
(7) Delete the old AUTOEXEC.BAT file.
(8) Rename the file just created.

*Note:* You can load resident programs in the Upper
Memory Block (UMB) by specifying the LOADHIGH
(LH) command in the AUTOEXEC.BAT file. See further
chapter 15.

From MS-DOS version 6.0, it is possible to work with
different startup configurations. Moreover, the startup
procedure can be influenced by means of the F5 and F8
function keys. If you press F5, you can skip the CON-
FIG.SYS and AUTOEXEC.BAT files. If you press F8,
you can move through the CONFIG.SYS file line by line,
and specify whether each command should be executed or not. If you have MS-DOS version 6.2, this
also applies to the AUTOEXEC.BAT file. In version 6.0,
it is only possible to either skip AUTOEXEC.BAT completely or to have it executed completely.

This makes it easier to examine the individual commands in the AUTOEXEC.BAT and CONFIG.SYS files.
Accordingly, you can isolate problems when your system configuration or other batch files are not operating
as you would wish.

There are two other startup commands in the MS-DOS
6.2 version: Ctrl-F5 and Ctrl-F8. These key combinations have the same effect as the F5 and F8 keys but
they also de-activate the DoubleSpace program at the
same time if this disk compression program has been
installed.

In versions 6.0 and 6.2, it is possible to de-activate the
F5 and F8 switches by specifying SWITCHES=/N in the
CONFIG.SYS file. If you wish to de-activate the Ctrl-F5
and Ctrl-F8 switches, you will have to make use of the
/SWITCHES option in DoubleSpace. For additional information about this, refer to DoubleSpace (section
13.5) and to the MS-DOS Help screens.

In addition, if you have the 6.2 version of MS-DOS, you
can run through **any** specified batch file by activating
the command interpreter and giving the command:

```
COMMAND /Y /C test.bat
```

where TEST.BAT represents the batch file you wish to examine. You then step through the batch file line by line. This is very useful if you are trying to debug batch files.

# 7    Using the harddisk

When preparing a harddisk for optimal use, you should be familiar with several procedures which you have not yet dealt with when using diskdrives:

■ Formatting the harddisk for the first time.
■ Creating a structure for the files.
■ Taking a number of safety measures.

Although, in daily use, instructions using the harddisk differ little or not at all from instructions using the diskdrive, the greater capacity makes it necessary to apply more regulations. Follow the advice which is given in various sections in this book. If something should go wrong with the harddisk, a great deal of data could all be lost at once.

> Make a copy on a diskette of the data on the harddisk (see section 7.3).
>
> Be extremely careful when transporting the computer - the hardddisk is very sensitive to bumps and jolts (see section 7.4).
>
> When you have switched off the computer, wait until you do not hear the harddisk rotating anymore before switching it on again.
>
> When using the FDISK, FORMAT, RECOVER and DEL *.* instructions, data can be lost very easily. Be extremely careful with these instructions.

## 7.1    Preparing a harddisk for use

If the computer dealer has not already done so, you will need to prepare the harddisk for use. The disk must have the so-called *low-level format*, which is generally the case with most disks. If problems occur in the execution of the processes outlined below, it is advisable to consult an expert.

**Partitioning the harddisk.** When working with MS-DOS, you can divide the harddisk into completely independent areas or partitions. This is useful if you wish to use different operating systems in your computer, such as OS/2 or UNIX. If you are working with an MS-DOS version previous to 4.0, partitions are also necessary in order to make full use of a harddisk which is larger than 32 Mb. From version 4.0 onwards, this is unnessary since the entire disk can be addressed. Further study of this subject matter lies outside the scope of this book - most readers will only use MS-DOS with the harddisk. If you install MS-DOS 5.0, 6.0 or 6.2 as the primary operating system on the harddisk, you can allow the SETUP installation program to carry out the partitioning immediately.

You must make at least one partition for the MS-DOS operating system on the harddisk. To do this, an *external system program* is necessary. This is loaded in the computer memory from the system diskette in drive A:.

**The FDISK instruction activates the program which partitions the harddisk.**

```
FDISK
```

FDISK      Fixed disk (harddisk).

If you start up the program for a harddisk already in use, you should first save all important data. The program deletes all data irretrievably.

The program generates a menu. Confirm standard option 1 to create a DOS partition. In the subsequent menu, the question will be asked as to whether the entire harddisk should be used for MS-DOS. Confirm the default answer (Yes) by pressing Enter. The program will ask you to place the system diskette in drive A: and to implement a warm start (reset). Subsequently, you only have to format the harddisk in the same way as a diskette.

*Example:* Create one partition for MS-DOS on the harddisk

```
A:\>fdisk                                              (1)

                        FDISK Options                  (2)

Choose one of the following:

1. Create DOS partition or Logical DOS Drive
2. Set active partition
3. Delete partition or Logical DOS Drive
4. Display partition information

Enter choice: [1]                                      (3)

Press Esc to exit FDISK                                (4)

Current fixed disk drive: 1                            (5)

Do you want to use the maximum available space for a
primary DOS partition and make it active? (Y/N)  ........ [Y]

System will now restart                                (6)
Place INSTALL diskette in drive A
Press a key when ready . . .
```

(1)  Drive A: is the current drive and the system diskette
     is located in this drive. This command activates
     FDISK.
(2)  The main menu of the program. The lines which are
     not relevant to this topic have been omitted.
(3)  The default option is [1]. In this example, you only
     have to confirm your choice by pressing Enter.
(4)  Press Esc if you do not wish to use any of the avail-
     able options. The program will then return to the
     DOS prompt, A:\>.
(5)  If you have chosen the first option, the menu will be
     replaced by this message. Confirm the standard
     reply Y, because only one partition should be cre-
     ated. In the case of more extensive configurations,
     more choices are available in (2) and (5).
(6)  If the system diskette is still located in drive A:\, you
     only need to press a random key. The program in-
     stalls the partition for MS-DOS and assigns Drive
     C: to it.

### Formatting the harddisk and copying the system files

You do not need a system diskette if your computer has a harddisk containing the system programs.

In section 4.3, we saw how system files can be copied to a new diskette simultaneously with formatting. The procedure is analogous in the case of the harddisk. Place the system diskette in drive A: and give the command:

```
A:\>FORMAT C:/S[/V]
```

The command formats the harddisk C: and then copies the system files from A: to C: using the /S option. In versions prior to 3.3 of MS-DOS, you have to specify the /V option along with the command if you also wish to allocate a name (of maximum eleven characters) to the harddisk. Otherwise, at completion, the program will ask for a name for the disk.

Subsequently, copy all external system programs from the system diskette to the harddisk:

```
A:\>COPY *.* C:
```

From this moment onwards, the operating system will use the files on the harddisk when starting up if drive A: is not locked. It does not matter whether a diskette is located in this drive or not. The computer's internal starting procedure always looks for the system files in drive A: first. If they are not found there, the computer switches to the harddisk and loads the operating system from there.

## 7.2    Managing the harddisk

In previous chapters, you have become acquainted with the most important commands for working with programs and data. It has also become clear how complex it may be to work with a large harddisk and a substantial directory structure. However, there are some utilities which can assist you with these tasks:

■ The MS-DOS Shell, which is a graphic user-interface for DOS programs (see chapter 10).
■ Microsoft Windows, a graphic user-interface for programs from both Windows and DOS.
■ A graphic user-interface of a different type.
■ Self-made menus.

A graphic user-interface enables you to work effectively with large applications. In addition, some programs, such as Word for Windows and Microsoft Excel only run under Windows. However, if you work with only a few programs, which mainly run under MS-DOS, it is not necessary to purchase a graphic user interface. In that case, it is more advisable to define a menu yourself in order to activate the applications quickly and easily.

*Example:* Organizing the harddisk; a word-processing program is to be automatically activated by means of a self-defined menu

In this example, we shall integrate the know-how gained from the previous chapters:

■ Dividing the harddisk effectively.
■ Using directories.
■ Using batch files.

The organizational structure of the harddisk is more orderly when the root directory contains only files which must be stored there (up to and including DOS version 3.3; from version 4.0 onwards, COMMAND.COM may be located in a subdirectory). These are the files:

■ The program file of the command processor COMMAND.COM.
■ The configuration file CONFIG.SYS.
■ The start-up file AUTOEXEC.BAT.

In order to create an efficient organization, it is advisable to group files together in directories according to their functions: DOS files, applications, text etc. This has the advantage that all sorts of procedures concerning files (COPY, DEL) remain limited to the file category in question.

In the example, we shall create a DOS directory for the system programs (external commands), using the command:

```
C:\>MD \DOS
```

Subsequently, copy all programs from the external commands to this directory.

**Important:** If you do not know whether a file should belong to the \DOS directory or not, it is extremely important to make a backup of *all* files in the root directory in a reserve directory (\SAFE). Use the commands 'C:\>MD\SAFE' and 'C:\>COPY *.* \SAFE'.

If you are confident of what should be done, give the command:

```
C:\>COPY *.* \DOS
```

(You can, of course, copy wrong files to another directory later and/or delete superfluous files.) If you use the (copy of the) original system diskette, the following command will ensure that all the necessary files will be placed in the DOS directory:

```
C:\>COPY A:*.* \DOS
```

Subsequently, delete all the system programs from the root directory. Do *not* do this using the general file pattern *.* because other kinds of files are also stored there. Delete the files one by one (C:\>DEL DISKCOPY.COM etc.).

In the same way, create a particular directory for each application and copy the files to these: \WP, \DBASE,

\LOTUS, etc. After all these manoeuvres, the root directory contains only directories. In the example, in addition to the \DOS directory, we have filled only the \WP
directory with the appropriate files.

Copy these three files from the DOS directory back to
the root directory:

```
C:\>COPY \DOS\COMMAND.COM
C:\>COPY \DOS\CONFIG.SYS
C:\>COPY \DOS\AUTOEXEC.BAT
```

In the example, the root directory appears approximately as follows:

```
C:\>dir                                   (1)

  Volume in drive C has no label
  Directory of C:\

DOS          <DIR>     17/11/93   10:56   (2)
WP           <DIR>     17/11/93   10:56
CONFIG   SYS      490 15/11/93   14:48
AUTOEXEC BAT      507 14/11/93   19:30
COMMAND  COM   47,845 09/11/93    5:00
        5 file(s)       48,842 bytes
                       276,480 bytes free

C:\>dir \dos                              (3)

  Volume in drive C has no label
  Directory of C:\DOS

.            <DIR>     17/11/93   10:56
..           <DIR>     17/11/93   10:56
ANSI     SYS    9,029 09/11/93    5:00
^C
```

(1) Displays the list of files in the root directory.
(2) The \DOS and \WP directories and the three es-
    sential system files.
(3) Checks the list of files of the \DOS directory, dis-
    continued by pressing Ctrl-C.

The CONFIG.SYS file is read and interpreted before
AUTOEXEC.BAT when the computer is started up. The
path is not yet installed (see chapters 1 and 6). This
means that the instructions in CONFIG.SYS to activate

programs and drivers must be equipped with the path because these programs are no longer located in the root directory.

Therefore, the command which activates the screen/keyboard driver in CONFIG.SYS must be changed from DEVICE=ANSI.SYS to:

```
DEVICE=C:\DOS\ANSI.SYS
```

In the same way, the command concerning the specific formats for date, time and unit of currency (from version 3.3 onwards) is:

```
COUNTRY=044,437,C:\DOS\COUNTRY.SYS
```

You can use the TYPE command (or press F8 when MS-DOS 6.2 is being started up) to examine the instructions in your CONFIG.SYS. If necessary, write a new version using the copy command 'COPY CON CONFIG.SYS' or change the old version using your word processor (see section 6.2).

Only include the COUNTRY instruction in CONFIG.SYS if you have the 3.3 version or more recent.

Subsequently, extend the path in AUTOEXEC.BAT with the directories \DOS and \WP. This enables you to activate the external system programs and the word processor later from a random directory. Here also, you may choose between writing the file once more using 'COPY CON AUTOEXEC.BAT' or changing the previous version using a word processor. The path instruction is then as follows:

```
PATH=C:\DOS;C:\WP
```

Conforming to the scheme at the beginning of this section, two directories should be created for text files: LETTERS and MEMO. Create these directories using the commands:

```
C:\>MD \WP\LETTERS
C:\>MD \WP\MEMO
```

If you have followed the examples, the following structure of directories and files is now present on the harddisk:

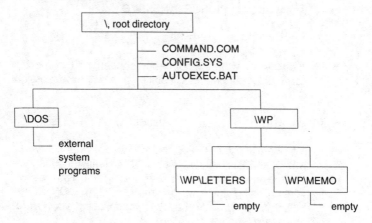

In principle, the contents of directories are not directly
accessible if you are not in the same directory. The
PATH instruction enables you to activate executable
files (programs) in a directory which is not current. The
APPEND instruction enables you to do the same with
other files in a non-current directory.

What are the benefits of working like this? If no path is
specified, a file is automatically saved in the current directory, even if the program which creates the file is located in another directory. Accordingly, letters and
memos are saved in the correct directory if you make
that directory active at the proper time. It is then very
easy to make a backup of a category of files on a diskette in drive A by using just one command: COPY *.*
A:.

In the example with which we are dealing at the moment, we shall make the \WP\LETTERS directory active
using a batch file, and we shall activate the WordPerfect

word processor from there. Thus, the letters which you then write will be saved in the \WP\LETTERS directory. When you quit the word processor, the operating system will continue with the batch file - switch to the root directory and clear the screen.
We shall create an analogous batch file for writing memos.

As an aid to memory for activating batch files, we shall write a text file with a menu screen (see section 5.2). This menu will appear on the screen when your computer is started up as a result of a TYPE instruction in AUTOEXEC.BAT. Write the menu using COPY CON, using EDIT from version 5.0 onwards or using a word processor.

```
+-------------------------------------------------+
|                                                 |
|            W O R D - P R O C E S S I N G        |
|            -------------------------            |
|                                                 |
|                 L = letters                     |
|                 M = memos                       |
|                                                 |
|                                                 |
|                                                 |
|         Choose a letter and press Enter         |
+-------------------------------------------------+
```

Save the text in the root directory under the name MENU.TXT. (Ensure that the word processor saves the text without the formatting codes, in ASCII format.) You can extend the menu later with other options, according to your own requirements.

The DOS command, TYPE MENU.TXT shows the menu on the screen at any chosen moment. It is best if you clear the screen beforehand using the command CLS. Add these commands to AUTOEXEC.BAT.

*Note:* To prevent batch file commands being displayed on the screen, specify ECHO OFF as the first instruction.

The last diagram in this section shows the contents of the new version of the AUTOEXEC.BAT file.

Each specified letter activates its own batch file: L.BAT and M.BAT. These batch files differ only in the directory which they activate.

It depends on your further computer pursuits whether it is more useful to include the \WP directory in the permanent path in AUTOEXEC.BAT, or to activate it using a new PATH instruction made with a batch file. The first method is more advantageous if you normally only use the word processor. The second method saves time for the operating system, since it does not have to look for \WP if you wish to use dBase for instance. These methods are illustrated in the example.

Due to the fact that the batch files differ so little from each other, the best way to deal with them is to write, copy and alter them using a word processor. This becomes more applicable the more you extend the menu.

The batch files contain the following instructions:

- Suppress the display of instructions.
- Switch to the work directory.
- Make a path to the directory containing the word processor, if it is not already present in the AUTOEXEC.BAT file.
- Start up the word processor.
- Switch back to the root directory.
- Clear the screen.
- Display the menu.

In the figure, the text from one of the batch files (L.BAT) is displayed.

```
C:\>type autoexec.bat                    (1)

echo off                                 (2)
path=c:\dos;c:\up                        (3)
prompt $p$g                              (4)
keyb uk 850 \dos\keyboard.sys            (5)
cls                                      (6)
type menu.txt                            (7)


C:\>type l.bat                           (8)

echo off
cd \up\letters                           (9)
path=c:\up;c:\dos                        (10)
up                                       (11)
cd\                                      (12)
cls                                      (13)
type menu.txt                            (14)
```

(1) Displays the contents of AUTOEXEC.BAT on the screen.

(2) Suppresses the display of commands on the screen. If you place an at sign (@) in front of ECHO, this will ensure that this command itself is not displayed.

(3) Installs the path to the directories.

(4) Shows the current directory in the prompt. This is normal in versions from MS-DOS 6.0 onwards.

(5) (In MS-DOS 3.3) Switches to the UK settings and the standard (USA) character set.

(6) Clears the screen.

(7) Displays the menu on the screen.

(8) Displays the contents of the L.BAT batch file on the screen.

(9) Makes the directory \WP\LETTERS current. (In the case of the M.BAT batch file, this is the \WP\MEMO directory.)

(10) Installs a new path. You will notice that the priorities of the directories have been switched.

(11) Activates the WordPerfect word processor.

(12) Switches to the root directory after quitting the word processor.

(13) Clears the screen.

(14) Displays the menu on the screen.

# 7.3 Protecting information on a harddisk

At various places in this book, we have emphasized that it is very important to safeguard information by keeping copies if it. You can use diskettes, a harddisk or cassette tapes (with a *tape streamer*) as storage media. This depends on your configuration.

The same instructions apply to both diskettes and harddisks when making backups - thus, for brevity, we shall refer to diskettes alone. Due to the fact that special hardware and a non-standard driver are necessary to save information on magnetic tape, we shall not deal with this possibility here.

**Safeguarding information by copying**. The simplest method of safeguarding information is to copy it to a diskette. This applies not only to files containing information but also to program files. Some manufacturers have saved their programs in such a way that they can only be copied back to the harddisk using a special program. In cases like these, it is of no use to make a copy on a diskette of the version on the harddisk.

The COPY command can be used for files in one directory on the harddisk. Using COPY, you can copy one file, a group of files or all files from a directory.

*Example:* Copying individual files, groups of files or all files from a directory to a diskette in drive A: (see illustration on the following page)

(1)  Switch to the OFFICE directory.
(2)  Copy the TMO1.TXT file from the current directory to the diskette in drive A:.
(3)  Copies all files with the .TXT extension to the diskette in drive A:.
(4)  The same as (3), but now for all files.
(5)  Switches to the root directory.
(6)  Copies the TMO.TXT file from a non-current direc-

tory to the diskette in drive A:. The operating system requires the path to the file.

(7) Copies all files in the non-active OFFICE directory to the diskette in drive A:.

```
C:\> cd text\memo\office               (1)

C:\TEXT\MEMO\OFFICE> copy tmo.txt A:   (2)

C:\TEXT\MEMO\OFFICE> copy *.txt A:     (3)

C:\TEXT\MEMO\OFFICE> copy *.* A:       (4)

C:\TEXT\MEMO\OFFICE> cd\              (5)

C:\> copy text\memo\office\tmo.txt A:  (6)

C:\> copy text\memo\office\*.* A:      (7)
```

**Copying a directory, including the files in the subdirectories.** From MS-DOS 3.2, there is an extended copy command which not only copies individual files, groups of files and all files in a directory, but also copies entire directories, *including* the subdirectories. In addition, this instruction can copy to a diskette of a different format. This is impossible using DISKCOPY due to the dissimilar format, and using COPY, it can only take place in progressive stages. The extended instruction enables you to copy complete branches of the harddisk directory tree to diskettes, using one command.

**The XCOPY instruction copies one or more complete directories, including the files in the subdirectories, from a harddisk or a diskette to another drive or another directory.**

```
XCOPY [d:]path/d:[path] [d:][path]
      [/A][/D:date][/E][/M][/P][/S][/V]
                                    [/W]
```

| XCOPY | Copy directory, including files. |
| [d:]path or d:[path] | Source directory or source drive. Specify at least one source directory, otherwise the command will produce an error message. The options between the square brackets are not compulsory. *Path* represents the complete path from the root directory. |
| [d:][path] | If you do not specify a destination drive and a destination directory, the directories or the files will be copied to the current directory (from where you activated XCOPY). |
| /A | Using this option, the command will only copy those files which have the *archive attribute*. The /A option does not alter the attributes of a file. |

**Explanation:** The archive attribute is one of the codes which is registered on the diskette along with the file name. Files may have more attributes, but this topic lies outside the scope of this book. This attribute is assigned to a new file and to a file which has been altered.

You can make the status of an attribute visible using the command:

```
ATTRIB [d:path]file_name
```

If the operating system replies with the letter A, the archive attribute of the file has been set.

You can set or remove this attribute yourself by using the commands 'ATTRIB +A file name' or 'ATTRIB -A file name', respectively.

If the Read Only attribute has been set, the file cannot be altered (ATTRIB +R file_name). Remove this blockage by specifying 'ATTRIB -R file_name'.

/D:date    The instruction copies only files which have been created since a given date.
Type the date according to the format you specified using the COUNTRY instruction in CONFIG.SYS. For the United Kingdom, that is dd-mm-yy.

/E    Empty. Using this option, you copy also the empty directories (without files). This option must always be accompanied by the /S option.

/M    Modify. The option has the same effect as /A, only, in addition, the archive attributes of the source files are deleted. This means that these files will only be copied at the next XCOPY instruction (with /A or /M), if they have been altered in the meantime.

/P    Prompt. Using this option, the instruction asks for each file whether it should be copied or not. Respond with y/Y or n/N.

/S    Sub. Copies one or more directories, including the subdirectories. The empty directories are only copied if you have also specified the /E option.

/V    Verify. Using this option, the instruction checks if there are differences between the originals and the copies.

/W    Wait. The command is only implemented after pressing a random key. This allows you the chance of placing an empty diskette in the destination drive, which is handy if you include the command in a batch file. You can cancel the command using Ctrl-C.

*Caution:* You should not use the XCOPY command if you have specified the APPEND/x command prior to this. If you wish to make regular use of this copy command, it is better to work with the PATH command instead of the APPEND command (see section 4.12).

*Example:* Copy the TEXT directory, as shown in the diagram, with the subdirectories LETTERS and MEMO and their files, from the harddisk C: to a diskette in drive

A: and then from the diskette in drive A: to a diskette in drive B:.

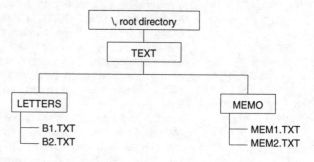

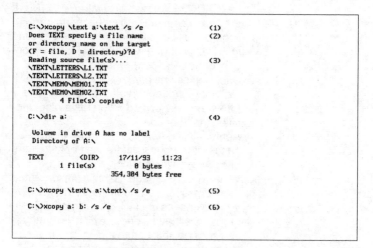

```
C:\>xcopy \text a:\text /s /e              (1)
Does TEXT specify a file name             (2)
or directory name on the target
(F = file, D = directory)?d
Reading source file(s)...                 (3)
\TEXT\LETTERS\L1.TXT
\TEXT\LETTERS\L2.TXT
\TEXT\MEMO\MEMO1.TXT
\TEXT\MEMO\MEMO2.TXT
      4 File(s) copied

C:\>dir a:                                 (4)

 Volume in drive A has no label
 Directory of A:\

TEXT        <DIR>     17/11/93   11:23
      1 file(s)           0 bytes
                    354,304 bytes free

C:\>xcopy \text\ a:\text\ /s /e            (5)

C:\>xcopy a: b: /s /e                      (6)
```

(1)  Copy the TEXT directory plus the TEXT\LETTERS
     and TEXT\MEMO directories from the harddisk C:
     to the diskette in drive A: under the same name,
     TEXT. The /S option copies all subdirectories of the
     specified directory. The /E option copies the empty
     directories in TEXT as well. The last option is
     superfluous since files are located in both direc-
     tories. There is no fixed order of sequence for the
     options.

(2) The program cannot deduce from the command whether the target is a directory or a file. If another backslash is located behind the target, TEXT, it can only be a directory. Then there is no prompt (see point 5).

(3) The program states that it is reading the source files and gives a list of the copied files, including their path.

(4) Due to the fact that there is not enough room in the figure to show the contents of the diskette in drive A:, we shall only display the file list in the root directory, without the headlines (we presume that the diskette was originally empty).

(5) The same command as in (1). The backslash behind the destination ensures that TEXT can only be interpreted as being a directory. The program does not have to ask for more information.

(6) Copies the \TEXT directory with all its directories and files from the diskette in drive A: to the diskette in drive B:. In this case, it is not necessary to specify the source directory, because no misunderstanding is possible. The same applies to the destination - if the diskette in drive B: is empty, there is no doubt as to where the directories and files should be saved.

**Protecting data using the BACKUP program (prior to MS-DOS 6.0).** It is rather laborious to make a complete copy of the harddisk using the standard copy instruction. You have to activate each directory separately in order to copy its files. In addition, you only copy the files using this method and not the tree structure of the directories. (Copying back is particularly tedious - first you have to reconstruct the tree and then work out which file on the diskette belongs to which directory on the harddisk.)

Another disadvantage is inherent in the copying process itself - the operating system gives an error message if a file on the harddisk does not fit on the target diskette. It would be an exceptional coincidence if the end of the file fitted exactly into the available space on the diskette.

MS-DOS provides a program which can deal with all the
problems mentioned above. Using this program enables you to:

■ Make a backup of all files and directories.
■ Write all data from the backup(s) back to the hard-
  disk.
■ Make a backup of a part of the files.
■ Make a backup of only those files which have been
  saved (altered) after a specified date.

The program states when the diskette is full. It will then
ask for another diskette and will subsequently continue
copying.

The destination diskette must already be formatted
(up to version 3.2).

Without the /A option, the files which are already located on the diskette will be deleted.

It is advisable to write successive numbers on the
diskette labels. The contents of the backup diskettes can only be written back in the same order of
sequence as they were written to the diskettes.

Up until MS-DOS version 5.0, the safeguard procedure
requires two *system programs* - one to make a copy of
the information and one to write the copy back to the
harddisk. Both instructions accept wildcards in the file
names.

**The BACKUP instruction activates a program which
makes a backup on diskette of information on the
harddisk (or vice versa)**

```
BACKUP [d1:][path][file.ext] d2:[/S][/M]
                     [/A][/D:date][/T:time]
  from MS-DOS 4.0 ALSO:
  [/L[:[d:][path][file]]][/F:byte]
```

BACKUP   Make a reserve copy.

d1:   Source drive.

file.ext   Name of a particular file of which you wish to have a copy.

d2:   Target drive.

/S   Subdirectories. Make a backup of all files and directories.

/M   Make only a backup of those files which have been altered since the previous backup instruction.

/A   Append. Add the backups to the files which are already located on the diskette.

/D:date   Make a copy of only those files which have been saved (altered) since the specified date

/T:time   Make a backup of those files which have been stored (altered) since the specified time.

/F:byte   The destination diskettes are formatted in the specified byte format for copying.

/L[:file]   After the copy process is concluded, a protocol file is created containing all the important data concerning the procedure just implemented, such as date and number of diskettes used. The protocol file may be placed in a different drive or directory. If no name is specified, the file will be assigned the name BACKUP.LOG.

*Example:* Making a backup of a harddisk on diskettes in drive A:.The copy program is located in the root directory on the harddisk (see illustration on the following page).

(1) Drive C: is current. The command activates the copy program which is located in the root directory. C: is the source drive, A: is the target drive. The /S option makes a backup of all the harddisk files and directories.

(2) The system registration requests the first diskette to be placed in the target drive. Ensure that the (formatted) target diskettes contain no indispensable

data. This will be deleted. The program states
where the information is located on the diskette. In
the example, there is only the root directory. The
command is implemented after striking a random
key.

```
C:\>backup c: a: /s                          (1)

Insert backup diskette 01 in drive A:        (2)

WARNING! Files in the target drive
A:\ root directory will be erased
Press any key to continue . . .

*** Backing up files to drive A: ***         (3)
Diskette Number: 01

\AUTOEXEC.BAT                                 (4)
\CONFIG.SYS
^C

C:\>backup c: a: /s/m                         (5)

C:\>backup c:\text\*.txt a:                   (6)

C:\>backup c: a:/s/d:24-09-93                 (7)

C:\>backup c:\basic\*.* a:/a                  (8)
```

(3) The program ascribes consecutive numbers to the
diskettes.
(4) The program first copies the root directory with its
files and then the directories successively with their
contents. In the example, the command is discontinued by pressing Ctrl-C.
(5) Copies all those files from the harddisk which have
been altered since the previous occasion a backup
was made.
(6) Makes a backup on diskettes of all files with the extension .TXT in the TEXT directory of the harddisk.
(7) Makes a backup on diskettes of all files which have
been altered since the 24th of September 1993.
(8) Copies all files from the BASIC directory from the
harddisk to the diskette in drive A: and adds them
to the files which are already located there.

**The RESTORE instruction activates a program
which writes the backup back to the harddisk from
diskettes which have been copied using BACKUP**

```
RESTORE d1: d2:[path][file.ext] [/S][/P]
                               [/M][/N][/D]
               [/B:date][/A:date][/E:time]
                                 [/L:time]
```

| | |
|---|---|
| RESTORE | Restore. |
| d1: | Drive of the diskettes containing the backups (source drive). |
| d2: | Drive to which the backups are to be written (target drive). |
| path | Destination directory for the back-ups |
| /S | Subdirectories. All files and directories. |
| /P | Prompt. The program asks permission to copy files back if they have the Read Only attribute on the target drive (or are more recently dated there). |
| /M | Modified. Writes back only those files which have been altered since the previous backup. |
| /N | Not. Writes back only those files which are no longer located on the target drive. |
| /D | Dir. Displays only the names of all files which are involved in this process; for instance, all text files which have been altered since the previous backup (*.txt/m) are shown but not written back. |
| [/B:date] | Before. Writes back only those files which have been altered prior to the specified date. |
| [/A:date] | After. Writes back only those files which have been altered since the specified date. |

| [/E:time] | Earlier. Writes back only those files which have been altered before the specified time. |
| [/L:time] | Later. Writes back only those files which have been altered after the specified time. |

*Example:* Write the backup files and directories from the diskette in drive A: back to the harddisk

```
C:\>restore a: c: /s                         (1)

Insert backup diskette 01 in drive A:        (2)
Press any key to continue . . .

*** Files were backed up 17/11/1993 ***      (3)

*** Restoring files from drive A: ***
Diskette: 01
\AUTOEXEC.BAT
\CONFIG.SYS
^C

C:\>restore a: c:\text\*.txt                 (4)

C:\>restore a: c:\basic /s                   (5)
```

(1) Writes all files and directories, which were copied to the diskette in drive A: using BACKUP, back to the root directory of the harddisk.

(2) The program requests the first backup diskette to be inserted in drive A:. Proceed by pressing any key.

(3) The program has registered that the correct diskette is in the drive and copies the files and the directories successively. The instruction is discontinued by pressing Ctrl-C.

(4) Copies all files with the extension .TXT from A: to the C:\TEXT directory.

(5) Copies all files and directories on the diskette in drive A: to the C:\BASIC directory. (This directory must already exist on the harddisk.)

**Protecting data using MSBACKUP (from MS-DOS 6.0 onwards).** Using the MSBACKUP program, you can transfer data on the harddisk to diskettes and copy them back again from the diskettes in a menu-driven operation. There is also a Windows version of this program under the name MWBACKUP. If you are mainly working with Windows, use this program. The operation of both programs is almost identical. Accordingly, we only need to outline the workings of MSBACKUP.

All directories and files, including the system files, can be archived. The program only runs on the harddisk. Normally it will be located in the DOS directory on the harddisk. The diskettes for the backups do not need to be formatted. Any data on the diskettes will be removed irretrievably. The diskettes are always fully written, even if a file is larger than the diskette. The program will then request additional diskettes.

The program can be operated using both the mouse and the keyboard. Choose the required options using the cursor keys. Press Enter to confirm these.

■ Activate the program from the prompt using the MSBACKUP command.

**Preparing the backup**

When you first start up the program, several tests will be carried out and the configuration determined. You must have two diskettes ready and available for this process. Clear instructions will be given on the screen. You will have to switch diskettes sometimes. You can modify default settings, if you wish, such as the required disk-drive. To do this, activate the appropriate option and adopt the required data from a list. Finally, the screen will look something like this:

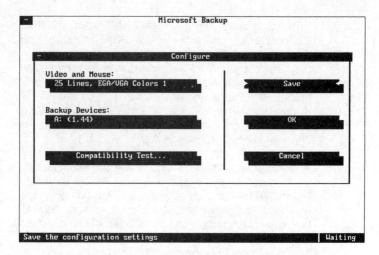

■ Save these settings using the Save button.

Subsequently, the window containing the MSBACKUP main menu will appear. This menu will appear on all future occasions when you activate the program:

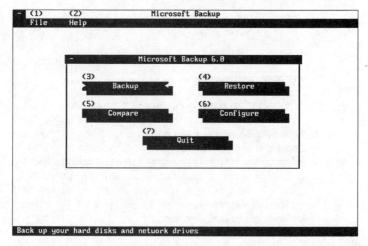

(1) The options in this menu enable you to open a different settings file, to save the present settings file

or to remove a file. In addition, you can print the configuration and install the printer.

(2) The options in this menu enable you to display information about the program. Press F1 for more information.

(3) Make a backup.

(4) Write the backup back.

(5) Compare backups.

(6) Modify the configuration.

(7) Close the program.

## Making backups

1. Select the menu option Backup and confirm this by pressing Enter or click on the option.

The Backup window then appears.

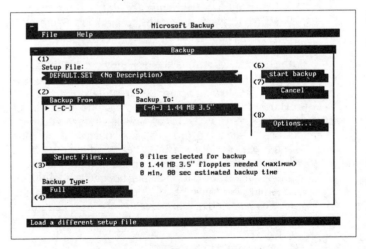

(1) The Default setup file. Select a different file if required.

(2) The drive is shown here from which a backup copy of data can be made. This applies to all or only certain data (files and directories) which are to be copied.

(3) If you only wish to copy certain directories or files, activate this option. A dialog box will appear showing the directory structure and the files stored there. Select the required directories and files.

(4) The Backup Types are Full (all files; after copying, the archive attribute is reset), Incremental (all files in which the archive attribute has been set to +A in the meantime; after copying, the attribute is reset to -A), Differential (as above, but now the backup attribute remains unchanged after copying).

(5) Select or confirm the diskdrive for the backups.

(6) Activate the backup process.

(7) Cancel.

(8) Select the required directories or files in the Options dialog box by clicking on them using the mouse or by moving to them using the cursor keys and activating them using the spacebar.

2. Select the required drives or files and the drive in which you wish to make the backups. Then start the backup process.

The program will request the diskettes one by one at the appropriate time. A catalog will be created on the last diskette, containing important information about the backups. If there are data on the diskette in the target drive, a warning will be given. You can then repeat, cancel or continue the process. Continuing the process leads to loss of data which is already on the diskette in the drive. When the backup procedure has been concluded, a message will be displayed, giving information concerning the backups, the number of diskettes, the capacity occupied and the duration of the procedure.

**Restoring the backups**

1   Activate the program using the MSBASIC command.

2   Activate the Restore option in the main menu.

The following window will appear:

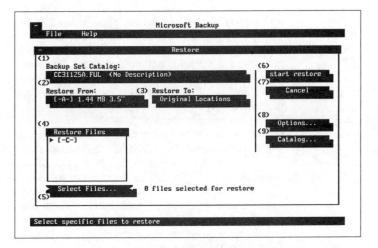

(1) The currently active catalog is shown here. Click on the button to display a window containing a list of possible catalogs. If the required catalog is present, load it. If you have made other backups in the meantime, you will have to retrieve the valid catalog from the last diskette of that backup procedure.

(2) Select the drive containing the backups which are to be written back.

(3) Select the destination for the files you wish to restore: Original Locations, Alternate Drives or Alternate Directories.

(4) The files which can be restored from the valid catalog are displayed.

(5) Select those files and directories you wish to restore from the active catalog.

(6) This command begins the restore procedure. This button is only active when files are selected.

(7) Discontinue the program.

(8) Open the Options dialog box and select the required settings by clicking on them or by moving to them using the cursor keys and activating them by pressing the spacebar.

(9) Activate this button to select the required catalog. Click on Retrieve in the subsequent window. Then click on the required drive. A message will appear

that the catalog is located on the last diskette. Insert the diskette and start up the procedure.

When the new catalog is active, this will be indicated by a tick mark. Quit the dialog box by selecting Cancel. Otherwise choose the Retrieve option.
The active catalog will be displayed in the Restore
window.

3.  If you have made various backups, you will have to
    select the appropriate catalog first. See point (9).
4.  Then activate the Restore Files option by selecting
    the Select Files option. The structure of the hard-
    disk is displayed. Select the required directory and
    activate it by pressing the spacebar. You can also
    select individual files in the other window. You can
    switch to the other window by pressing the Alt key.
5.  Start the restore procedure.

*Note:* When using MS-DOS 6.0 or 6.2, you can also restore backup files which have been created using a previous version of MS-DOS. Use the RESTORE command which was discussed in the previous section.

# 7.4    Protecting the harddisk during transport

A harddisk is very sensitive to jolts. If a harddisk is not
protected during transport, the write/read head can easily damage the magnetic layer of the disk. Not only can
data be lost, the mechanism which moves the head can
be deregulated, resulting in an inability of the operating
system to find information. Therefore, before you transport a computer with a harddisk, take the following
measures:

■  Make a backup of all data (see section 7.3)
■  Place the read/write head in a safe position.

To carry out this second safety measure, there are
utility programs which turn the read/write head to a safe

position. Consult the documentation about your computer to find the name of this program - common names are SHIPDISK, XPARK and PARK.

Some manufacturers supply the parking program on the diagnosis diskette in the manual. Place the diskette in drive A: and restart the computer. The diagnosis program will be activated and a menu will be displayed. Select the parking option.

Recent computers, particularly the laptops, automatically place the heads in a safe position as soon as you switch off the power. Consult the manual to find out if your computer also does this.

# 8    Other instructions

## 8.1    Interface settings for screen, printer and communication

The MS-DOS operating system contains an instruction which influences various interfaces and peripheral devices:

■ The screen (colour graphics adapter).
■ Printer (parallel interface).
■ Communications port (serial interface).

**The screen: number of characters per line**

It is occasionally convenient if the screen is able to display larger characters - for example, if you wish text to be read by a group of people. The screen has several modes: 80 or 40 characters per line, colour or black-and-white, and monochrome (only 80 characters).

**The MODE instruction specifies the screen mode**

```
MODE [display] [,r]
MODE CON [COLS=n][LINES=r]
```

MODE        Mode.
display     Number of characters, (colour) mode.
            40 or 80: the current (colour) mode remains active.
            BW40 or BW80: black-and-white display with 40 or 80 columns (CGA).
            CO40 or CO80: colour display with 40 or 80 columns.
            MONO: switch to monochrome adapter (80 characters per line only)

n      Number of columns displayed.

r    Number of lines (rows) displayed (25,43 or 50).
From MS-DOS 4 onwards: to display 43 or 50 lines,
ANSI.SYS must be included in CONFIG.SYS, by
means of the DEVICE=C:\DOS\ANSI.SYS command for example.

The MODE instruction on its own displays the current
settings of the peripheral devices.

**The printer: specifying the number of characters
per line and the space between the lines.**

**The MODE LPT instruction regulates the number of
positions per line and the number of lines per inch
used by the printer.**

```
MODE LPT#: [n][,[m][,P]]
```

MODE LPT   Printer mode (line printer).
#                 Number of the parallel printer port (1, 2 or
                  3). Instead of LTP1 you may also type PRN.
n                 Number of characters per line (80, 132).
m                 Line spacing (6 or 8 lines per inch, lpi).
P                 Permanent. This option ensures that the
                  operating system keeps on trying to send
                  characters to the printer if it is not yet
                  ready.

**Specifying the communications port.** You can connect a serial printer, modem, mouse or acoustic device
to the communications port (*serial interface, RS 232C
port*) of your computer.

You can only use a peripheral device with a serial connection if you regulate the computer interface to the
values specified by the manufacturer of the device. For
a *serial printer*, you have to specify both the following instructions. (In most cases, the printer is connected to
the parallel port.)

**The redirection version of the MODE instruction transports the output to the printer via the communications port.**

```
MODE LPT#[:]=COMn[:]
```

MODE LPT          Printer mode.
#[:]              Number of the printer (1, 2 or 3).
COMn[:]           Serial interface (COM1 or COM2).

**The MODE COM instruction regulates the communications port for serial (asynchronic) transmission.**

```
MODE COMn[:]baud[,[parity],[data bits],
                            [stop bits][,P]]
```

MODE              Regulating the mode.
COMn[:]           Serial interface (COM1 or COM2).
baud              Transmission speed (bits per sec-
                  ond). You only need to specify the
                  first two digits of the following valid
                  numbers: 110, 150, 300, 600, 1200,
                  2400, 4800, 9600, 19200.
parity            Each character if checked to ensure
                  proper transmission. The valid
                  values are: N (none, no parity bit),
                  O (odd, uneven parity), E (even,
                  even parity). The default value is E.
data bits         The number of bits sent per charac-
                  ter (7 or 8; the default value is 7).
stop bits         The end criterion (1, 1.5 or 2 bits -
                  the default value is 2 in the case of
                  110 baud, otherwise 1).
P                 E    Displays an error during the
                       status test of a connection
                       in working.
                  B    Indicates 'busy' to the oper-
                       ating system.
                  R    Indicates 'ready' to the
                       operating system.

N          Indicates 'none', that no
           new transmission attempt
           should be undertaken.

*Example:* Alterations are to be made to the settings
dealing with the screen, the printer and the communications port.

```
A:\>c: mode 40                        (1)

A:\>c: mode 80,r,t                    (2)

A:\>c: mode lpt1:132,8                (3)

A:\>c: mode lpt1:=com1               (4)

A:\>c: mode com1:12,n,8,1,p          (5)
```

(1)  The screen mode is set to 40 characters per line,
     with no change in the colour mode.
(2)  The screen mode is set to 80 characters per line,
     with no change in the colour mode.
(3)  The printer is set to 132 characters per line and 8
     lines per inch.
(4)  Output to the printer is sent via the communications
     port COM1.
(5)  The communications port is installed for a serial
     printer with 1200 baud, without parity control, 8
     data bits, 1 stop bit and without the routine which
     tests time-out errors.

## 8.2    Altering the prompt

The appearance of the system prompt differs according
to the supplier. The standard form displays the drive letter along with a 'greater than' sign. You can make the
prompt more informative by adding, for example, the
date, time, current directory, a chosen text etc. Using

so-called 'escape' functions, you can accentuate (parts of) the prompt, have them blink etc.

If you specify the instruction dealt with here, without parameters, the prompt will regain the standard form.

### The PROMPT instruction changes the form of the system prompt

```
PROMPT $x [$x]...
```

PROMPT    Without parameters, the operating system will continue using the standard prompt.

$    A dollar sign, the beginning code of a parameter. Without the dollar sign, the characters will be shown literally as text.

x    A character from the following list:
   d    date
   t    time
   p    current directory of the current drive
   n    current drive
   v    version of MS-DOS
   g    >, 'greater than' symbol
   l    <, 'smaller than' symbol
   b    ¦, pipe symbol
   q    =, equals sign
   h    back one space and delete previous symbol
   e    escape sign
   _    two symbols - CR plus LF (cursor to beginning of next line)

### Examples:

```
C:\>PROMPT $d $t$g        (PROMPT date, time>)
```

Result: Mon 01/11/93 15:56:26.32>

```
C:\>PROMPT $p$g           (PROMPT drive, directory>)
```

Result: C:\> (The standard prompt from MS-DOS 6.0 onwards)

```
C\>PROMPT
```

Result: C> (The standard system prompt prior to MS-DOS 6.0)

# 8.3    Assigning drive commands

The configuration with which you are working will not always have the same settings as those an application might expect. This can be problematic if the application expects a drive which your computer does not have. In a case like this, it is possible to allocate another letter to a certain drive. In this way, you can convert drive B: to drive C: or vice versa.

**The ASSIGN instruction registers a drive under another letter.**

```
ASSIGN x=y
```

ASSIGN       Allocate.
x              Original drive letter.
y              New drive letter.

**Example:**
```
C:\>ASSIGN C=B
```

# 9    Basic concepts

## 9.1    The working of the operating system

The processor is the heart of the computer. This is a collection of complex electronic switches which execute a great number of diverse calculatory, logical and organizational processes at high speed. The variation in problems which the processor must be able to solve is so large that it is not possible to include a suitable problem-solving method, in terms of an electronic component in the computer, for all cases. The system would be much too extensive and thus too expensive. In addition, it is not possible to make improvements to a solution method which is established in a chip. This could only be done by replacing chips or relocating them internally.

It is obvious that it is easier to distribute diskettes with an improved and more extensive version of the system programs than to supply all computers with a new set of processor chips. Computer programmers who are occupied with programs for the internal organization of computers are called system programmers.

The regulations and the organization of the processes needed to solve a problem are written in applications. The standard calculations in these changeable programs are executed by *operating programs* or *system programs* which, in turn, regulate the elementary steps carried out by the electronics in the processor. The collection of system programs which run the working of the computer is called the *operating system* or, in short, the system. (The word 'system' is generally used in the broader sense to include the hardware.)

**Components of a computer: an outline of the workings.** In order to understand the task of the operating system, we shall describe the most important computer components, categorized according to function.

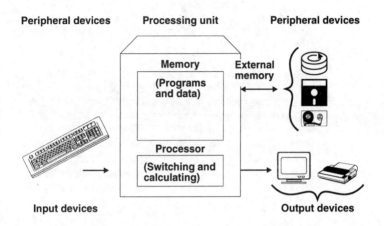

Peripheral devices     Processing unit     Peripheral devices

Memory   External memory

(Programs and data)

Processor

(Switching and calculating)

Input devices            Output devices

A complete computer, a device for electronic data processing (EDP), consists of two groups of components:

- the central processing unit (CPU)
- the peripheral devices.

The central processing unit consists mainly of:

- one or more processors
- the working memory.

Important peripheral devices are:

- input: keyboard, mouse, scanner etc
- output: screen, printer, loudspeaker etc
- external memory: magnetic disk, optic disk (CD ROM), magnetic tape etc.

The tangible EDP system devices are called *hardware*. Programs are called *software*. (In the extended meaning, lists and collections of data also fall into the 'software' category.)

Programs and information are entered using the keyboard or a scanner (previously also using punch cards and tape). If these have previously been entered in a

way legible to the computer, they can also be read from
an external storage medium, such as a harddisk or cassette tape etc.

Programs are mostly started up from the keyboard by
entering their name. The processor and the operating
system interpret the instructions in the program and implement them.

Information and the contents and results of programs
can be displayed on a monitor (screen), using a printer
or a graphic plotter in the form of letters and numbers,
as a picture, or in the form of an acoustic or optical signal.

Programs and original information need not be entered
every time they are to be used if they have already been
saved on a storage medium (diskette, cassette tape,
harddisk). This makes it easier to exchange information
and results.

**The tasks of the operating system.** The operating
system consists of a collection of programs. These programs, of course, can only be executed when they have
been loaded into computer memory. For this reason,
they are loaded automatically into memory when the
computer is started up, mostly from the harddisk, sometimes from diskette.

The system programs are loaded in a specific area of
the working memory. This is then no longer available to
applications. Many commands are stored in a chip with
a permanent memory. This applies particularly to the
start commands in the initial loading program (the *boot-
strap loader*). This program loads the operating system.
Other elementary routines are located in the BIOS chip
(Basic Input Output System).

The computer is confined to reading in the permanent
memory (Read Only Memory, ROM). This is in contrast
to the Random Access Memory (RAM) in which both
reading and writing can take place.

There are also computers which have the entire operating system in ROM. Then the system no longer requires loading from an external storage medium, but the system does have to make a copy in working memory. This occurs much more quickly than reading from disk.

Some operating systems load only the most frequently-used system programs in working memory (*internal commands*); other commands are then only loaded when they are requested (*external commands*).

As soon as the most important operating system programs are loaded, they take control of the processes in the computer. The figure on the following page indicates the direct influence exerted by the operating system.

An operating system must execute the following duties:

- Managing and controlling the execution of a program.
- Managing the input and output of information.
- Managing files on external media.
- Managing peripheral devices.
- Implementing the instructions of the user.
- Registering errors in the devices and in the operation of these.
- Saving, adjusting and stating date and time when required.
- Making conversion and test programs accessible.
- (Sometimes) managing simultaneous usage of the computer from different workstations in a network.
- (Sometimes) implementing different programs simultaneously (multitasking).
- Activating utility programs to safeguard information.

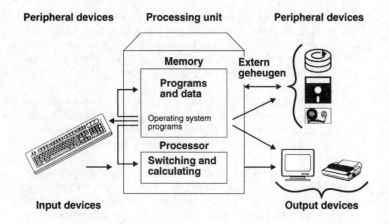

These duties are carried out by routines at two different levels:

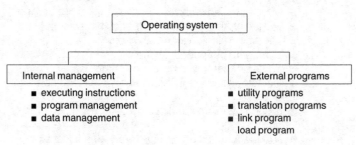

Some programs are needed constantly by the computer - they form the so-called *kernel* (IO.SYS, MSDOS.SYS) of the internal management. These procedures can be divided into three groups of routines with different functions:

■ Executing user commands *(job control)*.
■ Implementing a program: starting up, implementing measures, discontinuing, quitting, dealing with errors, management of virtual memory (storing parts of memory on harddisk), managing multitasking, managing multiple usage, etc. *(task control)*.
■ Managing the transport of data between system unit,

the storage media and other peripheral devices *(data control)*. Errors which occur in this process are also registered here.

*Utility programs* also play an important part, but they do not have to remain constantly in memory.

■ External instructions often execute recurring standard duties: copying, sorting, data transport, testing hardware and software.

There are, in addition, programs which mainly concern programmers:

■ Translation programs (assembler, compiler, interpreter) which convert legible commands (source code) into an executable program in machine code which suits the processor (object code).
■ A Linkage Editor combines a number of objects with standard routines which are stored ready-made in a library.
■ Load programs shift program modules (overlays) back and forth between working memory and external memory. In addition, there are programs which manage memory extensions.

**MS-DOS compared to other operating systems.** The demands on an operating system are mainly dependent on the capacity and speed of the hardware. The capabilities of a computer always depend upon the combination of the hardware and the operating system. When assessing the capabilities of a computer system, one should take into account:

■ calculation speed
■ storage capacity and writing and loading speed
■ availability of virtual memory
■ availability of multi-user facilities
■ availability of multitasking facilities.

In the light of these features, computers are divided into four categories according to size: mainframes, minicomputers, personal computers and home computers. The first two categories generally differ only in processing speed and memory capacity. In the latter two categories, also called microcomputers, there is seldom talk of configuration in a multi-user environment or of a system which works with multitasking. However, the most recent types of personal computers, ATs, tend more and more towards the minicomputer in terms of features.

The MS-DOS operating system has been developed for personal computers (PC, XT, AT). Up until version 3.0, MS-DOS was only usable in a single-user environment. Multitasking and virtual memory management has only become possible with the OS/2 operating system which is distant family of MS-DOS. It is possible to use MS-DOS in a system from a higher size category if that computer works with a set of instructions which emulates the DOS instructions.

The most important rivals to MS-DOS are:

| | |
|---|---|
| UNIX | This is a universal multi-user operating system (AT&T); XENIX (IBM); SINIX (Siemens). |
| DR DOS | Digital Research. |
| OS/2 | This is an operating system with a graphic user interface (IBM). |

# 9.2    MS-DOS structure and working

As mentioned in the first chapter, the letters MS, in the name MS-DOS, are an abbreviation of the name of the manufacturer, Microsoft. The letters DOS represent 'disk operating system'. The magnetic storage disk may be a harddisk, which is also called a fixed disk, or a floppy disk (diskette). We shall now only refer to diskettes, but the information also refers to operations using the harddisk. (Chapter 7 deals specifically with harddisks.)

The MS-DOS operating system was developed for the Intel microprocessors 8088 and 8086 Intel, but it is also compatible with the more powerful successors, 80186, 80286, 80386, 80486 and 80586 from the same firm.

MS-DOS is also usable on computers with processors from other manufacturers if the specific hardware routines are emulated by extra system programs.

The MS-DOS operating system is generally supplied along with the computer. The computer starting-up routine loads the most important system programs. Subsequently, these take charge of the management for implementing instructions and programs. This way of working is time-consuming, but it has the advantage that the operating system can be easily replaced by an improved version (see section 9.1).

The MS-DOS operating system consists of the following programs:

IO.SYS              Management of input and output.
MSDOS.SYS           The system kernel.
COMMAND.COM   The command interpreter.

The internal system programs IO.SYS and MSDOS.SYS cannot be found on the system diskette using the DIR command. They have the *hidden* file attribute. They are registered when the CHKDSK command is executed (see section 4.6). The third essential system program is the *command interpreter* COMMAND.COM. This program is visible in the normal list of files.

The three essential programs remain in memory as long as the computer is switched on - they are *resident*. Nevertheless, there is a difference, within the modules of COMMAND.COM, between 'essential' and 'important'. Components in the latter category may be replaced in memory, if necessary, by other programs. If you quit a program which has overwritten parts of COMMAND.COM and return to the operating system, you

will receive a request to place the system diskette in the
current drive if you have a computer without a harddisk.
The operating system can then reload the missing
parts:

```
Place diskette with COMMAND.COM in drive A:
```

In the case of a harddisk the computer loads the program automatically, if the circumstances correspond to
those outlined in chapter 7. If you do not wish to give
commands using external instructions, you can remove
the system diskette from the diskdrive and insert a diskette with an application.

**Instructions on the system diskette.** The COM-
MAND.COM program examines all input when the computer has been started up and compares the command
text to an internal list of reference words. If a word coincides with a word on the list, the corresponding module
in COMMAND.COM is activated and carried out immediately. Instructions which belong to the resident part
of the operating system are called *internal instructions*.
These instructions are readily accessible because they
are already located in memory - they only have to be
activated.

In the case of a reference word which does not occur on
the internal list, the instruction may refer to an external
DOS command or to an application. COMMAND.COM
searches in the directory of the current drive for a program containing the specified name. If it is located
there, the program is loaded into memory and activated.
The advantage of system programs which are only
loaded when they are explicitly named is that a large extent of memory remains available for applications.
These system programs are called *external instructions*. Thus, you can only use them when the MS-DOS
system diskette is placed in the current diskdrive (unless the files are located on a harddisk and you have installed a path to them).

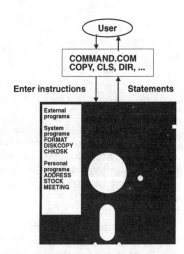

If COMMAND.COM cannot find the instruction name in a directory on the system diskette, this means that the requested program is unavailable (or the name has been specified erroneously). The command interpreter then states:

```
Bad command or file name
```

Change an erroneous command by entering it once more, correctly. If necessary, replace the current diskette with a diskette containing the desired program. Accordingly, it is important to inexperienced users that an application explicitly states when another diskette is required. There is a list of internal and external commands in the appendix.

**MS-DOS and computer type.** The fact that two computers have the same processor does not mean that they react in exactly the same way to the MS-DOS operating system. There are differences according to manufacturer, particularly in the interfaces between the hardware and the main MS-DOS system programs. The manufacturers qualify their goods using two differing descriptions:

- compatible with MS-DOS
- completely (100%) compatible with the IBM PC or
  with the industry norm.

The first claim merely means that methods of instruction specification and the results of the system programs are similar.

The second claim means that the applications which have been developed for the IBM PC will work in the machine in question, without any problem. It remains to be proved whether this is true or not for all applications which you may acquire.

Even without MS-DOS, personal computers already contain a limited operating system. The *basic input output system* (BIOS) consists of routines which manage the input and output at the most fundamental level (thus, 'basic'). The BIOS forms the link between the hardware and the IO.SYS input and output program of the operating system. The BIOS and IO.SYS together load the remaining main system programs in memory from the startup disk.

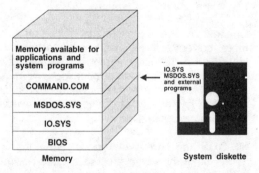

| Memory available for applications and system programs |
| COMMAND.COM |
| MSDOS.SYS |
| IO.SYS |
| BIOS |

Memory

IO.SYS
MSDOS.SYS
and external
programs

System diskette

If the BIOS of a compatible computer is not identical to that of an IBM PC, this must be compensated by IO.SYS. For a long time, small differences were necessary in order to allow clones to circumnavigate the IBM copyrights. This entails that the complete operating system of one computer is not automatically usable on another. The IO.SYS program straightens this out so that the two other main system programs are interchangeable (unless the manufacturer has altered something here too).

## 9.3    Input devices

Under the MS-DOS operating system, personal computers are mostly operated in conjunction with the keyboard. In the configuration, there are additional mains switches and specific switches on the devices: brightness and contrast on the monitor, line length and font on the printer etc.

During the last couple of years, the *mouse* has become extremely popular. If you shift this operating device over the table, a rubber ball underneath rolls along two small wheels which measure the distance moved. These measurements are translated into movements of the *cursor* on the screen. This shows the current working position. The shape of the cursor (block, arrow) differs according to the program. Using this, you can select an object or an option in a list (menu). By pressing one of the buttons on the mouse, you can give the instruction to execute the corresponding task: marking, deleting, drawing etc. The mouse was previously a device which was particularly used in graphic programs. Nowadays, the mouse is being increasingly used as an indication device in a menu system, replacing typed instructions via the keyboard. A driver must be installed for the mouse on the computer. This is supplied along with the mouse.

The *joystick* is available to operate computer games. This input device works in roughly the same way as the mouse. The movements of the joystick produce guide signals which relocate the movable object in the game. The buttons cause actions which differ according to the game.

**Keyboard.** Most manufacturers of compatible computers make use of the keyboard layout which was designed by IBM; for this reason we shall deal only with this type.

Since 1983 IBM has brought three types of keyboard on to the market: PC, AT02 and AT03 (advanced technology). (The abbreviation AT, with the same meaning, is now also used for the most recent type of personal computers, 80286-80586.) The AT03 type is also called the MF (multi-functional) keyboard. Due to the fact that the AT02 type was only in supply for a short time, most clone manufacturers have adopted the PC and MF keyboards as standard.

PC keyboards are now only supplied with PCs and XTs. Personal computers of the XT technology type are PCs which are suitable for a harddisk. Nowadays, MF keyboards are widespread with all types of personal computers.

**Keyboard compatibility.** It is not possible to just replace one kind of keyboard with another. In principle, each type of keyboard requires its own driver, but there are also MF keyboards nowadays which have a switch enabling you to change from the PC/XT mode to the AT mode.

**Keyboard and character set.** Normally, keyboards generate the American character set. This is troublesome for languages with tildes, accents and other special signs (French, German, for example). Keyboards for these countries often deviate in terms of layout and have other lettering on the keys. Using an appropriate keyboard driver, you can link a suitable character set to your keyboard (see chapter 7 concerning the DEVICE instruction for CONFIG.SYS). In addition, the keyboard driver adjusts the registration of the date and time to the national standard.

**Groups of keys.** Four groups of keys with different functions are located on the keyboard:

■ typewriter keys
■ numerical keys

■ operation keys
■ special keys and function keys.

**The typewriter keys.** The numbers and letters in the typewriter keypad work in exactly the same way as on a normal typewriter. The Shift keys change a letter to a capital letter, or to the upper character if two characters are shown on the key. In order to type a number of capitals successively, you can switch to the upper case by pressing CapsLock - this mode has no effect on the special characters on the number keys or on the punctuation marks. A small lamp will light up when the capital letter mode is active. In this mode, you can produce small letters by holding down Shift.

The hard carriage return on a typewriter (begin new line) is represented on a computer by the Enter key (may also read 'Return' and/or show an arrow pointing leftwards with short vertical extension).

**The numeric keypad.** The numeric keypad at the right-hand side of the keyboard facilitates the typing of numbers because you can type them with one hand. Normally these keys have the function of moving the cursor on the screen. Only when the numeric mode has been switched on using the NumLock key, will these keys generate numbers. There is also a small light to indicate this mode. Press NumLock again to switch back to the normal mode.

The following keys in the numeric keypad have functions in text editing:

■ on the 2, 4, 6 and 8 keys, there are arrows for moving the cursor. Under MS-DOS, only the leftwards arrow (delete) and the rightwards (move) have effect. The Backspace key in the typewriter block can also be used to delete characters to the left.
■ on the 0 key, there is also Ins (insert). This function produces an empty position in the text in order to insert a character. This also applies to the text of the

previous instruction in the input buffer of MS-DOS (see chapter 2).
■ on the decimal point key, there is also Del (delete). This function deletes the character at the current position. Under MS-DOS, you delete characters to the right in the input buffer.

The remaining number keys in this pad produce no effect under MS-DOS. Their further functions depend upon the application. In a word processor, that is mostly as follows:

| | | |
|---|---|---|
| Home | (7) | cursor to beginning of the line |
| End | (1) | cursor to end of the line |
| PgUp | (9) | move to the previous (screen) page |
| PgDn | (3) | move to the next (screen) page |

On MF keyboards, between the typewriter pad and the numeric keypad, there is a set of keys with positioning functions similar to those in the numeric keypad. The advantage of these is that they are logically grouped and that they remain available when working in the numeric mode.

**Operation keys.** Adjacent to the numeric keypad on PC keyboards, there are two keys with the names:

| | |
|---|---|
| Scroll Lock/Break | stop screen contents (output) rolling |
| Print Screen (PrtSc) | transport screen contents to the printer |

On an MF keyboard these functions are divided over three keys:

| | |
|---|---|
| Print Screen | print screen contents |
| Scroll Lock | has no function under MS-DOS |
| Pause | interrupt command (for example, scroll) |

In the upper left-hand corner and along the bottom, you will find the following operation keys:

Esc    return to the previous activity
Ctrl   control, regulate
Alt    alternate, another code

On MF keyboards there are two Ctrl and Alt keys. In some applications it does make a difference whether you use the right or the left key. This also applies to Shift. We refer you to chapter 2 for an outline of the operation keys under MS-DOS.

In applications, these keys mostly acquire another meaning:

Esc              quit the main program or the current module
Alt+other key(s)    generate another character
Ctrl+other key(s)   execute an operating instruction

**Function keys.** There are two vertical rows of five function keys on the PC keyboard. On an MF keyboard, there is a row of twelve function keys at the top. Their function depends to a large extent on the application (often the help menu is activated by F1). There are few programs which use F11 and F12.

Under MS-DOS, only the keys F1 to F6 have a function when entering instructions (see chapter 2).

**Note:** In principle you may redefine each key, allocating it a different effect, but in order to do this, the ANSI.SYS keyboard/screen driver has to be adjusted. (ANSI: American National Standards Institute.) To do this, you really require a thorough knowledge of programming using ASSEMBLER, but nowadays you can also purchase utilities which can assume this task. It is also possible to define a key otherwise, using an ANSI command (escape sequence). However, it lies outside the scope of this book to deal with this topic more extensively.

# 9.4    Disk memory

We mentioned in section 9.2 that it is possible to operate a personal computer using the system diskette. In
general, it is also necessary to store the programs you
write or the data you calculate permanently on external
storage media. If you do not do so, these will be lost as
soon as you switch off the computer.

A harddisk has the advantage over a diskette in that it
works at a greater speed and has a much larger capacity. The price of harddisks has decreased to the extent
that almost all personal computers are now equipped
with them. PCs with only one diskdrive are beginning to
become a rarity.

The great advantage of diskettes is that they can easily
be transported and that they provide cheap and flexible
storage of backups of programs and information. Although replaceable harddisks are increasingly coming
into use, most users still work with diskettes. For this
reason, we shall we shall pay special attention to diskettes in this section.

**Disk management under MS-DOS.** MS-DOS manages disks using a letter, beginning with A. The second
diskdrive is normally referred to as B and the first harddisk is always C, even if there is only one diskdrive. The
position and relative situation of the diskdrives in the
system unit differs according to type. This may have tedious consequences if you save files on the wrong diskette when using an unfamiliar computer.

You can allocate another letter to a drive by using the
ASSIGN command. In order to activate a program or to
load a data file, you generally have to specify the letter
of the source drive in the instruction. However, this is
not necessary if the source drive is the current drive (i.e.
the drive whose letter is shown in the system prompt on
the screen. Instead of 'A:\>DIR A:' you can simply type
'A:\>DIR'.

**Saving programs and data.** The contents of a program or a collection of data is written to a diskette as a *file* with its own name. The information concerning files (name, size, position, attributes, date etc) is registered in a separate part of the diskette. The contents of the file are written in the data section of the diskette in binary form.

The contents of a file are not directly legible. Only an application program, which has been activated in memory, is able to load, interpret and display a file.

If a file on a diskette is an executable file (program file), it can only become active when it has been loaded in memory by an instruction and then started up (see chapter 1).

New diskettes are not yet ready to receive information - there are no markings allowing the information to be retrieved. The preparation of a diskette is called *formatting*. MS-DOS has a program called FORMAT which carries out this operation. This program makes circular magnetic tracks on which the information is written in miniscule magnetic patterns. Each track is divided into sectors - the quantity differs according to the type of diskette.

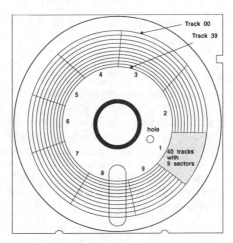

**Types of diskette.** In compatible personal computers, four types of diskette are now in use, each having its own specific demands on the diskdrives, according to size and/or write-density.

From MS-DOS 2.0 onwards:
a) 5.25 inch diskettes with double density (DD, 360 Kb).

From MS-DOS 3.0 onwards (instead of or in addition):
b) 5.25 inch diskettes with high density (HD, 1.2 Mb).

From MS-DOS 3.2 onwards (instead of or in addition):
c) 3.5 inch diskettes with double density (DD, 720 Kb).

From MS-DOS 3.3 onwards (instead of or in addition):
d) 3.5 inch diskettes with high density (HD, 1.44 Mb).

**Type A, the standard diskette for PCs and XTs**
Personal computers with the 8088 or 8086 processor have, as a rule, at least one diskdrive. Mostly, they have a second diskdrive or, in the case of an XT, a harddisk. Diskettes with the following features should be placed in the diskdrives:

| | |
|---|---|
| 5.25 inch | diameter of the diskette |
| double-sided (DS or 2) | information written on both sides |
| double density (DD) | information written in double density form |
| 48 tpi | |

MS-DOS formats this diskette in the following way:

■ 40 tracks on each side
■ each track is divided into nine sectors
■ each sector has a capacity of 512 bytes (characters).

This means that the capacity of this diskette is 2x40x9x512=368,640 bytes. That is 360 Kb (1024 bytes is one Kb).

Some older types of diskdrive are only able to write on one side of the diskette. These drives can format one side for 180 Kb. To do this you must give the FORMAT command with the /1 option.

In the oldest versions of MS-DOS (1.0 and 1.1) diskettes were formatted with eight instead of nine sectors. Diskettes like these can be formatted using more recent versions of FORMAT if you specify the /8 option. Single-sided capacity is 160 Kb, double-sided is 320 Kb.

**Type B, the standard diskette for ATs**
The more recent personal computers with the 80286, 80386 or the 80486 processor use diskettes with greater write density. ATs (advanced technology) use diskettes with the following features:

| | |
|---|---|
| 5.25 inch | diameter of the diskette |
| double-sided (DS or 2) | information written on both sides |
| high density (HD) | information written with high density |
| 96 tpi | 96 tracks per inch |

If no options are specified, from version 3.0 onwards, FORMAT will format these diskettes in the following way:

- 80 tracks on each side
- each track divided into fifteen sectors
- each sector has capacity of 512 bytes (characters).

This means that the capacity of this diskette is $2 \times 80 \times 15 \times 512 = 1,228,800$ bytes. This is 1.2 Mb (1 Mb = 1024 Kb = $1024 \times 1024$ bytes).

**Caution:** HD diskettes which have been formatted for high density cannot be read by diskdrives for normal density (DD). The other way around is generally possible - a 1.2 Mb diskdrive is almost always able to read 360 Kb diskettes.

In most 1.2 Mb diskdrives it is possible to format DD diskettes if you use the FORMAT command with either the
/4 option or the combined option /T:40 /N:9 (see section
4.3). These diskettes have, of course, a capacity of 360
Kb. On your own computer, a diskette which has been
formatted in such a way will cause no problems, but if
you use it to exchange information on someone else's
computer, there is a chance that reading errors may
occur. Especially on other PCs and XTs, there is the
chance that the diskette will (appear to) be illegible. This
is due to the fact that the method of writing is different
when using an AT than when using PCs and XTs. In addition, the writing and reading heads may differ a little
with respect to their positioning.

Practice shows that many of these faults can be
avoided if the diskettes are formatted in the diskdrive
which has to read them later.

Never format a DD diskette in a HD diskdrive without
using the options mentioned above.

Depending upon the diskdrive and the quality of the diskettes, it is sometimes possible to format a capacity
greater than 360 Kb, but these diskettes cannot be used
on another computer because they are not legible there.

**Type C, the small diskettes for personal computers**
From version 3.2 onwards, MS-DOS can work with 3.5
inch diskettes for personal computers. These diskettes
can be used along with 5.25 inch diskettes, or instead of
them. 3.5 inch diskettes are not only smaller and therefore handier in portable computers (laptops), they also
are protected by a much more sturdy plastic casing.
These diskettes have the following features:

| | |
|---|---|
| 3.5 inch | diameter of the diskette |
| double-sided (DS or 2) | information written on two sides |
| double-density (DD) | information written with double density (most manufacturers do not specify this) |
| 135 tpi | 135 tracks per inch |

If no options are specified, FORMAT will format these diskettes in the following way:

- ■ 80 tracks on each side
- ■ each track divided into nine sectors
- ■ each sector has capacity of 512 bytes (characters).

This means that the capacity of this diskette is 2x80x9x512 = 737,280 bytes. That is 720 Kb.

**Caution:** 3.5 inch diskettes cannot be used in a 5.25 inch diskdrive.

### Type D, the small diskettes with high write density
From version 3.3 onwards, MS-DOS also uses 3.5 inch diskettes with high write density. These diskettes have the following features:

| | |
|---|---|
| 3.5 inch | diameter of the diskette |
| double-sided (DS or 2) | information written on both sides |
| high density (HD) | information written with high density |
| 135 tpi | 135 tracks per inch |

If no options are specified, FORMAT will format these diskettes in the following way:

- ■ 80 tracks on each side
- ■ each track divided into eighteen sectors
- ■ each sector has a capacity of 512 bytes (characters).

This means that this diskette has a capacity of 2x80x18x512 = 1,474,560 bytes. That is 1.44 Mb.

In most 1.44 Mb diskdrives, it is possible to format normal DD diskettes if you give the FORMAT instruction with the combined option /T:80 /N:9. These diskettes have, of course, a capacity of 720 Kb. (The remarks concerning the legibility of type B also apply here.)

If you attempt to format a DD diskette in a HD drive

without the options mentioned above, this may be successful. If you are fortunate, these diskettes will not cause problems on your own computer, but there is a large chance of encountering problems when using them in other computers. Most diskdrives will not accept the instruction because they identify the type of diskette by the square hole in the HD diskette casing (opposite the write protection sleeve).

**Caution:** It is impossible to read or to write a HD diskette in a diskdrive for normal write density (DD).

**Exchanging information via diskettes.** Diskettes are a very handy means of transporting programs and information files from one computer to another. This can only take place, of course, if the diskettes used are compatible with the diskdrives in both computers. The way in which the information is stored on the diskette depends upon the diskdrive and the storage format which the operating system uses. In order to be able to use diskettes which have been formatted under MS-DOS to transport files, it is necessary that both computers be constructed according to the industry standard.

Whether the transported *programs* also work on the second computer is another matter. The software compatibility of a computer depends on the hardware and the permanent components of the operating system (see section 9.2).

Passive *data files* do not cause problems with computers which are not fully compatible, as long as they have been saved in ASCII format (American Standard Code for Information Interchange).

**The treatment of diskettes.** When using diskettes, nothing can go wrong as long as you treat them with care. The 5.25 inch diskettes, in particular, are vulnerable to pressure, bending, dirt, high or low temperatures and magnetic fields. The diskettes mostly bite the dust only after a reasonable length of time unless they have been badly treated. 3.5 inch diskettes are less sensitive to mechanical maltreatment due to the sturdy plastic casing and the sleeve over the opening for the write/read head. This is, however, no reason to carry them loosely in a jacket pocket full of breadcrumbs.

**The following good habits also apply to advanced users!**

- Make a backup of important information and programs.
- Place a diskette in its holder directly after use.
- Do not touch the write surface.
- Write the label while it is still on the sticker sheet. Do not erase on the diskette.
- Keep and transport diskettes in a plastic or hard cardboard box.
- Do not allow diskettes to be influenced by extremely high or low temperatures. Be wary of dust and cigarette ash. Keep the diskettes away from strong magnetic fields (telephone, electromotors, electromagnets).

**Copying, copy protection, copy programs.** In principle, it is possible to copy, alter and delete the operating system, other programs and data files to, or on, a formatted diskette using one of the DOS instructions.

Some software manufacturers protect the copyright on their applications by making copying more difficult by using a programming trick, a deviating storage format or a physical blockage on the diskette. Copying is then no longer possible using the standard MS-DOS instructions. In practice, a new copy protection is always decoded quite quickly, and an appropriate copy program appears on the market.

Of course, it remains a fact that illegal copying is a form of stealing. Copying for third parties is only allowed if you have received explicit permission for this.

**Write protection.** You can protect diskettes against unintentional overwriting by using a write protection. In the case of a 5.25 inch diskette, you can tape over the

notch with an opaque sticker. In the case of a 3.5 inch
diskette, you can open the little sleeve to activate the
protection. A protected disk can be read, but nothing
can be written to it.

If you attempt to write on a diskette with write protection,
the operating system gives an error message:

```
Write protect error writing drive A
Abort, Retry, Fail? _
```

Place an unprotected diskette in the drive (or remove
the protection) and reply with R (Retry).

Make a habit of protecting diskettes containing important programs or data immediately after saving, by applying a sticker or by opening the protection sleeve.

Put away a diskette only after you have attached a label
indicating the most important files and the date of saving. Write the information on the label first and then attach it to the diskette in order to prevent the pressure of
writing damaging the diskette surface.

# 9.5    Files

A collection of information can only be saved in the form
of a file.

- A *file name* consists of a maximum of *eight* alphanumeric characters or other allowed characters. A file
  name may have an extension consisting of a point
  and a maximum of *three* characters. For example:
  FILENAME.DAT
  HOUSE.111
  12345678.XYZ

- Internally, MS-DOS fills up short names and short or
  missing extensions with spaces. You have already
  seen in the file lists that the point of the extension is
  not shown. For example:

| LETTER.TXT | LETTER____ TXT |
| INTER92.3 | INTER92_ 3__ |
| NOW | NOW_____ ___ |

■ You may write file names using small or capital letters. Internally, MS-DOS uses only capitals.

■ A file name may only occur once on the same diskette (unless in different directories). The same file name may, of course, occur on different diskettes. Files may have the same name if the extension differs. For example:
NOTES.001
NOTES.002
NOTES.003

In versions prior to 3.0, file names may not contain characters with accents (ASCII codes above 127). This is permitted in more recent versions (for instance, using Alt+number), but this is not applicable to all characters. For this reason, you should only use normal letters and, of the special characters, only the hyphen or the underlining.

**The following characters are not valid in file or directory names:**

. , ; : = + < > [ ] / \ | * ?

*A name may not include spaces, even at the beginning.*

A distinction can be made between data files and program files.

**Data files** are (ordered) collections of numeric, alphanumeric and graphic characters (the ASCII codes from 0 to 255) which are stored in such a way that they can be interpreted by an application.

Imagine an article (for a well-read daily newspaper) has been written using a word processor and has been saved under the name REP.TXT. The letters, punctua-

tion marks and numbers in the article make up the data
in the REP.TXT file. Using the word processor, you can
reproduce the data later on the screen or on the printer.

```
Data file: REP.TXT
----------------------------------------------------

Police are considering whether charges can be
brought against the Rap group Gr-Gr-Groin on ac-
count of their latest single 'Show your bottoms
in the House of Commons'. The single, taken from
the LP 'Another Brain Cell Would Make One' con-
tains the allegedly offensive line "Show Black
Rod your wig". Spokesman for the group, Mr Reg
Nostril, remarked at the opening of his brother's
new glue factory, "We cuff care don't a," before
collapsing into the back seat of his limousine.
```

Other sorts of data files contain, for example, numbers
from spreadsheets or picture elements (pixels) from
graphic images.

**Program files** consist of a collection of commands
which can be registered in two different ways.

Command file: If, for instance, you use the BASIC language to write a program which calculates interest, you
will use commands which you yourself are able to read.
Commands which people can read without expert
knowledge of program language is called *source code*.
This type of file can be written, altered and saved using
a word processor in the same way as a text file.

Object file: A computer cannot directly execute commands written in the form of legible text. They have to
be translated first into much smaller commands in a
code which the computer can process. The result consists of ones and zeros only. This is machine code or
*object code*. These data can also be saved as a file, an
object file. A program which is available as an object file

can be directly executed by the computer. This is an executable program. Depending on the programming language, the translation program is called a *compiler* or an *assembler*. There are languages which translate the commands one by one at the moment the program is being executed in working memory: the object code is temporary. These types of language behave as an interpretor and accordingly are referred to as *interpreter* languages. There are compilers and interpreters for some programming languages such as BASIC, dBASE and C.

The contents of a file can be displayed using a DOS command or a word processor (see section 3.8). For most users, the display will only be legible if the file has been saved in ASCII format (text file and source code). Compiled and assembled files (object files) appear to consist of a hotch-potch of strange signs on the screen. These types of files can only be decoded using specific utilities.

| Program file | Program file |
|---|---|
| INTEREST.BAS | INTEREST.EXE |
| (program text) | (object code) |
| ------------------------------- | ------------------------------- |
| 10 INPUT K,P,D | 1001110111011010 |
| 20 LET R=K*P*D/(100*360) | 1110101010001001 |
| 30 PRINT R | 1010101111001111 |
| | 1001000000101101 |

**Reserved file names and extensions.** Under MS-DOS, several names are reserved for special files, devices, temporary files and utility files. If you use these names for your own files, there is a strong possibility that MS-DOS will interpret these according to the special, reserved significance. This may lead to loss of data.

The following names are used by MS-DOS as a utility file in the redirection of data, in the linkage of program modules and in the restoration of damaged files:

```
%PIPE        NUL       FILEnnnn.CHK
@...         VM.TMP    FILEnnnn.REC
```

The nnnn characters represent numbers from 0000 to 9999.

The following names are reserved for the peripheral devices with which MS-DOS can work:

```
AUX    COM1    CON    LPT1    PRN
       COM2           LPT2
                      LPT3
```

The extensions listed below are automatically added to a file name by MS-DOS, a translation program or an application. In most cases, you are not able to influence this process. You will often encounter them in directory lists.

```
.$$$    .BAS    .COM    .HEX    .MAP    .REL
.ASM    .BAT    .CRF    .LIB    .OBJ    .TMP
.BAK    .BIN    .EXE    .LST    .REF
```

**Grouping file names according to a pattern.** Normally, a separate command is required for each file which you copy or delete.

*Example:* Imagine that you wish to copy four text files from diskette A to diskette B. Four commands are needed to do this.

In cases like this, MS-DOS provides the possibility of combining commands by means of non-defined characters. These are called *wildcards*. A question mark takes the place of one (any) character, and an asterisk represents all subsequent characters from the current position onwards.

In this way, the four copy commands in the example can be unified in one command:

```
COPY A:LETTER?.TXT B:
```

*Caution:* This command will also copy the LETTER9.TXT file although this may not be the intention. See also the example in section 4.4.

If you also wish to copy the backups of these files (with the extension BAK), you can replace the extension with an asterisk:

```
COPY A:LETTER?.* B:
COPY A:LETTER*.* B:
```

**More examples:**
The first column of the table displays examples of files which can be combined in one name by means of the wildcards. The combined name is shown in the second column:

| Files | File pattern |
| --- | --- |
| LETTERAB.TXT...LETTERXY.TXT | LETTER*.TXT |
| PROGRAM.101...PROGRAM 123 | PROGRAM.1?? |
| All BASIC programs | *.BAS |
| All files with the name DOC | DOC.* |
| All files | *.* |

**Obvious file names.** Always give a file a meaningful name, so that you (roughly) know what the contents are without having to have them displayed. The standard extensions which applications and translation programs (compiler, interpreter, assembler) assign will assist you in this.

Examples of meaningful names:

ADDRESS.BAS     BASIC program which deals with
                adresses
MEMBERS.ADD     members address file
GASMETER.Y93    gas meter figures 1993
AGENDA.TXT      heading of meeting agenda
UGHH4393.TXT    inlaws coming to dinner 4th of
                March 1993
MMMM4993.123    plans for evening out with new
                boy/girlfriend

# 9.6     Installation of hardware and software

Before you can begin using an AT computer which has
an 80286, 80386, 80486 or 80586, it is necessary to install and register the hardware components using a
special start-up program. Fortunately, this is generally
done by the manufacturer or the supplier. We shall not
discuss here what the program demands and performs,
we shall only make a couple of remarks.

**Actually installing the hardware.** An AT configuration
can consist of several components, for example, two
diskdrives, two harddisks, various serial and parallel interfaces, a video card for a monochrome or colour
screen, working memory with capacity between 512 Kb
and 16 Mb or more. Without special measures, MS-
DOS is only able to address 640 Kb memory directly.
For all components, you must consult the manuals and
other documentation.

**Configuring the hardware.** The computer components
can only work when they are aware of each other's existence. They must be registered using a utility. This
utility is mostly located on the system diskette under the
name SETUP, or it is stored in a small memory which
saves the information with the assistence of a battery
(CMOS memory), or in the ROM BIOS.

Activate the utility on the diskette using the SETUP instruction, or directly from the permanent memory using the key combination Ctrl-Alt-Esc. If the program is not present in your system, you must acquire it.

The SETUP utility procedure differs according to type, but the program on the Advanced AT Diagnostic Disk from IBM has functioned as an example in most cases. It implements the following tasks (among others):

■ checks the system
■ registers the system components
■ physically formats the harddisk.

### Installing MS-DOS 5.0

If you wish to replace your present MS-DOS version by version 5.0, you can select one of two programs:

■ MS-DOS 5
■ MS-DOS 5 upgrade

The normal version is only required if no MS-DOS has been installed on your computer as yet. If you already running a DOS version between 2.11 and 4.01, the upgrade will suffice. The greatest difference between the program versions is that the first diskette in the normal version is the startup diskette. This diskette is not necessary in the upgrade version because the computer can activate itself.

In both cases, the installation is implemented by the SETUP program. With the upgrade version, you will have to activate this yourself (enter SETUP); with the normal version, this will take place automatically when the computer is started up. The installation is simple and is carried out automatically. You only need to select the required installation. When upgrading, you must have two diskettes available in order to save the existing configuration data. The old DOS version can be stored in the OLD_DOS1 directory on the harddisk if required or on diskettes.

### Installing MS-DOS 6.0 or 6.2

You can install MS-DOS 6.0 or 6.2 on a computer where there is an old version of MS-DOS (this is called an *upgrade*), and also on a computer where no MS-DOS is active as yet.

If there is no operating system installed (or a different operating system), insert the diskette 1 Setup in disk-drive A: and start up the computer. Follow the instructions on the screen closely. If a different operating system is installed, Setup will ask if this should be removed. At this point, it is possible to discontinue the installation or to attempt to install MS-DOS 6.0 or 6.2 in addition to the other system. If OS/2 or Windows NT is active on your computer, discontinue the process by pressing F3 and read the information in the README.TXT file on system diskette 1. To do this, give the command TYPE README.TXT ¦ MORE or print the file on the printer by means of the command TYPE README.TXT > PRN.

If there is a version of MS-DOS on your computer already, start up the computer, insert diskette 1 Setup in drive A: and give the command SETUP. Then follow the instructions on the screen closely. During the installation, you must have two diskettes (or one 3.5 in. HD diskette) readily available in order to store the most important components of the old version. Label the diskettes UNINSTALL (1+2). If problems with MS-DOS 6 versions arise after installation, you can always reinstate the old situation by inserting the first of the UNINSTALL diskettes in drive A: and start up the computer.

The Setup program registers the system configuration: the DOS version, the DOS directory and the video card. Accept the default values or alter them by selecting an option from the list. If Windows is installed on the computer, you can determine whether the Backup, Undelete and Anti-Virus utility programs should also be installed for Windows, only for Windows, only for MS-DOS or not at all. The operation of the various versions is largely identical. The installation program will also determine the Windows directory if necessary, but you can also specify this yourself. When you have acknowledged all messages, the installation will begin and then continues automatically. You only need to switch the UNINSTALL (or installation) diskettes when requested.

Then you can work with the new operating system. If you have installed utility programs for Windows, this will be displayed in the Microsoft Tools group window.

You can also *update* your 6.0 version to 6.2. To do this, you require the appropriate diskettes. This procedure is basically the same as that described above. Keep in mind that the *update* to 6.2 can only be made from 6.0 and not from an older version.

# 10   Working with the MS-DOS Shell

## 10.1   MS-DOS Shell: Structure and routines

The MS-DOS Shell utility program is a standard component of the MS-DOS 5.0, 6.0 and 6.2 versions. MS-DOS Shell is a graphic user interface which envelops the program kernel. This simplifies the operation of the various programs. The drives, directories and data are represented by icons and names in windows and lists. You can operate the entire system from these windows and lists by means of easy key combinations or using the mouse. For instance, you can:

- Operate the drives for the diskettes and harddisk.
- Activate MS-DOS commands and applications.
- Copy and delete files and groups of files.
- Create and delete directories.
- Switch between various activated programs using the task list.
- Adjust the graphic display of the MS-DOS Shell.
- Activate utility programs.

Start up the MS-DOS Shell using the following command:

DOSSHELL

One of the following windows subsequently appears on the screen. The display depends on the settings in the *Options* menu. These can be changed by opening *Options* and selecting *Display*.

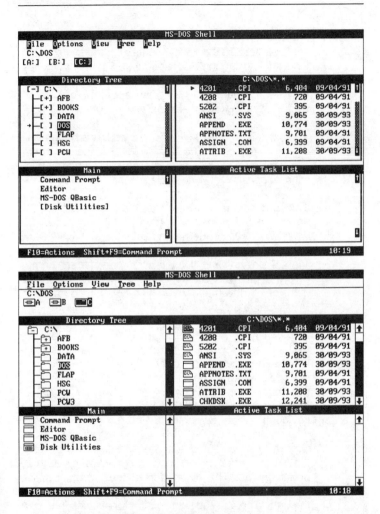

If neither of these windows appears on the screen, perhaps the wrong MS-DOS version has been installed on your computer. You can easily check this by typing the VER command behind the prompt. If necessary, first install MS-DOS 5, 6.0 or 6.2 before continuing (see section 9.6).

It may also be possible that no valid path has been installed to the DOS directory containing the system files.
Check this using the PATH command. If the directory is
not shown in the search path, you will have to define a
new search path or specify the appropriate directory
when activating the MS-DOS Shell (see section 4.12).

The only difference between the windows is the graphic
display of the icons. The first window is in the text mode;
this type of display is possible on any computer. The
window consists of various elements.

**Title bar and menu bar.** The title bar containing the
name *MS-DOS Shell* is located at the very top of the
window. Directly underneath this is the so-called menu
bar containing the five pull-down menus, *Files, Options,
View, Tree* and *Help.* If you click on one of these names
or press the corresponding key combination (Alt+first
letter or F10), a menu containing commands appears.
Press Esc to quit the menu.

**Drives.** Under the menu bar, the drives available in the
system are shown. The currently active drive is highlighted and located above the other drives. A minimum
of three drives are shown, even if the computer only has
two. If the computer has more, these are also indicated.
You can activate another drive using the mouse or a
key combination (cursor key + Enter).

**Directory Tree.** The directories and files are shown in
the middle of the screen. You can move to this area by
pressing Tab. The directories of the currently active
drive are displayed at the left and the files it contains at
the right. The currently active directory is highlighted. A
plus sign in the symbolic display of a directory indicates
that the directory has subdirectories. A minus sign indicates that the subdirectories are currently being shown.

The files of the currently active directory are displayed
in the right-hand window. The upper bar of the window
indicates the active directory. If the *.* file pattern is
shown here, this means that all files in the currently ac-

tive directory are being displayed. Directories can be activated and programs started up using the mouse or key combinations (cursor + Enter).

**Program area.** The lower area of the screen shows a list of programs and program groups. Programs which are frequently used can be started up using the mouse or key combinations (Tab, cursor, Enter). It is also possible to activate several programs at once and subsequently switch back and forth between them (see section 10.5).

The second figure shows the MS-DOS Shell in the graphic mode. The drives, directories and program groups are represented by icons instead of square brackets and names. You can specify the appropriate method of display when activating MS-DOS Shell. If your computer has graphic facilities, start up MS-DOS Shell along with the /G parameter, otherwise with the /T parameter. You can also specify the display mode when working with the MS-DOS Shell. We shall return to this topic shortly.

# 10.2 Operating the MS-DOS Shell

The MS-DOS Shell can be operated using both the mouse and the keyboard. A selected object (menu option, directory, file name or program) is displayed inversely in the case of monochrome screens and in another colour with colour monitors.

### Operation using the mouse

(Refer to section 6.3 if you wish to install the mouse). Using the mouse, you are able to select any object on the screen straightaway. The object is immediately activated by clicking on the left-hand mouse button. One click activates a file name or a menu option. If you wish to start up a program file, press the left-hand button twice in rapid succession, a *double click*. If you wish to

leave a menu, place the mouse pointer anywhere outside the menu frame and click once.

At the right-hand side of the Directory Tree, flanking the
window, there is the so-called *scroll bar*. You can use
this to scroll the window in order to view more of the
contents. Place the mouse pointer on one of the arrows
and click once to move the list one line up or down. You
can hold the mouse button down to scroll the window
until you reach the required position. This can also be
done by placing the mouse pointer on the scroll block
between the arrows and by *dragging* it (click and hold
down, move the pointer up- or downwards), releasing it
at the correct position.

When you wish to quit the MS-DOS Shell, click on File
in the menu bar and then on the *Exit* menu option.


**Operation using the keyboard**

In addition to the names in the menu bar, you can also
select all areas in a window using the Tab key. You can
return to a previous window area by pressing Shift-Tab.
In lists and in the drive area the elements are selected
by means of the cursor. Pressing Enter will subsequently activate the highlighted element.

The menu bar is activated using the Alt key. An option
from an opened menu is selected using the cursor keys,
and subsequently activated by pressing Enter. An option can also be activated by typing the letter highlighted
in the option. Quit menus and the menu bar by pressing
Esc.

If you wish to leave the MS-DOS Shell, press F3 or Alt-
F4.

## 10.3   The menu bar

When you move from one area in a window to another using the Tab key, you will notice that the Tree menu disappears from the menu bar when the program list is activated. This menu has no function for the program list. The other menus can be used in all areas.

The most important functions of the operating system can be executed using the commands in the menus. These deal chiefly with drives, directories and files. Before applying a command to a specific object, you first have to select the object.

*Example:* Display the contents of a file.
(You can, of course, also use the mouse when implementing this example. Follow the instructions and click on the appropriate options.)

- Activate the Directory Tree window using the Tab key.
- Select the DOS directory (or other directory) using the cursor keys.
- Using the Tab key, switch to the window containing the file list.
- Select the README.TXT file (or other legible file) using the cursor keys.
- Press the Alt key. The *File* menu on the menu bar is activated.
- Press Enter to open the *File* menu.
- Place the cursor on the *View File Contents* option and press Enter.

The contents of the file are displayed on the screen. If the contents are shown in hexadecimal form, you can change these to a text display by selecting *Ascii* from the *Display* menu or by pressing the F9 key.

- Quit the text window by pressing the Esc key or by selecting *Restore View* from the *View* menu.

This entire procedure can be shortened considerably by pressing F9 immediately after selecting the required file.

The options which are displayed in grey in the menus cannot be activated for the selected object. In some menus, certain options are followed by three dots. This means that a dialog window will appear when this option is chosen. Other options are accompanied by a key combination which will activate that option from outside the menu. The underlined or otherwise accentuated letters in a name can be used to directly activate the option.

The various menu options are described in section 10.6. In addition, supplementary information can be gained for each selected object by pressing the F1 key.

## 10.4  Working with directories and files

Several examples of the facilities provided by the MS-DOS Shell for working with directories and files are given below.

*Example:* Create the \TEST subdirectory in the root directory on harddisk C:.

- Activate the Directory Tree window using the Tab key. Ensure that the root directory has been selected.
- Press the Alt key and then Enter to open the *File* menu.
- Select the *Create Directory* option using the cursor keys. Press Enter. The *Create Directory* window appears. Type the name of the new directory in the *New directory name* box: TEST. You do not need to type a backslash. The program does this.

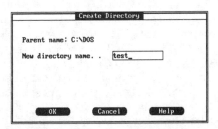

Confirm the name by pressing Enter.

The new directory is included aphabetically in the Directory Tree list. If you now select this directory, the message 'No files in selected directory' appears in the files window.

*Example:* Alter the name TEST to TRIAL.

■ Activate the Directory Tree window using the Tab key.
■ Select the directory whose name you wish to alter.
■ Select the *Rename* option from the *File* and press Enter. The *Rename Directory* dialog box appears.
■ Type the new directory name and press Enter.

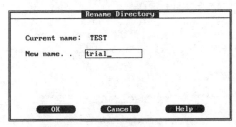

The directory receives a new name and is adopted alphabetically into the Directory Tree once more.

*Example:* The README.TXT file is to be copied from the \DOS directory to the \TRIAL directory.

■ Activate the Directory Tree window.
■ Select the \DOS directory.

■ Switch to the file list window using the Tab key.
■ Select the README.TXT file (or other required file).
■ Select the *Copy* option from the *File* menu and press
  Enter. The *Copy File* dialog box appears containing
  two text areas. The first contains the selected file;
  underneath, a destination is suggested. This is nor-
  mally the currently active directory. In this case, this
  must be altered.
■ Change the contents of the *To:* text line to
  \DOS\TRIAL and press Enter.

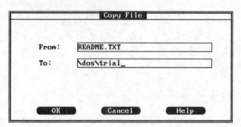

The file is copied to the new directory. Subsequently,
select the \TRIAL directory and check the result.

*Example:* The README.TXT file is to be linked to the
MS-DOS editor, EDIT.

■ First proceed as in the previous example.
■ From the *File* menu, select the *Associate* option and
  press Enter. The *Associate File* dialog box appears.
  If the name EDIT is not shown on the text line, type it.

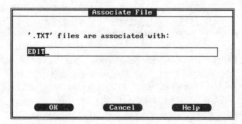

Confirm by pressing Enter. All files with the TXT extension will be subsequently linked to the DOS editor.

Press Enter while the README.TXT file is selected. The editor is then activated and the README.TXT file is opened. Quit the editor (see section 11.2) to return to the MS-DOS Shell.

*Example:* Deleting a file.

■ Activate the file list window using the Tab key.
■ Use the cursor keys to select the name of the file you wish to delete, README.TXT for instance.
■ Press the Del key. The *Delete File Confirmation* window appears.

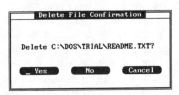

This window provides the possibility of confirming the deletion using *Yes* or revoking it using *No* or *Cancel*. *Yes* is the default setting. If you press Enter the deletion is implemented.

■ Activate the *No* option by pressing the Tab or cursor key and press Enter.

*Example:* Start the WordPerfect word processor from the file list window. Or choose a different word processor, EDIT from MS-DOS for instance. In this example, all files belonging to the program are located in the \WP51 directory. The program file is WP.EXE. But you can start up any other program with the extension EXE, COM or BAT.

■ Activate the Directory Tree window.
■ Select the \WP51 directory.
■ Switch to the file list window using the Tab key.
■ Select the WP.EXE file using the cursor keys.
■ Press Enter to start up the program.

```
     Directory Tree                    C:\WP51\*.*
 ┌─┬─ VENTURA              ↑   ▒ UGAUND   .FRS     4,896  01/08/91  ↑
 │ ├─ WINDOWS                  ▒ VIDEO7   .VRS     8,129  01/08/91
 │ ├─ WIN_APPS                 ▒ WP       .DRS   490,022  01/08/91
 │ ├─ WP                       ▒ WP       .EXE   229,376  17/09/91
 │ ├─ WP51                     ▒ WP       .FIL   617,332  17/09/91
 │ ├─ WPC                      ▒ WP       .LRS    25,298  05/08/91
 │ ├─ WPDOC                    ▒ WP       .MRS     6,072  17/09/91
 │ ├─ WPWIN                    ▒ WP       .PIF       545  05/08/91
 │ └─ XL                   ↓   ▒ WP       .QRS    17,034  17/09/91  ↓
```

# 10.5    Working with programs

Several programs have already been included in the list
of programs. By selecting *Command Prompt* from the
*Main* group or by pressing Shift-F9, you can switch to
familiar DOS prompt. There you can give a DOS command in the familiar way. When you have implemented
the task, you can return to MS-DOS Shell by typing
EXIT. The *Editor* option activates the text editor available since MS-DOS 5. The *MS-DOS QBasic* option activates the MS-DOS Basic program (also from version 5
onwards). The [Disk Utilities] option is shown between
square brackets to indicate that this refers to a group of
programs. Activate this option to have a look at the contents of this group: Disk Copy, Backup Fixed Disk etc.

*Note:* The examples discussed below can only be carried out if the *Program/File Lists* option in the *View*
menu is activated. This is normally the case, but if only
the Directory Tree window and the file list window are
shown, open the *View* menu and select *Program/File
Lists* (Alt-V, F). In the examples you can, of course, use
the mouse instead of the key combinations given. Select the relevant objects using the mouse pointer and
click on the left-hand mouse button. Confirm the data
entered in dialog boxes by clicking on OK.

**Starting programs from the program list.** A method
of starting up a program has already been outlined.
However, it is much easier and quicker to do this from
the program list.

*Example:* Starting up the MS-DOS editor from the program list (operating the editor is dealt with in chapter 11).

■ Activate the program list using the Tab key.
■ Select the name Editor using the cursor key and press Enter.

Prior to the program being started up, a dialog window appears on your screen in which you can type the name of a file to edit or which is to be created.

■ Skip the window by pressing the Enter key.

The editor is started up. We shall leave this again immediately:

■ Remove the opening screen by pressing Esc.
■ Select the *Exit* option from the *File* menu (Alt-F, x) in order to return to the MS-DOS Shell.

**Using the program group.** Programs which are frequently used may be gathered together under one name. This provides a clearer overview when working with these programs. Whenever you open a group, the corresponding programs are displayed in the window.

*Example:* Open the *Disk Utilities* program group.

■ Activate the program list.
■ Select the *Disk Utilities* group using the cursor keys and press Enter.

The program list is now called *Disk Utilities* and displays the corrresponding commands. In addition to these commands, the *[Main]* group is also shown. If you select this and press Enter, you will return to the previous *Main* program list. If you wish to activate one of the programs, select the required name and press Enter. When the program has been executed, you will automatically return to the MS-DOS Shell. If you wish to gain additional information about a certain command, press F1.

**Adding a new program or new program group.** It is possible to add new programs to the Main group or other groups. A new program or group of programs is automatically added to the currently opened group.

*Example:* The WordPerfect word processor is to be added to the Main group. (Choose a different program if you prefer.)

■ Open the *Main* group. It does not matter which program is currently selected.
■ Activate the *New* option in the *File* menu.

The following dialog window appears:

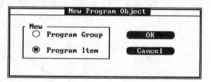

The *Program Item* option is automatically selected. Confirm this using Enter.

Another dialog window appears:

```
┌──────────────────────── Add Program ────────────────────────┐
│                                                             │
│  Program Title . . . . [                                 ]  │
│                                                             │
│  Commands  . . . . . . [                                 ]  │
│                                                             │
│  Startup Directory . . [                                 ]  │
│                                                             │
│  Application Shortcut Key        [                       ]  │
│                                                             │
│  [X] Pause after exit       Password . . [             ]   │
│      OK        Cancel         Help        Advanced...       │
└─────────────────────────────────────────────────────────────┘
```

When you have specified the relevant data, press Tab to move on to the next area.

■ Program Title: Type *Word Processor* here. This title will subsequently appear in the program list.
■ Commands: Type here the command to start up the word processor.

*Note:* If no search path to the directory containing the word processor has been registered in AUTOEXEC.BAT or anywhere else, you must specify here the complete directory path for the file, for instance: C:\WP\WP.EXE.

You only need to specify the following data if they are necessary. You can skip them by pressing Enter.

- Startup Directory: Specify the directory to which the word processor is to be linked. The directory must already exist.
- Application Shortcut key: This is a key combination you can use in the Task List (see below) in order to activate the word processor from a different program. Hold down the Ctrl key and press W. The combination Ctrl-W appears in the text box.

The key combination may consist of one of the special keys Ctrl, Alt or Shift together with another key of your choice. When using this combination later, you must first press and hold down the special key and then press the chosen key. It is also possible to combine two special keys with another key. The combinations shown below are not permitted because they have a special, reserved significance:

| | |
|---|---|
| Ctrl-M | Shift-Ctrl-M |
| Ctrl-I | Shift-Ctrl-I |
| Ctrl-H | Shift-Ctrl-H |
| Ctrl-C | Shift-Ctrl-C |
| Ctrl-[ | Shift-Ctrl-[ |
| Ctrl-5* | Shift-Ctrl-5* |

*) this is the number 5 key on the numeric keypad at the right of the keyboard.

- Pause after exit: This option is normally activated. This means that the system does not immediately switch back to the MS-DOS Shell when the program is terminated. A short pause is included in order to give the program a chance to display a final message

on the screen. By pressing a key, you return to the
MS-DOS Shell.
- Password: Specify a password here so that the pro-
gram may only be used by authorized people.

Activate the *Advanced* button (Tab, Enter) in order to
summon a dialog box with additional options. You can
type a help-text with a maximum length of 255 characters which will be shown when the program is selected
in the program list and F1 is pressed. The minimum
memory capacity required is also specified here and the
minimum and maximum extended memory required
when using task swapping. You can also specify a number of parameters here to be applied in task swapping.
If you require supplementary information, press F1 for
context-related help.

*Example:* A program group called *Accounts* is to be
added to the *Main* group. The (fictional) programs *Accounts Texts* and *Tables* are to be placed in this group.

- Activate the *Main* group. It does not matter which pro-
gram is selected.
- Activate the *New* option in the *File* menu.
- Activate *Program Group* (use cursor keys) in the *New
Program Object* window and press Enter.

The following dialog box appears:

```
┌────────────────────────────────────────┐
│              Add Group                  │
│ Required                                │
│  Title . . . .   [_____]     │
│ Optional                                │
│  Help Text . .   [_____]     │
│  Password  . .   [_____]           │
│                                         │
│   ( OK )      ( Cancel )    ( Help )     │
└────────────────────────────────────────┘
```

- Type *Accounts* as the title.
- If you wish, you can enter a help text (maximum 255
characters) in the next text area. This will be shown

when the title of the program is selected in the program list and F1 is pressed. In addition, you can specify a password in order to restrict access to the program to authorized users.

When you have confirmed these data by pressing Enter, the title of the group is added to the list of programs. Now add two programs to this group, the word processing program *Accounts Text* and the spreadsheet program *Tables*. (These programs are fictional - add any programs of your own choice.)

■ Select the new group using the cursor keys and press Enter.
■ Add the two programs to the program group as described above. If you wish to work with the examples below dealing with task swapping, assign the Shortcut key combinations Ctrl-A (Accounts Text) and Ctrl-T (Tables) to these programs. This is done by pressing the chosen keys. You must specify the command required to start up these programs; this would be WP for instance in the case of WordPerfect.

**Altering the data of a program or program group.** Data concerning programs or program groups which you have added to the program list can be altered whenever you wish.

*Example:* Determine a different startup directory for the *Tables* program in the *Accounts* group.

■ Open the *Accounts* group by moving the cursor to Accounts and pressing Enter.
■ Select the *Tables* program.
■ Activate the *Properties* option from the *File* menu. In the *Program Item Properties* window which is identical to that in which the data were entered, place the cursor on the Startup Directory line, type the new directory and press Enter.

**Copying a program to another group.** A program can easily be copied to a different group.

*Example:* Copy the *Disk Copy* program from the *Disk Utilities* group to the *Main* group.

■ Activate the *Disk Utilities* group and select the *Disk Copy* program.
■ Activate the *Copy* option from the *File* menu.
■ Select *Main* as destination using the cursor keys, press Enter and then press F2.

In this way, the program is copied to the *Main* group and displayed there under its own name.

**Removing a program or group of programs from the list.** Removing a program can be done very easily, but a program group can only be removed when it contains no programs. The programs are not physically removed from the disk, the name is only removed from the list.

*Example:* The *Disk Copy* program which was copied in the previous example is to be removed from the list.

■ Select the *Disk Copy* program using the cursor keys and press Del. A dialog box appears in which you must confirm or cancel the operation.
■ Accept the default setting (*Delete this item*) by pressing Enter.

**Starting up various programs simultaneously and switching to these programs.** Using the MS-DOS Shell, it is possible to start up various programs simultaneously and to switch back and forth between these programs. When you switch to another program the memory and screen data of the active program are stored in the buffer of the harddisk and the data concerning the program which is to be activated are read in from the harddisk. Task swapping works as follows:

*Example:* The programs *Accounts Text* and *Tables* are to be started up in order to be able to switch back and forth between these programs.

■ Open the *Options* menu using Alt-O, select the *Enable Task Swapper* option and confirm this using Enter. A spot appears next to the option to show that this option is active (check by opening the menu again; close by pressing Esc). A repetition of this action switches the Task Swapper off again.

The program list is now divided into two windows. The list of active programs is displayed in the right-hand window. Each activated program is included in this window. When you have terminated the program it is cleared from the list. It is also possible to place the program in the list without starting it up. Both methods are described below.

■ Select the title *Accounts Text* in the *Accounts* group and press Enter. The program which is linked to this (WordPerfect for instance) is started up.
■ Quit the program using the key combination Ctrl-Esc. The title of the program and the defined shortcut key are shown in the list.
■ Now select the *Tables* program and press Shift-Enter. In this way, the program is placed in the Active Task List without starting up the program.

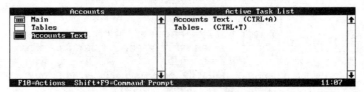

Before it is possible to switch back and forth between the two programs, the second program has to be started up:

■ Select the *Tables* program from the Active Task List and press Enter.

The program is now started up. Just for practice, enter some data and switch to the first program:

■ Press the key combination Shift-Alt-Esc.
■ Type some data in this program too, and then switch to the other program using the key combination Alt-Esc.

Thus, using Alt-Esc you can switch to the next program and using Shift-Alt-Esc you can switch to the previous program. If you press the same key combination twice, that will have the same effect as Ctrl-Esc: back to the MS-DOS Shell. However, the programs remain active in the background. A program in the Active Task List is started up by selecting it and simply pressing Enter.

In order to switch between programs, the shortcut keys which you defined are even more convenient:

■ If the *Accounts Text* program is active, you can switch to the *Tables* program by pressing Ctrl-T. Return using Ctrl-A.

A program can also be activated from the program list or from the Command Prompt. If this is done more than once, the name of the program is shown twice in the Active Task List. The second time it is followed by a dot, the third time by two dots and so on.

When you no longer need a program, remove it from the Active Task List by terminating the program. You can also clear it from the list by selecting it using the cursor keys and then pressing Del. The MS-DOS Shell warns, in a dialog box, that the program is still active. You can then confirm or cancel the removal.

## 10.6    The menu commands

The menu bar is activated using the Alt key. Subsequently, one of the menus can be selected by pressing Enter or Cursor Down. A menu can also be opened by pressing Alt and then the accentuated letter (see the figure below).

(1)  Open a selected program file.
(2)  Open a dialog box in which you can specify the start command for a program.
(3)  Print the contents of a file.
(4)  Links the selected file to a program so that the program is started up when this file is activated. The program then opens the file immediately, for instance a word processor opens a text file.
(5)  Looks for a specific file, on the entire disk if necessary.
(6)  Examine the contents of the selected file.
(7)  Move the selected file to a specified directory and remove it from the original directory.
(8)  Copy the selected file to a specified directory or drive.
(9)  Delete the selected file.
(10) Assign a different name to the specified file or directory.
(11) Change the attributes of the selected file: Hidden, System, Archive, Read Only.
(12) Create a new subdirectory under the activated directory.
(13) Select all files in the file list to, for instance, copy, move or delete them all at once.
(14) Undo the selection.
(15) Quit the MS-DOS Shell.

```
┌─────────────────────────────────────┐
│ Options                             │
├─────────────────────────────────────┤
│ Confirmation...                 (1) │
│ File Display Options...         (2) │
│ Select Across Directories      (3) │
│ Show Information...             (4) │
│ Enable Task Swapper            (5) │
│ Display...                      (6) │
│ Colors...                       (7) │
└─────────────────────────────────────┘
```

(1) Determine, in the subsequent dialog box, whether the Delete and Replace functions and the Mouse Operation should be confirmed before implementation.

(2) In the *File Display Options* box, determine the criteria used to display the files in the file list. Normally this is *.* in ascending order. If you only wish to see files with the TXT extension, for example, change this pattern to *.TXT.

(3) Activate this option to be able to select files in different directories simultaneously, so that you can copy them to a diskette for instance. The option is active if a spot is shown in front of it.

(4) Display detailed information about the selected file and the immediate environment, such as attributes, directory and disk.

(5) Activate the facility of switching between activated programs. This is described extensively in the previous section.

(6) Summon an options list for the screen display mode of MS-DOS Shell. The number of options depends on the graphic capabilities of the computer. The normal current VGA cards provide three options for text display and five for graphic display. Try out an option by selecting it using the cursor keys and then press the *Preview* button. In this way, you can view various possibilities before deciding on the display you prefer. Quit the *Preview* screen using Esc.

(7) Summon an options list for screen colour, depending on the graphic capabilities of the computer. To select a colour, proceed as in (6).

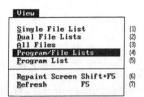

(1) Show only the two upper windows, Directory Tree and file list on the screen. This enables you to examine several files at once.

(2) Shows the two upper windows on both the upper and lower parts of the screen. Accordingly, you can examine file names from different drives or directories at one time.

(3) Remove the Directory Tree and program list from the screen and enlarge the file list window. The information window displaying data about the individual files is also shown alongside. The files are shown in the order of sequence defined in the *File Display Options* in the *Options* menu. You can browse through the file list using the cursor or the mouse. If you click on a file name, the corresponding data appear in the information window.

(4) Restore the original display.

(5) Display only the program list along with the Active Task List.

(6) Redraw the screen after an alteration.

(7) Redraw the screen after disk switch.

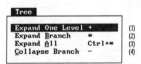

(1) Display the subdirectories of the selected directory at the first level. The plus sign in the directory icon is changed into a minus sign. If using the mouse, place the pointer on the plus sign of the directory and click once to display the subdirectories. Click once more to remove them again; the minus sign is replaced by a plus sign.

(2) Display all subdirectories of the selected directory
    at all levels.
(3) Display all directories at all levels.
(4) Remove the display of directories at the current
    level. If you wish to remove the display of all direc-
    tories at all levels, you must first select the root di-
    rectory in the Directory Tree window.

**Help**

The Help menu provides information about the operation of MS-DOS and the MS-DOS Shell. The operation
of the Help menu is self-evident. Context-oriented help
is gained by selecting the object in question and pressing F1.

# 11 Compiling and editing text using EDIT

## 11.1 The editor routines

The editor is a standard component of the package from MS-DOS 5 onwards. It can be used to compile, edit, save, copy and print straightforward, simple texts. The editor is especially useful for creating batch files in general and the AUTOEXEC.BAT and CONFIG.SYS files in particular.

In contrast to the large word processors such as Word-Perfect or Word, texts made using EDIT are not laid out: they have no alignment and no special attributes for the characters, such as italics or underlining. The editor is simple to use and accordingly is ideally suited to the operation system functions.

The EDIT editor replaces the EDLIN program which was supplied with versions prior to MS-DOS 5.

## 11.2 Starting up and closing down the editor

**Starting up the editor.** Start up the editor either from the command line using the command EDIT (confirm using Enter) or from the MS-DOS Shell using the mouse or the keyboard. Place the mouse pointer on the name Editor in the Program List and double click, or select Editor using the Tab key to activate the Program List and highlight it using the cursor. Press Enter.

If you cannot start up the editor, that may be due to one
of the following reasons:

■ MS-DOS 5, 6.0 or 6.2 has not been installed. Give
  the command VER at the command line to discover
  the current MS-DOS version.
■ The system directory (normally \DOS) does not contain
  the files EDIT.COM, EDIT.HLP and QBASIC.EXE.
  Check this by applying the commands DIR
  \DOS\EDIT.* and DIR \DOS\QBASIC.*. You need
  QBASIC because the editor is a part of this programming language.
■ The directory path to the system programs has not
  been correctly specified. Check the search path by
  giving the command PATH (see section 4.12).

When you have started EDIT, the following screen appears:

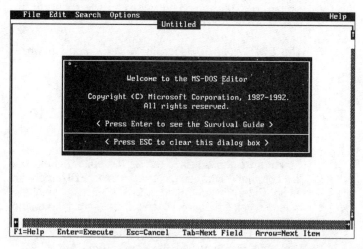

You are provided with a short introduction if you press
Enter, and you can close the window by pressing Esc.

■ Press Esc to close the window.

This dialog box is not shown if you start up the editor along with a file name. If, for instance, you wish to edit the AUTOEXEC.BAT file, you can activate the file directly by giving the command *EDIT AUTOEXEC.BAT*. The following elements are also shown on the screen:

| | |
|---|---|
| The menu bar | The menu bar is located at the top of the window. It contains the four menus. |
| The title bar | The title bar is located under the menu bar. It displays the name of the file to be edited. Initially, this will be *Untitled*. |
| Work area | The majority of the screen area consists of the work area in which you can type and edit your text. |
| Scroll bars | At the right-hand side and along the bottom of the screen, there are scroll bars which enable you to scroll lengthy texts over the screen. Place the mouse pointer on a scroll bar and click once to shift the text one line or column. Hold the mouse button down to scroll several lines or columns. You can drag the scroll block in order to move the text over the screen in larger segments. |
| Status bar | Indicates methods of operation and the current cursor position. |

**Closing the editor.** The editor can only be closed using the *File* menu:

■ Press Alt-F to open the *File* menu.
■ Select *Exit* by pressing x or by clicking on it with the mouse.

If you have not saved the text, a dialog window appears, providing the possibility of doing so. Select the required option and press Enter or click once with the mouse. If you selected *Yes*, a dialog box appears for saving the file.

# 11.3    Working with the editor

**The menu bar.** The menus on the menu bar are o-
pened using the mouse or a key combination. You can
then select the required option from the opened menu.
The key combinations consist of the Alt key (to activate
the menu bar) and the Cursor Right or Cursor Left to select the required menu name. This can be done more
quickly by pressing the Alt key and then the accentuated letter of the menu name. An option is selected by
pressing the accentuated letter of the option or by moving the cursor to the required option and pressing Enter.
Or you may click once using the mouse.

**Entering text.** The text is typed in the editor just as you
would do on a typewriter. A line is concluded by pressing the Enter key; the text does not automatically wrap
round to the next line as is common when using word
processors. If the line is longer than the screen is broad,
the window is shifted over. A maximum of 254 characters can be entered on one line.

**Saving text.** The command *Save* from the *File* menu
enables you to save a text you have typed. If you specified a name when you started up the editor, the text will
be saved directly. Otherwise a dialog window will appear in which you must assign a name to the document.
The same window appears if you select the *Save As*
option. You can also use the *Save As* option to save the
text under another name without having to remove the
original file.

*Example:* Three lines of text are to be saved under the
name TEST1.

- Start up the editor using the EDIT command.
- Press Esc to skip the opening screen.
- Type a few lines in the work area. Conclude each line
  by pressing Enter before reaching the right-hand
  edge of the screen.
- Select the *Save As* option from the *File* menu.

■ Type the name TEST1 in the File Name box in the subsequent dialog window.

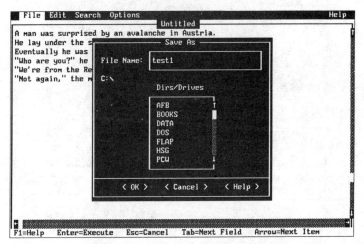

The file is saved under the specified name in the directory which is displayed immediately under the text box. You can specify a different directory by moving the cursor to Dirs/Drives list (press Tab) and selecting the required drive and directory using the cursor keys and Enter.

The name *Untitled* is then changed to *Test1*.

*Note:* If the name already exists in the selected directory, a dialog box appears providing the possibility of overwriting the existing file (Yes), selecting another name (No) or discontinuing the process (Cancel).

**Opening an existing text file.** It is possible to open an existing file in the editor work area at any time.

*Example:* The text file TESTS.TXT from the root directory of the harddisk is to be opened and adjusted.

■ Select the *Open* option from the *File* menu. The *Open* dialog window appears containing the names of drives, directories and files.

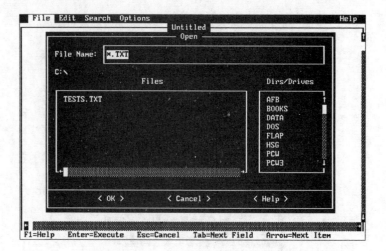

The File Name text box shows the *.TXT file pattern as the default setting. All files with this pattern are then automatically displayed in the Files list.

If the required file is shown in the Files list, select it as follows:

■ Use Tab to switch to the Files list and select the file using the cursor keys.
■ Press Enter to open the file. If using a mouse, double click on the file to select it and open it in one go.

If the file is located in a different directory or on a different diskdrive, select the required drive and/or directory from the Dirs/drives box first:

■ Use Tab to switch to the Dirs/Drives list and use the cursor to move through the directories and drives to select the required option. Using the mouse, drag the scroll block at the right-hand side of the list.
■ Confirm your choice by pressing Enter, or double click on the option.
■ Two dots indicate that a subdirectory is currently selected. Double click on the two dots to activate the

parent directory, or select them using the cursor keys and press Enter.

The required directory is activated and the Files list displays the corresponding files in accordance with the specified file pattern. This pattern can be altered by typing over the text in the File Name text box.

Select the file from the Files list as described above.

**Editing text.** The most important key combinations used in text editing are listed below.

### Moving the cursor

| | |
|---|---|
| Using the mouse: | Place the mouse pointer at the required position in the text and click once on the left mouse button. |
| Using the keyboard: | |
| Cursor keys | Move the cursor one position in the text. |
| Home | Places the cursor at the beginning of the line. |
| End | Places the cursor at the end of the line. |
| Ctrl-Cursor Left | Places the cursor at the beginning of the previous word. |
| Ctrl-Cursor Right | Places the cursor at the beginning of the next word. |
| PgDn | Moves the cursor downwards one screen page. |
| PgUp | Moves the cursor upwards one screen page. |
| Ctrl-Home | Places the cursor at the beginning of the text. |
| Ctrl-End | Places the cursor at the end of the text. |
| Tab | Places the cursor at the following tab position. |

**Deleting characters**

Del                         Deletes the character currently
                            under the cursor.

Backspace                   Deletes the character immedi-
                            ately to the left of the cursor.

**Inserting**

Ins                         Activates the insert mode. The
                            cursor then assumes a different
                            form. It will become either a
                            stripe or a block depending on
                            its original form.

**Selecting text**

Using the mouse             Place the pointer at the starting
                            position, hold down the left-
                            hand mouse button and drag
                            the pointer to the end position.

Using the keyboard
Shift-cursor keys           The text is selected in the direc-
                            tion of the cursor keys.

Shift-Home                  To the beginning of the line.
Shift-End                   To the end of the line.
Shift-PgUp                  One screen page upwards.
Shift-PgDn                  One screen page downwards.
Shift-Ctrl-End              To the end of the file.
Shift-Ctrl-Home             To the beginning of the file.

Cancel the selection by pressing any one of the cursor
keys, or by clicking with the mouse at a different position.

**Deleting selected text**

Using the mouse             Click on the *Edit* menu and se-
                            lect the *Clear* option.

Using the keyboard
Del                         Press the Del key to delete the
                            text.

## Moving selected text

The text is first placed in the Clipboard by means of the *Cut* option from the *Edit* menu. It can then be inserted at any other chosen position.

| | |
|---|---|
| Using the mouse | Click on the *Edit* menu and then on *Cut*. |
| | Click on the target position in the work area. |
| | Click on the *Edit* menu and then on *Paste*. |

| | |
|---|---|
| Using the keyboard | |
| Shift-Del | The text is moved to the Clipboard and removed from the screen. |
| cursor keys | Place the cursor at the target position. |
| Shift-Ins | The text is taken from the Clipboard and placed at the target position. |

## Copying selected text

The text must first be moved to the Clipboard by means of the *Copy* option from the *Edit* menu. It can then be copied to any chosen position.

| | |
|---|---|
| Using the mouse | Click on the *Edit* menu and then on the *Copy* option. |
| | Click on the target position in the work area. |
| | Click on the *Edit* option and then on the *Paste* option. |

| | |
|---|---|
| Using the keyboard | |
| Ctrl-Ins | The text is moved to the Clipboard but also remains visible on the screen. |
| Cursor keys | Place the cursor at the target position. |
| Shift-Ins | The text is taken from the clipboard and placed at the specified position. |

**Inserting text fragments or merging text files.** If you wish to insert a text fragment or an entire text from one file into another, proceed as follows:

■ Open the first file from which you wish to extract a section.
■ Select the section you wish to adopt.
■ Move the selected section to the clipboard using the *Cut* menu from the *Edit* menu.
■ Open the file to which the section of text is to be moved by selecting the *Open* option from the *File* menu. Answer No to the question whether you wish to save the altered text.
■ Insert the contents of the Clipboard into the text by means of the *Paste* option from the *Edit* menu.

**Printing text.** If you wish to print the entire text or a selected section of text, proceed as follows:

■ Select the text section if necessary.
■ Select the *Print* option from the *file* menu. The following dialog box appears:

```
                ─── Print ───
        ( ) Selected Text Only
        (•) Complete Document


   < OK >   < Cancel >   < Help >
```

The first or second option will be activated depending on whether you have selected a section of text or not. You may change your mind if you wish. Select the other option using the cursor keys and then use Tab to select OK, Cancel or Help. Press Enter to confirm.

**Finding and replacing text.** Using the editor, you can search for and, if necessary, replace pieces of text in a document. Proceed as follows:

■ Select the *Find* option from the *Search* menu. The *Find* dialog window appears.

■ Type the required text in the *Find What:* text box. Confirm this using Enter or click on OK.

If the text really exists, it will be automatically found and selected. If the text occurs several times, you can use the *Repeat Last Find* option from the *Search* menu to search further. This can also be done more quickly and easily by pressing the shortcut key F3. Once the end of the file has been reached, the search will begin again at the beginning.

You can also specify in the dialog window whether the search should take capitals and small letters into account when searching and whether the word sought is a whole word or part of a word.

To replace one piece of text with another, proceed as follows:

■ Select the *Change* option from the *Search* menu.

In the subsequent dialog window, type the text to be found in the *Find What:* text box and the text which is to replace it in the *Change To:* text box. In addition, you can determine whether all changes are to be confirmed or all occurrences replaced in one go.

## 11.4 Configuring the editor

**Defining the directory path for Help.** Normally the EDIT.HLP file is located on the same disk and in the same directory as the editor (C:\DOS for instance). In that case, you do not need to alter any settings. However, if this file is located in a different directory, you should define the access to the file as follows:

■ Activate the *Options* menu using the Alt-O key combination and select the *Help Path* option. A dialog window appears.
■ Type the appropriate directory path, including the drive, in the text box.

■ Confirm this using Enter or click on OK.

By selecting Help here, you can gain additional information about this dialog window. See also section 4.12.

**Specifying the screen display.** The *Display* option from the *Options* menu enables you to determine the colours for the screen display, i.e. the text and the background. In addition, you can specify whether you wish to use the scroll bars, and also the distance between the tabstops.

*Example:* The colours are to be defined as follows: the text is to be white and the background blue. The scroll bars are to be shown and the distance between the tabstops is to be set to 8.

■ Select the *Display* option from the *Options* menu.
■ Use Tab to activate the various windows and specify the settings as follows using the cursor keys: Foreground White and Background Blue. If using the mouse, you only need to click on the relevant choices.
■ Press Tab to move to the Scroll Bars options and press the spacebar to activate [X] or de-activate the setting. You may also click on the option.
■ Move to the Tabs section by pressing the Tab key. If Tabs is not set to 8, type an 8 here.
■ Confirm the settings by pressing Enter or click on OK.

# 12 Protecting data under MS-DOS 5.0, 6.0 and 6.2

## 12.1 The concept of protection

The necessity of data protection has been discussed in chapters 4 and 7. But do keep in mind: no matter how advanced the data protection actually is, it is not possible to recall data which have been lost due to hardware problems or which have been overwritten by other data.

Section 4.7 outlined the workings of the RECOVER program which was also available in earlier versions of MS-DOS. Data security has been extended with the following facilities from version 5.0 onwards:

- Erroneous formatting of the harddisk can be rectified under certain circumstances.
- Deleted files can be restored under certain circumstances.
- The system information pertaining to a new, partitioned hardisk can be stored on diskette (see section 7.1). This can be used to rectify certain errors on the harddisk.

## 12.2 Rectifying erroneous formatting

New harddisks and diskettes must be formatted before they can be used. But used harddisks and diskettes can also be formatted in order to, for instance, create a new directory structure. You must always be extremely careful when formatting a disk. Even advanced users make the mistake of unintentionally formatting a disk, leading to the loss of valuable information.

**Conditions of rectifying a formatting process.** It is possible to rectify unintentional formatting under MS-DOS from version 5 onwards, but certain conditions must be satisfied:

■ The formatting must have been performed by means of the normal formatting command or the quick format command. If you used the /U parameter when formatting, the formatting *cannot* be undone.
■ After formatting, there should be (preferably) no new data stored on the disk. Therefore, try to rectify the formatting *immediately* after discovering the mistake.
■ The diskette may not be fully in use up to the last byte (message: 0 bytes free). If this message is given, you should first remove a file in order to create space on the disk.

**Safe formatting.** The normal formatting command and the quick format command are both safe types of formatting which can be undone if the other conditions are fulfilled. In this method of formatting, MS-DOS makes an *image* file which is hidden and which contains an image of the structure of the directories and files. If the formatting has to be undone, MS-DOS restores the original structure by means of the information in this file.

**Creating a separate image file.** It is also possible to create the image file separately, without formatting. This has two advantages:

■ The image file registers the information concerning files and directories at a time which you specify.
■ The image file can be used to store information about files and used later to restore deleted files.

**From MS-DOS 5 onwards, the MIRROR command enables you to create image files on disk.**

```
MIRROR [d1:d2:...] [/1] [/td[-number]]
                          [/u] [/partn]
```

d1:d2:...         The drives for which the image files are to be created. The image files for the specified drive are stored in the visible file MIRROR.FIL and in the invisible file MIRORSAV.FIL.

| | |
|---|---|
| /1 | Overwrites an existing image file which is not kept as a backup (MIRROR.BAK). |
| /td[-number] | This option starts up, simultaneously with the image file, a program which stores information about deleted files in a file which keeps track of the deletions. The program is resident and remains active until the computer is switched off. Type the appropriate letter instead of the *d* shown here. Instead of *number*, specify the maximum number of deleted files which are to be registered in the file. This ranges from 1 to 999. The default values are: |

Diskettes:  360 Kb: 25 files
               720 Kb: 50 files
               1.2 Mb: 75 files
               1.44 Mb: 75 files

Harddisks:  20 Mb: 101 files
              32 Mb: 202 files
              more than 32 Mb: 303 files

| | |
|---|---|
| | If you wish to keep track of file deletion for more than one drive, for A: and C: for instance, you must specify this straightaway: MIRROR A: C: /ta /tc. |
| /u | This option terminates the program which keeps a record of the deletions. This is only possible if no other resident programs are loaded. Do not apply this option if you are not sure about the situation. |
| /partn | This option saves the partition data of the harddisk on a diskette (see section 12.4). |

Note: If your computer has a harddisk, you can specify this option when starting up the computer. In that case, starting up will take a little longer, but the possibility of rectifying faults is increased. Accordingly, include the following command in AUTOEXEC.BAT:

```
MIRROR C: /tc
```

To do this, start up the MS-DOS editor along with the
AUTOEXEC.BAT file and add this command to the last
line. Save the command using Alt-F, S and quit the editor using Alt-F, X.

*Example:* A diskette (3.5 inch and 1.44 Mb) is to be
safely formatted in drive A:. Subsequently, an image file
is to be created, stored and displayed on another diskette with the same capacity in drive A: (see the figure
below).

```
C:\>format a:                                    (1)
Insert new diskette for drive A:
and press ENTER when ready...

Checking existing disk format.
Saving UNFORMAT information.
Verifying 1.44M
Format complete.

C:\>format a:/f:720                              (2)
C:\>format a:/q                                  (3)

C:\>mirror a:                                    (4)

Creates an image of the system area.

Drive A being processed.

The MIRROR process was successful.

C:\>dir a:

MIRROR   FIL       6,656 25/11/93   13:15        (5)
```

(1)  The normal formatting command produces a safe
     formatting. The message indicates that the file and
     directory data are stored, although the information
     is hidden; it is stored invisibly on the diskette.
(2)  The command also produces a safe formatting.
     However, the capacity must correspond to the orig-
     inal capacity of the disk, in this case 720 Kb.
(3)  The quick format is also safe.
(4)  This command produces a separate image file on
     the diskette in drive A:. In fact, the image file ac-
     tually consists of two files, a visible and an invisible
     file. The data stored are identical to those in the
     safe formatting process.
(5)  This command displays the visible image file. The

other information on the diskette is not displayed here.

**Rectifying formatting under MS-DOS 5.0, 6.0 and 6.2.** Using the following command, it is possible to rectify an unintentional formatting of a diskette or harddisk, under the conditions mentioned above. This command can also be used if you have unsuccessfully attempted to recover files using the RECOVER command (see section 4.7)

```
UNFORMAT D:[/J][[/U][/L][/TEST][/P]]
                        [[/PARTN][/L]]
```

| | |
|---|---|
| d: | The drive for which the formatting must be undone. |
| /j | Checks whether the data are located in the image file and are suitable for recovery. If this option is given, no other option may be used. |
| /u | Attempts to rectify the disk without using the image file created using the MIRROR command. That can be advantageous if the image file is so old that it lacks many recent modifications. |
| /l | Attempts to recover subdirectories and the files stored in these, if there is no image file. This is less safe than using the image file. |
| /test | Displays only the names of the files which can be recovered if no image file exists or if it is not going to be used. |
| /p | Also prints the command messages on the printer. |
| /partn[/l] | Under MS-DOS 5, writes the partition table (saved on diskette) back to the harddisk. The /l option displays the partition data on the screen. |

## 12.3   Recovering deleted files

**Recovering files under MS-DOS 5.** Occasionally, files
are deleted unintentionally by giving the DEL command.
These files are not immediately lost. The DEL command only replaces the first character of the file name
and makes space available on disk for other files. As
long as this space has not been occupied by other files,
a deleted file can be recovered. This is very easy if,
using the MIRROR command, a file has been created
beforehand to record the deletions. This is then sufficient for recovery.

**The UNDELETE command will probably enable you
to recover deleted files if you apply it as soon as
possible after the deletion.**

```
UNDELETE [[d:][path]file][/list / all]
                              [/dos /dt]
```

d:path    The drive and, if necessary, the directory con-
          taining the files to be recovered.

file      This is a specific file or a group of files (using
          the wildcards * and/or ?). There must be no
          spaces between drive, directory path and file
          name.

/list     The names of deleted files to be recovered are
          shown but not yet recovered.

/all      Recovers all deleted files without any further
          action on your part. Without this option, all file
          names are displayed and you can specify sep-
          arately whether you wish to recover any par-
          ticular file.

/dos      Does not make use of the Deletion-tracking
          file. The program tries to recover the files using
          information from the root directory and the
          FAT.

/dt       When recovering, this option makes use of the
          Deletion-tracking file.

■ If there is no Deletion-tracking file for the recovery
process, the first letter of the file name will be missing. If the /ALL option is not specified, all file names
will be shown and you can add the missing letter
yourself. If the /ALL option is applied, each first letter
is automatically replaced by a number sign (#) and if
this coincides with an existing file, the characters %,
&, 0, 1, ...are used. You can then change the name of
the file using the RENAME command.

■ If an existing file is used, containing data about the
deleted files, the first letter of the file name is replaced
with the proper character. If the /ALL option is applied, the names of all files are automatically restored.

*Example:* Delete all files on the diskette in drive A:,
check the deletion and then recover all the deleted files.
There is no file containing information about the deletions.

```
C:\>del a:*.*                                            (1)
All files in directory will be deleted!
Are you sure (Y/N)?y                                     (2)

C:\>dir a:                                               (3)
MIRROR   FIL       6,656 25/11/93   13:15                (4)

C:\>undelete a:                                          (5)
Directory: A:\                                           (6)
File Specifications: *.*

    Delete Sentry control file not found.

    Deletion-tracking file not found.

    MS-DOS directory contains    3 deleted files.
    Of those,    3 files may be recovered.

Using the MS-DOS directory method.

    ?OSE            44 25/11/93 13:20   ...A  Undelete (Y/N)?y
    Please type the first character for ?OSE   .  : n

File successfully undeleted.                             (7)
```

(1) This command deletes all files on the diskette in
    drive A:.
(2) Respond Yes to the confirmation question.
(3) Check the contents of the diskette.
(4) All files have been deleted except MIRROR.FIL.

This file cannot be deleted because the operating system has allocated the *Read Only* attribute to the file. (You can display the file attributes by giving the ATTRIB command, see section 10.6.)

(5) This command is given to recover the files on the diskette in drive A:.

(6) The program states that three files may be recovered.

(7) The files found are displayed separately with a question mark instead of the first letter. You can determine whether you wish to recover each individual file and also which character should replace the question mark. This need not be the original character.

*Example:* Delete all files once more and recover them all automatically

```
C:\>del a:*.*                                    (1)
All files in directory will be deleted!
Are you sure (Y/N)?y

C:\>undelete a:/all                              (2)

C:\>dir a:

MIRROR    FIL      6,656 25/11/93    13:15       (3)
#OSE                 44 25/11/93    13:20
#EAD                 39 25/11/93    13:25
#OOT                 26 25/11/93    13:25
        4 file(s)         6,765 bytes
                        718,848 bytes free
```

(1) The files are deleted.

(2) The program along with the /ALL option recovers the files automatically.

(3) The missing first character of each recovered file is replaced by a number sign (#).

*Example:* A program is started up along with the MIR-ROR a:/ta command in order to create a file which records deletions on the diskette in A:. Subsequently, four files on a diskette are deleted. Then a new file is stored on the diskette. The deleted files are now to be recovered.

```
C:\>undelete a:                                                    (1)

UNDELETE - A delete protection facility
Copyright (C) 1987-1993 Central Point Software, Inc.
All rights reserved.

Directory: A:\                                                     (2)
File Specifications: *.*

    Delete Sentry control file not found.

    Deletion-tracking file contains    4 deleted files.            (3)
    Of those,    4 files have all clusters available,
                 0 files have some clusters available,
                 0 files have no clusters available.

    MS-DOS directory contains    3 deleted files.                  (4)
    Of those,    3 files may be recovered.

Using the Deletion-tracking method.                                (5)

      KNEE              23 25/11/93 13:55   ...A Deleted: 25/11/93 14:00
All of the clusters for this file are available. Undelete (Y/N)?   (6)
```

(1) The command to recover the files on the diskette in drive A:.
(2) The command, without additional selection criteria applies to all deleted files. If you only wish to recover text files, for instance, specify *.TXT as a selection criterion.
(3) The file recording deletions displays four deleted files including all clusters.
(4) However, only three files were found in the directory since one of the files has been replaced by a new file. The three files may be recovered.
(5) Because the /DOS option was not specified along with the command, the Deletion-tracking file is used in the recovery process.
(6) The file names from the file are shown individually on the screen because the /ALL option was not specified. You can specify individually which files are to be recovered.

**Recovering files under MS-DOS 6.0 and 6.2.** The facility of recovering files under MS-DOS 6 has been improved in comparison to previous versions. In addition, there is a version of the recovery program for Windows. This enables you to recover files by means of menu options.

Both programs provide three different levels of security:

■ Sentry control
■ Deletion-tracking
■ the standard method.

**UNDELETE for MS-DOS.** Sentry control is the highest security level. Deleted files are placed in the SENTRY directory and recovered from there if necessary. The number of deleted files which can be stored depends on the capacity of the disk. The program reserves roughly 7 percent for deleted files. Each file which is then deleted is then written over the oldest file in the SENTRY directory. The program requires approximately 13.5 Kb working memory.

In order to have a continual record of deletions on the disk, include the following command in the AUTOEXEC.BAT file:

```
UNDELETE /S[drive]
```

You only need to specify a drive if you wish to record deletions on a drive other than the currently active one. The following command recovers deleted files:

```
UNDELETE /DS[drive] [/ALL]
```

If you do not specify the /ALL option, you will have to determine individually which files are to be recovered.

Deletion-tracking is the second security level. Only the most important data from each deleted file are stored in the PCTRACKR.DEL protocol file. Accordingly, the program requires less disk capacity.

Include the following command in the AUTOEXEC.BAT file in order to keep a record of deletions on the disk using this method.

```
UNDELETE /T[drive]
```

Deleted files are restored using the following command:

```
UNDELETE /DT[drive] [/ALL]
```

In the case of the standard method of recovery, you do not need to include a special command in AUTOEXEC.BAT; this is always active. However, deleted files can only be recovered with any certainty if no other files have been written to the disk.

More information concerning UNDELETE can be acquired using the MS-DOS help function. Type HELP UNDELETE.

**UNDELETE for Windows.** When the Windows programs for MS-DOS 6.0 or 6.2 have been installed, a group window for Microsoft Tools is created in the Windows Program Manager window. The icon representing the Undelete program shows a bin from which a piece of paper is being extracted. In addition, the File Manager contains the option *Undelete* in the *File* menu.

If you activate one of these functions, the Microsoft Undelete window appears on the screen displaying the menus *File, Options* and *Help*. Several command buttons are located under the menu bar. The names of the deleted files, if any, are shown in the middle of the window.

If you wish to install deletion security, open the *Options* menu and select the *Configure Delete Protection* option. Activate the required level in the subsequent window. The figure below provides an example.

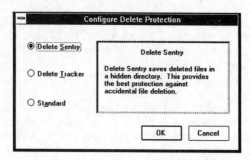

If you click on Delete Sentry, another window appears
in which you can specify which files are to be saved, the
period of time they are to be saved, the maximum disk
capacity for the files and the drives for which the protection is applicable.

Deleted files can be recovered as follows: select the
data of the deleted file in the Microsoft Undelete window
and click on the Undelete button.

Include the following command in the AUTOEXEC.BAT
in order to have the Sentry control continually active:

```
UNDELETE /LOAD
```

The program makes use of settings in the UN-
DELETE.INI file which is a text file in which you yourself
can also make modifications. More information concerning the UNDELETE.INI file can be gained from the
MS-DOS help function.

## 12.4 Saving the harddisk partition data

A harddisk must be partitioned for use. If the harddisk
on your computer has not yet been partitioned, this will
have to be done (see section 7.1).

Under MS-DOS 5, when preparing the harddisk, you
can save certain partition data on a diskette by means
of the following command:

```
MIRROR /PARTN
```

Then insert a diskette in drive A: or in a different drive if you alter the standard letter. When this has been done, keep this diskette beside the MS-DOS diskettes.

If your computer cannot gain access to the harddisk for some reason or other, the harddisk may be defective. Using the partition data on diskette it may be possible to rectify the fault:

```
UNFORMAT /PARTN
```

You must specify the diskdrive from which you wish to rectify the data. Follow the instructions given on the screen.

*Example:* The partition data of the harddisk are to be saved on diskette.

```
C:\>mirror /partn                                             (1)

Disk Partition Table saver.                                   (2)

The partition information from your hard drive(s) has been read.

Next, the file PARTNSAV.FIL will be written to a floppy disk.  Please
insert a formatted diskette and type the name of the diskette drive.
What drive? A                                                 (3)

Successful.

C:\>dir a:                                                    (4)

 Volume in drive A has no label
 Volume Serial Number is 3534-18ED
 Directory of A:\

PARTNSAV FIL        2,048 25/11/93   14:15
        1 file(s)           2,048 bytes
                    1,316,544 bytes free
```

(1) The command to save the partition data.
(2) System message.
(3) Proposal to store the partition data on the diskette in drive A:. Confirm by pressing Enter or change the drive if required.
(4) Check the diskette in drive A:. The file has been saved successfully.

# 13 Utility programs from MS-DOS 6.0 onwards

From version 6.0 onwards, MS-DOS provides several utility programs which previously had to be purchased separately and were supplied in packages, such as PC Tools and Norton Utilities. Utility programs can fulfil the following useful functions:

- Linking computers
- Reducing the computer energy consumption
- Searching for and eliminating viruses
- Optimizing file management on disks
- Increasing disk capacity.

Utility programs for data security, recovery of deleted data and the detection and elimination of viruses are also available for Windows (see section 9.6 and 13.6).

## 13.1 Linking computers

Users who have two computers, for example a normal desk computer and a laptop, often require to exchange data and programs between the computers. Up until now, that had to take place by means of diskettes or using a special program. From MS-DOS version 6.0 onwards, that can be done by means of the standard programs INTERLNK and INTERSVR which are now supplied along with MS-DOS.

Here is a concise description of these facilities:

- Data and programs can be exchanged between computers.
- Most programs are interchangeable.
- The drives of the other computer can be used in addition to those on your own computer.

**Hardware requirements for linkage.** The two computers must be linked to each other by means of a cable connected to the parallel or serial ports. If the parallel port is used, the transmission will take place more quickly than if the serial port is used. Cables used to link serial ports are called nulmodem cables and are specially wired for computer linkage. Most computers have one parallel port to which the printer is connected in general, and two serial ports. The mouse is generally connected to one of these. If you wish to link the two computers frequently, it is convenient to make use of the free serial port to avoid having to switch cables repeatedly.

You can recognize serial ports by the 9 or 25 pin plugs. Accordingly, many nulmodem cables have a 9 pin plug at one end and a 9 and a 25 pin plug at the other. A separate extension plug can also be used to convert a 9 pin plug to a 25 pin plug.

**Making the connection.** The most simple method of making a connection between two computers is when one computer makes its harddisk and diskettes (and Printer) available for use by the other. The drives are then redirected. In that case, the former is referred to as the *server* and the latter as the *client*. If nothing else is specified, the extra drives are assigned the first available letters. If both computers have a harddisk C:, the client is able to make use of two harddisks after linkage, C: and D:. When being used by the client, the server cannot be independently used and displays only messages concerning the link.

If you wish to redirect more drives, you must ensure that there are sufficient drive names available on the client. Normally, only one drive more than is physically present in the system is kept available for this task. Using the command LASTDRIVE in the CONFIG.SYS file, you can register additional drives in the system (see section 6.3). Imagine your computer has three drives, A:, B: and C:. When linked, 3 + 1 will become available (D: is added). If you wish to redirect three drives from a server, the maximum number of drives must be increased to

6, i.e. A: to F:. To do this, include the command LAST-DRIVE=F in the CONFIG.SYS file.

The link between the computers is made as follows:

1.  Connect the serial or parallel ports of the two computers using the appropriate cable.

2.  To make the link, the MS-DOS 6 programs IN-TERSVR and INTERLNK are required on both computers. If necessary, copy these to the harddisks of the computers. If you have connected the computers to one another via a nulmodem cable, you can copy the programs from one computer to the other by giving the following command: INTERSVR/RCOPY. The server will then display the message that you must configure the serial port on the client. Depending on the port, the command will be as follows, for instance: MODE COM1:2400,N,8,1,0 and CTTY COM1.

3.  Install the INTERLNK program as the operating program in the CONFIG.SYS files on both computers. For instance: DEVICE=C\DOS\INTERLNK.EXE as the last line in the file. If necessary, also add the command LASTDRIVE=X, where X represents the last possible drive.

    *Note:* When you adopt a new command into CONFIG.SYS, you must restart the computer in order to activate the command.

4.  Use the INTERSVR command to define on the server which drives are to be available to the client and which are not. If no parameters are specified, all drives will be made available. The program automatically registers which drives on the server can be redirected. If you only wish to redirect drive C: and not A: and B:, give the command INTERSVR C:/X=A /X=B. Information concerning the redirected drives and printers appears on the server screen. Modifications made on the client using the INTERLNK command are also shown on the server.

5. Activate the link from the client by giving the command INTERLNK.

These settings are adequate for a great number of applications. But if you wish to specify additional settings, you can include these in CONFIG.SYS when installing the INTERLNK program or specify them when giving the commands INTERSVR and INTERLNK. The MS-DOS help function provides more information about this. Give the command HELP INTERLNK or HELP INTERSVR.

**Working with the link.** When the link has been made, you can address the server drives and printers (if they have not been excluded) from the client. It then seems as if they are part of the client computer. Only the access time is longer, because the transport of data takes place via the ports. The COPY, XCOPY and MOVE commands can also be used in the normal way. Applications which are located purely on the server can now be started on the client.

*Note:* The commands CHKDSK, DEFRAG, DISKCOMP, DISKCOPY, FDISK, FORMAT, MIRROR, SYS, UNDELETE and UNFORMAT cannot be applied to redirected drives.

**Breaking the link.** The link between the two computers is broken by pressing the key combination Alt-F4. You can no longer address the other drives from the client. The allocation of a drive can be revoked by giving the INTERLNK command along with the letter of the allocated drive and an equals sign, for instance, INTERLNK F=. Subsequently, you can make a new allocation by specifying INTERLINK F=C, for example.

*Example:* Link two computers by means of a nulmodem cable. MS-DOS 6 is installed on both computers. The configuratiion files of both computers is to be extended with the menu option *Data Exchange*. This menu option enables the INTERLNK.EXE program to be installed on each computer. On the server, only drive C: is to be redirected to the client and the diskette drives are to be excluded from the link. On the client, the server drive is available under the name D:. Printers connected to the server may be used by the client.

The server configuration file and the redirection command is as follows:

```
C:\>type config.sys                                                (1)

[menu]                                                             (2)
menuitem=Standard
menuitem=RAM drive
menuitem=Data Exchange

[common]                                                          (3)
DEVICE=C:\DOS\HIMEM.SYS
DEVICE=C:\DOS\EMM386.EXE NOEMS HIGHSCAN
BUFFERS=30,0
FILES=30
DOS=HIGH,UMB
FCBS=4,0
DEVICEHIGH /L:1,12160 =C:\DOS\SETVER.EXE
DEVICEHIGH /L:1,37520 =C:\DOS\VGA\UTILS\FASTBIOS.SYS
DEVICEHIGH /L:1,2000 =C:\DOS\VGA\UTILS\EANSI.SYS
STACKS=9,256
COUNTRY=044,437,C:\DOS\COUNTRY.SYS
SHELL=C:\DOS\COMMAND.COM C:\DOS\   /P
DEVICEHIGH /L:1,44496 =C:\DOS\DBLSPACE.SYS /MOVE

[Standard]                                                        (4)

[RAM drive]                                                       (5)
DEVICEHIGH=C:\DOS\RAMDRIVE.SYS 8192 512 1024 /E

[Data Exchange]                                                   (6)
LASTDRIVE=N
DEVICE=C:\DOS\INTERLNK.EXE



C:\>intersvr c: /x=a /x=b                                         (7)
```

(1) The server configuration file is displayed on the screen. The client file contains the same commands.

(2) The texts behind the MENUITEM command are shown on the screen when the computer is started up. In order to link the computers, the *Data Exchange* option should be selected. Subsequently, the Common and Data Exchange blocks are processed.

(3) The Common block containing commands belonging to all configurations.

(4) The standard configuration contains no other commands than those in the Common block.

(5) In this configuration, a RAM drive is installed in extended memory with a capacity of 8 MB.

(6) These commands are given for the Data Exchange. Since only one drive is being redirected, the number of drives on the client does not need to be increased. This line has only been placed here as a test. The INTERLNK.EXE program is automatically installed in extended memory if this is possible. Accordingly, the DEVICEHIGH command is not necessary.

(7) The activation command for the redirection. In this case, this is only for drive C:. The diskette drives are excluded from the redirection.

The screen on the following page appears on the server:

(1) Drive C: with a capacity of 180 Mb and the printer port LPT1 of the server are available to the client.

(2) The client is not yet registered. Additional information is not yet available.

(3) The current action during transmission is displayed, for instance, reading.

(4) The port being used is shown here, for example, COM2.

(5) Unless you specify otherwise, the default speed of 115,200 characters per second is shown here.

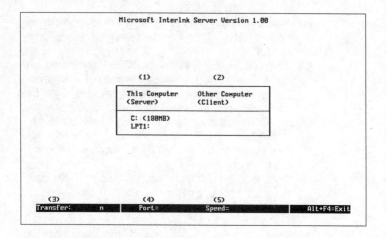

On the client, the allocation of drives and ports must be activated using the INTERLNK command.

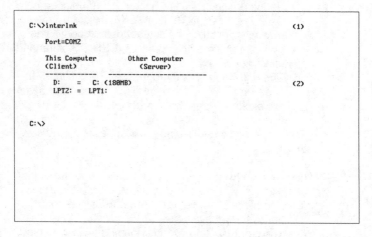

(1) If no parameters are specified, the allocations are automatically adopted.
(2) Drive C: on the server receives the name D: on the client. The server printer port can be addressed from the client using LPT2. The printer can be excluded from the link by means of the IN-TERSVR/NOPRINTER command on the server.

The redirection is disconnected by pressing the Alt-F4 key combination. If you cancel an allocation on the client, for instance using the command INTERLNK F=, the program is not ended on the server. Instead, a message appears on the screen:

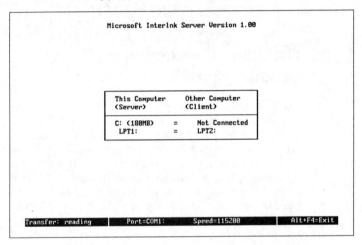

On the client, you can only address the F: drive after you have registered it once again. The following figure illustrates how this is done:

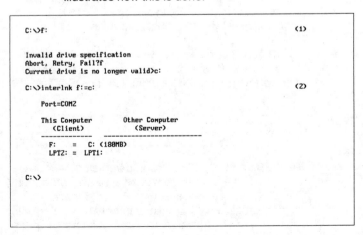

(1) Unsuccessful attempt to address the disconnected
    server drive. You can remove this message by
    pressing F (Fail). A drive which is physically pres-
    ent must then be specified.
(2) Drive C: on the server is assigned the name F:.
    This redirects the printer port once more.

## 13.2    Reducing the computer energy consumption

The POWER.EXE utility program provided by MS-DOS
6.0 and 6.2 makes it possible to reduce the energy consumption when they are switched on but not performing
any tasks. Leaving aside the fact that energy-saving is
always worthwhile, this program is especially functional
for computers which run on batteries such as laptops.
Each piece of energy saved makes this type of computer independent of mains supply. According to Microsoft, the energy saved should amount to something like
5%. In the case of computers which are APM-specified
(Advanced Power Management), this is said to be
around 25%.

*Note:* Some battery-driven computers are supplied with
a power-saving program. In that case, the POWER program may not lead additional saving. Try it out.

**The POWER command activates the energy-saving
program for PCs which are running but inactive.
The command should be placed in the CONFIG.SYS
file.**

```
POWER [adv:[max|reg|min] [std] [off]]
```

POWER                    If no other parameters are given,
                         the command displays the current
                         status of the Power Manager.
adv:max|reg|min          Determines the energy-saving with
                         regard to the requirements of the

applications (the default setting is REG). MAX means that the maximum energy-saving is achieved. If the applications run more slowly because of this, you can try MIN.

std                Produces additional saving for computers which support APM.

off                Switches the energy-saving off.

**Procedure.** Install the POWER program in the CONFIG.SYS configuration file (see section 6.2) by typing *EDIT config.sys* behind the system prompt. Type the line DEVICEHIGH=C:\DOS\POWER.EXE at the end of the file and save the file using Alt-F, S. Quit the editor (Alt-F, X), and start up the computer anew. This activates the function.

*Example:* Adopt the energy-saving command in CONFIG.SYS and start up the computer again. The status is then to be shown on the screen.

```
   ...
Microsoft Power Manager version 1.0                    (1)
(C) Copyright Microsoft Corporation 1986, 1993
   ...


C:\>type config.sys                                    (2)
         ...
[Standard]
DEVICEHIGH=C:\DOS\POWER.EXE
   ...



C:\>power                                              (3)

Power Management Status
-----------------------
Setting = ADV: REG
CPU: idle 90% of time
```

(1) The system indicates that the Power Manager has been installed.
(2) Display the configuration file. An extract from the CONFIG.SYS file is shown.
(3) This command displays the current energy status. REG indicates the average time the computer is not actively being used. The Central Processing Unit is idle 90% of the time.

# 13.3　Detecting and eliminating viruses

Viruses are small programs, invisible to the user, which make alterations in programs and data, causing potentially serious damage. They are deliberately created and distributed with that aim in mind. The distribution takes places via diskettes and bulletin boards. A virus settles in the working memory or on the harddisk of the computer and begins its destructive activities. Sometimes it remains inert until a certain programmed date, wherupon it suddenly becomes active. Other viruses become active when a particular program is started up or a certain function is implemented. Viruses possess the tedious property of spreading to other users via programs and data, so that they can gain new opportunities to carry out their undermining work.

**Detecting viruses.** Some viruses are harmless: they produce interesting figures on the screen but they do not destroy anything. But many viruses are dangerous and are capable of devastating months of work. If you repeatedly encounter certain irregularities in the system which cannot be explained by faults in the software or hardware, your computer may be harbouring a virus.

**Avoiding infection.** You can protect your computer against viruses by means of several simple organisational measures:

■ Do not insert diskettes whose origins are unknown in the diskdrives and carry out data transmission.
■ Only install programs from the original diskettes. In-

fections may occur in the factory but this is very unlikely.

- Do not lend your original diskettes to others.
- Apply write-protection to new program diskettes before use (see section 9.4).
- Always make backups of your data files so that you can fall back on these in the case of infection and loss of data. If these files also become infected, you will have to transfer the information to paper for instance, and read the information in again using a scanner.
- When installing MS-DOS 6.0 or 6.2, create a startup diskette using the MSAV program (see section 9.6). In this way, you have a good chance of eliminating even the most stubborn viruses.

**Detecting and eliminating viruses using a program.**
MS-DOS 6.0 and 6.2 provides three programs for eliminating viruses:

- MSAV.EXE: detecting and eliminating viruses from MS-DOS.
- MWAV.EXE: detecting and eliminating viruses from Windows.
- VSAFE.COM: permanent virus alert.

The MSAV and MWAV resemble one another very closely in terms of operation. You can install the Windows version when installing MS-DOS, but this can also be done later (see section 9.6).

New viruses are continually brought into circulation. Accordingly, it is advisable to acquire an update of the program regularly.

**Procedure under MS-DOS.** Check your computer system for viruses as follows:

1. If necessary, go to the DOS directory using **cd DOS**. Give the following command behind the DOS prompt:

```
MSAV
```

The data in the currently active drive are read and the program window appears on the screen. The harddisk is normally the currently active drive.

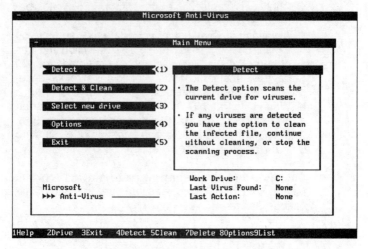

(1) The first menu option is accentuated or highlighted. You can select the other options using the cursor keys. Any outline of each option is given in the right-hand window when the option is highlighted. An option is activated by pressing the Enter key, or click on it using the mouse (see section 10.2).

(2) The currently active drive is scanned for viruses. Any virus found will be eliminated.

(3) Selects a different drive.

(4) A dialog window appears in which you can specify certain options. You can gain more information about the individual options by pressing F1. Select them using the cursor keys and activate them using Enter.

(5) Closes the program.

2.   If you only wish to check the system, select the *Detect* option.

The working memory and the currently active drive are examined for viruses. As soon as a virus is detected, a message appears on the screen with the name and type of virus. After the check, an information window appears containing the diagnosis.

3.  Select the *Detect & Clean* option when you think or know that your computer is harbouring a virus.

In this case also, the window displayed above will appear, but now the data are shown in the *Infected* and *Cleaned* columns.

4.  If you wish tó check a different disk, for instance a diskette, select the *Select new drive* option. Proceed as described above.

**Procedure under Windows.** If you wish to check the computer for viruses when running the Windows graphic user interface, proceed as follows:

1.  Start up Windows using the command WIN.

2.  Open the Microsoft Tools group window by double-clicking on the icon. The following window appears containing the utility programs which are available since version 6.0 of MS-DOS.

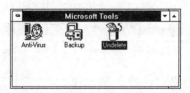

3.  Double-click on the Anti-Virus icon. The Microsoft Anti-Virus program for Windows appears.

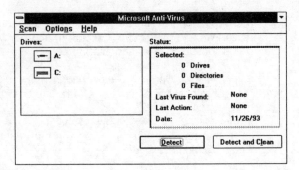

4.   Click, using the left-hand mouse button, on the icon of the drive you wish to check. The directories of the drive to be checked are read in.

5.   Click, using the left-hand mouse button, on the *Detect* option if you only wish to examine the drive for viruses.

The working memory is first checked, then all directories and files on the chosen disk. Both procedures are graphically displayed on the screen. If a virus is found, a corresponding message is shown on the screen. When the check has been carried out, a window containing a diagnosis appears, similar to that under MS-DOS.

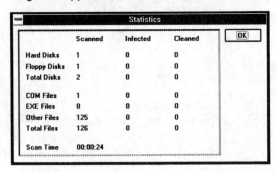

6.   Click, using the left-hand mouse button, on the *Detect and Clean* option in order to remove the viruses simultaneously. If a virus is found, a mes-

sage to this effect is show on the screen indicating the name and location. By clicking on the relevant button, you can choose whether to clean up the virus, to stop or continue the program. At the conclusion of the process, a window appears, similar to that shown above.

7. Close the program by double-clicking on the symbol in the upper left-hand corner of the window.

Using the *Scan* and *Options* menus in the Microsoft Anti-Virus window, you can specify certain settings if required. By pressing F1, you can gain more context-oriented help concerning these settings.

### Checking automatically

It is also possible to check the working memory and the disks when the computer is started up (under either DOS or Windows).

**Automatic check under MS-DOS.** To do this, place the command MSAV in the AUTOEXEC.BAT automatic startup file (see section 5.5). Special parameters enable you to adapt the program to your configuration. To gain a concise description of these parameters, activate the MS-DOS help function using MSAV /? or HELP MSAV (more extensive).

**Automatic check under Windows.** In Windows, proceed as follows:

1. Open the Microsoft Tools group window.

2. Select the *Anti-Virus* icon without starting up the program (a single click).

3. Open the *File* menu from the Program Manager and select the *Properties* option.

The Program Item Properties dialog window of the Anti-Virus program appears. The command line contains the command MWAV.EXE. If that is not the case, you will have to search for this file using the *Browse* button and place it in the text box. If, for instance, you wish to check the C: harddisk for viruses when starting up the computer in Windows, proceed as follows:

4.   Specify C: behind the MWAV.EXE command (space between) and press Enter.

5.   Drag the Anti-Virus program icon to the Startup group window so that it is executed directly each time Windows is started up.

**Protecting the computer against infection**

You can protect the system against infection by known viruses by means of the VSAFE.COM program. Most viruses cause certain alterations in the working memory or on the startup disks. Particularly favoured locations are the executable files (COM, EXE) and the operating system kernel in the boot sector of a startup disk. The program registers the alterations which have taken place in these essential components of the system. Alterations in the working memory can also be carried out by network programs. Check this before proceeding to examine the network configuration for a virus. If necessary de-activate the VSAFE program first.

In order to have the computer permanently checked, you must include the VSAFE program in the AUTOEX-EC.BAT file (see section 5.5). If you wish to make the program permanently active under Windows, add the command LOAD=MWAVTSR.EXE to the WIN.INI file. Accordingly, the statements made by VSAFE will be displayed in Windows.

The VSAFE program can be de-activated using the Alt-V key combination. An information window then appears with an explanation of the warnings given by

VSAFE. VSAFE can be removed using the Alt-U key combination. The following figure shows the statements produced by the active VSAFE program and by the information window activated by Alt-V.

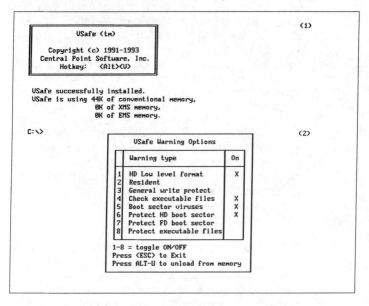

(1) The VSAFE statement at the program startup. You can load the program in conventional memory, or in extended memory using the command LH VSAFE. The program occupies 23 Kb. The information window is summoned by pressing the Alt-V hotkey.

(2) The information window indicates which functions are active. The harddisk, for instance, is protected against low-level format. You can alter the individual options using the number keys 1 to 8. Remove the program from memory if required using the key combination Alt-U.

It is possible to gear the check to your own configuration. The required parameters are described in the MS-DOS help function. Type HELP VSAFE.

# 13.4   Optimising file management on disk

When you save data on a harddisk or on diskette, the various file clusters are placed successively on the disk. Modification of the files means that the files are extended, reduced or deleted. MS-DOS always stores new clusters at positions which are available or which have become available as a result of deletions. This maximizes the disk capacity. Eventually however, this leads to the situation in which the clusters are physically no longer in the ideal order of sequence. They have become spread out over the entire disk. This makes little difference to the files themselves because the clusters are linked to one another logically. But addressing these files becomes more time-consuming because the reading and writing heads have to be moved to different positions more often. This spreading of a file over the disk is referred to as *fragmentation.*

In order to improve the speed of access to a disk, it is advisable to *defragment* the disk now and again. In the case of diskettes, you can do this quite easily by copying the disk contents to another disk using the COPY command (see section 4.4). In the case of a harddisk, a defragmentation program is necessary to reorganize the files stored on disk.

From MS-DOS version 6.0 onwards, the DEFRAG program is available for this purpose.

*Note:* No problems have arisen during tests on different computers. The addressing was considerably quicker after optimization, especially in the case of large text files. Nevertheless, prior to optimization, it is advisable to make a backup of all important files on the disk. Depending on the frequency of use, it is advisable to implement the defragmentation approximately once a month.

**Application.** Proceed as follows to defragment a harddisk:

1.   Remove all files from the harddisk which you no longer need (see section 4.9).

2.   Check the harddisk for any faults using the command CHKDSK /F and convert lost clusters to files (see section 4.6). Check the contents of these files and delete them if necessary.

3.   Then start up the DEFRAG program as follows:

```
DEFRAG
```

The program appears in a window on the screen. You can select various options by means of the cursor keys and Tab or the mouse.

4.   First select the drive, for instance the harddisk C:. The program states that it is reading and analysing the data on disk and then indicates the percentage of the disk which is not fragmented. The recommended optimization method is shown.

5.   If the program recommends optimization, confirm this by selecting the *Optimize* button. You can also makes specifications for the program first by selecting *Configure*.

*Example:* The harddisk C: is to be optimized by defragmenting the files. The configuration menu is to be shown.

When the DEFRAG command has been given behind the DOS prompt, the disk data are read and the following window appears:

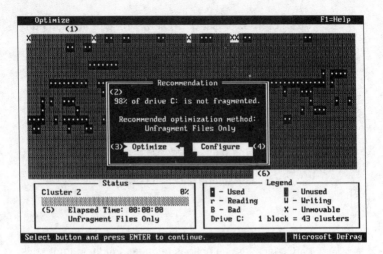

(1) The clusters are shown in the window by means of the symbols which are explained under point (6). The more unused space there is between the clusters, the greater the fragmentation.

(2) The percentage indicates the non-fragmented disk capacity in relation to the entire disk capacity.

(3) Activate this button to start the optimization.

(4) Activate this button to make certain specifications first.

(5) Information, in the form of a percentage bar and a clock, concerning the optimization to be implemented.

(6) Explanation of the symbols representing the clusters on disk.

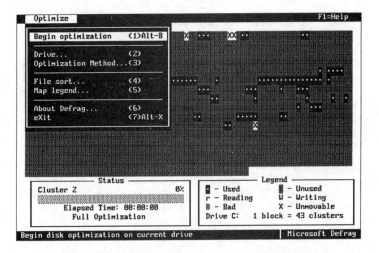

(1) Start the optimization.
(2) Select a different drive in a dialog window.
(3) You can choose either a complete optimization or an optimization of files.
(4) You can determine the order of sequence in which the files are to be sorted. Normally, they are un-sorted. The options include sorting according to name, extension, date and time and size. You can also determine whether the sorting should occur in ascending or descending order.
(5) Provides an explanation of the symbols used to in-dicate the division of the disk capacity.
(6) Gives information about the programmer.
(7) Terminates the program.

During optimization, a graphic display illustrates the re-organization of the disk. The clusters which have been dealt with are shown in colour. Depending on the extent of the fragmentation, the reorganization can take minutes or even hours.

## 13.5    Increasing disk capacity

From version 6.0 of MS-DOS onwards, it is possible to
virtually double the normal capacity of harddisks and
diskettes by means of the **DoubleSpace** program. This
is done by compressing the data without physically altering the disk. The compression program retards the
reading and writing speed a little.

Text files in particular are stored in a rather extravagant
manner using the common methods of saving. The
compression program makes more efficient use of the
available space, which produces the effect of having
more capacity.

For example, the following sentence includes the 'at'
string:

The fat cat sat up.

DoubleSpace compresses this sentence by replacing
the repeated 'at' string (including the space) with a
cross-reference to the first 'at'. Thus:

The fat c#s#up.

where 'at' is represented here by #.

When files are copied to other disks, the compression is
undone, which means that it remains possible to copy
files from a compressed harddisk to diskettes for instance.

*Note:* Disk compression cannot be undone immediately
in version 6.0. Before decompressing a disk, you must
transfer *all data* which you wish to retain to another disk,
delete the compressed files on the compressed disk and
transfer the copied files back again. In version 6.2, you
can uncompress a drive by invoking the DoubleSpace
program along with the /UNCOMPRESS option. Notice,
however, that it is not possible to undo the installation of
MS-DOS 6.0 or 6.2 by means of the UNINSTALL dis-

kette if the startup disk has been compressed after the installation. Prior to compressing the harddisk or diskette, it
is advisable to make backups of the data. If your computer is running in a network, you will have to log in to the
network first in order to specify the diskdrives.

**The compression**

The first time you use the program, an installation
procedure is implemented. In this, you can choose
either *Express Setup* or *Custom Setup*. The first option
will format the computer harddisk without further specifications. The latter option enables you to determine
yourself exactly what is to be compressed.

Subsequently, the following processes are executed
automatically. The disk is checked for scattered clusters
using the CHKDSK program, the CONFIG.SYS file is
supplemented with the command DBLSPACE.EXE
which organizes the workings of the DBLSPACE.BIN
program. Then all files on the disk are compressed and
transferred to a CVF (Compressed Volume File) called
DBLSPACE.000.

The disk is divided into two areas: a compressed and an
uncompressed part. Both areas are regarded as separate drives by the system. The compressed area is the
drive with the extended capacity and it retains the name it
had prior to the compression (C: for example). You can
continue working with this as you did previously. The uncompressed area is smaller and receives a new name,
H: for example (representing *host drive*). You do not
need to actually make use of this drive, although it can be
used to save files which you do not wish to compress. For
instance, the Windows permanent swap file does not
work properly when it is compressed. Other files which
must be stored here after compression are those used to
operate the compressed disk. This involves the IO.SYS
and MSDOS.SYS system files and the compression file
DBLSPACE.000. The file names are hidden so that they
cannot be removed unintentionally.

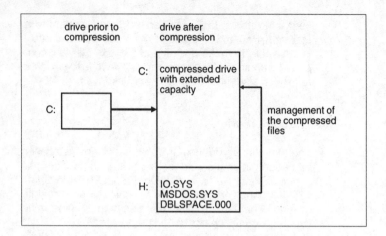

In order to implement the compression, there must be a minimum of 1 Mb available on harddisk, and 200 Kb on diskette.

*Example:* The capacity of a harddisk in drive C: is to be increased by compressing the files. The compression program has not been applied to this disk previously.

Proceed as follows:

1.  Give the compression command behind the DOS prompt:

    ```
    DBLSPACE
    ```

    The DoubleSpace Setup program is then activated and an introduction window appears. Press Enter to proceed or press F1 for more information. You can discontinue the process by pressing F3.

2.  Press Enter. You may now choose between the *Express Setup* and the *Custom Setup*.

3.  Select the default setting *Express Setup* by pressing Enter. A window is displayed indicating approximately how long the process will take. However,

the complete procedure will take even longer because the compressed disk is subsequently defragmented. The process is continued by pressing D, F1 provides additional information and F3 discontinues the program. You can return to the previous screen by pressing Esc.

4.  Press D. DoubleSpace begins. The disk is first checked by starting up the computer again. The programs are then compressed and the defragmentation is carried out. During the entire process, you will be informed of what is going on. Finally, a message window appears providing information concerning the process and the disk capacity.

5.  Press Enter. The CONFIG.SYS and AUTOEXEC.BAT configuration files (and the WIN.INI file if Windows is present) are adjusted, and the computer is started up again. The drive with the extended capacity can now be used.

**Checking the drive.** You can now check the result of the compression.

*Example:* The root directories of both drives, C: and H: are to be displayed, and then information concerning DoubleSpace is to be given.

```
C:\>dir                                        (1)

 Volume in drive C is DOS6_CCC
 Volume Serial Number is 1CF5-1F54
 Directory of C:\


DOS          <DIR>     17-05-93     14:26
WINDOWS      <DIR>     17-05-93      8:58
...
AUTOEXEC BAT     289 13-05-93     10:16
CONFIG   SYS     429 13-05-93      9:23
     23 file(s)        75235 bytes
                    43761664 bytes free
```

```
C:\>dir h: /a                                                    (2)

 Volume in drive H is HOST_VOOR_C
 Volume Serial Number is 1A81-AC08
 Directory of H:\

IO       SYS     40646 19-05-93    12:00
MSDOS    SYS     38184 19-05-93    12:00
CHKLIST  SM         81 16-06-93    11:48
DBLSPACE BIN     51252 19-06-93    12:00
DBLSPACE INI        91 23-07-93    16:00
DBLSPACE 000 90765312 02-08-93     9:02
        6 file(s)      90895566 bytes
                       13871104 bytes free


C:\>dblspace /info                                               (3)
DoubleSpace is checking drive C.

Compressed drive C is contained on uncompressed drive
H: in file
H:\DBLSPACE.000.


        Disk space used:               109.31 MB
        Average compression ratio:     1.7 to 1


        Free space:                    41.73 MB
        Estimated compression ratio:   2.0 to 1


        Total capacity:           151.05 MB
```

(1)  The directory listing of drive C:. The number of free
     bytes is shown at the bottom. This is substantially
     more than previously. It seems as if the files have
     not undergone any modification.
(2)  The directory listing of the the uncompressed drive
     H:. The /a option is required to display the hidden
     files (see section 3.2). As you see, the
     DBLSPACE.000 file, with its 90 Mb, contains all the
     compressed files of the old drive C:. The DBL-
     SPACE.BIN and DBLSPACE.INI files are also lo-

cated here. The former file is loaded from this drive when the computer is started up. The INI file contains the currently active settings of the compression program (see below).

(3) This command produces information about the capacity of the compressed disk. Of the 151 Mb available capacity on the disk, 109 Mb is being used for compressed data. The remaining available space cannot be determined exactly because the system does not yet know the type of data to be compressed. DoubleSpace estimates the available space as being 41 Mb in an estimated compression ratio of 2 to 1. The eventual available space may be smaller if the compression ratio turns out to be different.

**Drive management.** When you have installed the compression program, you can use it to manage disks. In this way, you can compress new harddisks and diskettes, connect (*mount*) and disconnect (*unmount*) compressed disks and alter the size of the compression ratio. In addition, you can request all information concerning the compressed disks. All these functions can be implemented in the DoubleSpace window.

*Example:* The capacity of an empty, formatted diskette is to be enlarged.

Proceed as follows:

1. Insert the formatted diskette in the appropriate drive.

2. Start up the compression program:

```
DBLSPACE
```

The DoubleSpace window appears:

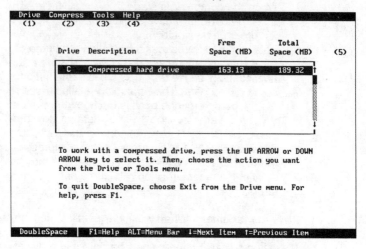

(1) Activate the menu bar using the Alt key and select the required menu using the cursor keys or by pressing the accentuated letter on the name. The following options are available in the *Drive* menu:

| | |
|---|---|
| *Info* | Gives information about the drives shown in the list (5). |
| *Change Size* | Changes the size of the drive. |
| *Change Ratio* | Changes the compression ratio as the basis for determining the available space. |
| *Mount* | Establishes a connection between a compressed volume file and a drive letter. |
| *Unmount* | Breaks the connection between the CVF and the drive letter. |
| *Format* | Format the compressed drive selected from the list (5). |
| *Delete* | Deletes the selected compressed drive and the associated CVF. |
| *Exit* | Terminates the DoubleSpace program. |

(2) The options from this menu enable you to compress additional drives:

*Existing Drive*    Compresses another drive which is added to the computer, for instance a diskette.

*Create New Drive*    Creates a new compressed drive on the available space of an existing uncompressed drive.

(3) The options in the *Tools* menu provide the following possibilities:

*Defragment*    Defragments the selected drive.

*Chkdsk*    Checks the disk structure of the selected compressed drive.

*Options*    There must be sufficient letters available for the compression. You can determine here the last letter reserved for DoubleSpace, for instance H:. You can also specify the number of drives you wish to be able to mount after starting up the computer.

(4) This menu provides detailed information about all menu functions. Context-oriented information can be acquired by selecting a certain object and then pressing F1. Moreover, most dialog windows provide a Help button.

(5) The list of compressed drives. If the list contains several drives, you must first select the drive appropriate to the required process.

3. Select the *Existing Drive* option from the *Compress* menu.

The program automatically examines all diskette drives for diskettes to be compressed. Information concerning the current and the estimated available space is displayed on the screen.

4.  Select the relevant diskette if necessary and press
    Enter. You will then be informed how long the com-
    pression will take. You will also be warned at the
    same time that the compression cannot be directly
    undone.

5.  Press D to implement the compression. The dis-
    kette is checked and then compressed. Sub-
    sequently, the diskette is automatically *mounted*
    i.e. connected to the system. A mounted diskette
    can be recognized by the fact that the data are in-
    cluded in the options list of the DoubleSpace win-
    dow (see (5) in the figure above). An empty 5.25
    inch 1.2 Mb diskette has a capacity of 2.18 Mb after
    compression; a 3.5 inch HD diskette has a capacity
    of approximately 2.63 Mb.

**Connecting and disconnecting drives.** Compressed
drives have to be connected to the system before they
can be used. In the case of harddisks, that only needs
to be done if they have been previously disconnected.
Diskettes are different, because they are switched regularly. After each switch, the diskette has to be connected to the system first before you can work with it.
The connection of a compressed drive to the system
can also be undone. However, do not unmount the
harddisk which functions as the startup disk for the
computer!

In version 6.2, mounting and unmounting of compressed diskettes is done automatically. In version 6.0,
however, you must mount and unmount diskettes yourself. The following, therefore, applies to version 6.0
only.

*Note:* A compressed diskette which is not connected to
the system normally contains only the file with the name
READTHIS.TXT and the available space is registered
as zero. If you check the diskette using CHKDSK, a
message appears indicating that the entire available
space is being used for a hidden file. The command DIR
/a shows that this file is DBLSPACE.000. The READ-

THIS.TXT file indicates how you can connect the compressed diskette to the system.

Connecting and disconnecting (mounting and unmounting) a compressed diskette can not only take place using the options in the above menu but also using a command behind the DOS prompt:

```
DBLSPACE [[/mount] [/unmount] drive]
                                  [/list]
```

mount       Connects the drive.
unmount     Disconnects the drive.
drive       The name of the drive which is to be connected or disconnected.
list        Displays the current connections.

More information can be gained using the MS-DOS 6.0 or 6.2 Help function. Type HELP DBLSPACE.

*Example:* A compressed diskette is to be checked prior to and after connection to the system.

```
C:\>dir b:                                              (1)

 Volume in drive B has no label
 Volume Serial Number is 2F4B-10F3
 Directory van B:\

READTHIS TXT      312 02-07-93   10:07
        1 file(s)         312 bytes
                            0 bytes free

c:\>type b:readthis.txt                                 (2)

This disk has been compressed by MS-DOS 6 DoubleSpace.

To make this disk's contents accessible, change to the drive that
contains it and then type the following at the command prompt:
```

```
    DBLSPACE/MOUNT

(If this file is located on a drive other than that containing
the compressed disk, then the disk has already been mounted.)


C:\>dblspace /mount b:                                            (3)

DoubleSpace is mounting drive B.
DoubleSpace has mounted drive B.


C:\>dir b:                                                        (4)

 Volume in drive B has no label
 Volume Serial Number is 11D0-3207
 Directory of B:\

EXMPL   123      8128 29-06-93   16:08
        1 file(s)        8128 bytes
                      2277376 bytes free


C:\>dblspace /list                                                (5)

Drive  Type                    Total Free  Total Size  CVF Filename
-----  ----------------------- ----------  ----------- ----------------
  A    Removable-media drive   No disk in drive
  B    Compressed floppy drive  2.17 MB      2.18 MB   G:\DBLSPACE.000
  C    Compressed hard drive   41.72 MB    151.08 MB   H:\DBLSPACE.000
  D    Available for DblSpace
  E    Available for DblSpace
  F    Available for DblSpace
  G    Floppy drive             0.00 MB      1.16 MB
  H    Local hard drive        13.23 MB     99.92 MB


C:\>dblspace /unmount b:                                           (6)

DoubleSpace has unmounted drive B.
```

(1) The directory listing of the unmounted diskette with the text file only. The available capacity is zero.

(2) The text file supplies the information necessary to mount the diskette.

(3) The diskette is mounted. The program states the result.

(4) After the connection has been made, a new directory listing is requested. This indicates one file on the compressed area of the disk. The text file no longer appears in the directory listing. The capacity of the 1.2 Mb diskette has been substantially increased.

(5) An overview of the drives in the computer system. This indicates two compressed drives (C and B) and one uncompressed drive. The CVF files on the compressed disks can be regarded as separate drives (G and H). There are three reserved drives.

(6) The diskette in drive B is unmounted.

As mentioned above, DoubleSpace in version 6.2 normally mounts all removable drives automatically, even when Windows is running. In version 6.0, you had to specify the /MOUNT command in each case. You can switch automatic mounting off if you wish to save memory. To do this, use the DBLSPACE /AUTOMOUNT=0 command or go to the Automount option in the Options dialog box (start DoubleSpace, select Options from the Tools menu). To activate it again, specify DBLSPACE /AUTOMOUNT=1. New settings only become effective after you have restarted your computer.

**Optimizing memory.** If you wish to continue working with compressed disks, you must examine your CONFIG.SYS file to check if the DBLSPACE.SYS operating program for compression has been optimally specified. If the computer possesses high memory area, it is advisable to include the program in CONFIG.SYS as follows: DEVICEHIGH=C:\DOS\DBLSPACE.SYS. Use the DOS editor to enter this specification or use the MemMaker program to optimize computer memory (see chapter 15).

**Undoing the compression.** Disk compression, as mentioned, cannot be immediately undone. Normally, in fact, this is not necessary. But if you wish to do so, proceed as follows:

1.  Copy all data from the compressed files to diskettes.

    If you have two computers with large harddisks and a transmission cable, install the INTERLNK program (see section 13.1) and start up the computer with the compressed disk as the client and the other computer as the server. You can subsequently address the server drives from the client. If the compressed drive is C: and the server drive is referred to as D: on the client, the command to copy the files (to the DUPLIC directory for instance) is as follows:

    ```
    C:\>XCOPY *.* D:\DUPLIC\ /S /E
    ```

    Depending on the amount of data, the contents of the compressed disk are transferred to the other harddisk in one or two hours.

2.  Then copy the COMMAND.COM system file to the uncompressed area of the disk (to the host drive) using the command: COPY COMMAND.COM H:. The IO.SYS and MSDOS.SYS are located as hidden files on this drive. The computer makes use of these to start up again when the compression has been undone.

    If you wish to use the second computer again along with the INTERLNK program to return the copied files, create a CONFIG.SYS configuration file on the host drive using the command: DEVICE=INTERLNK.EXE. Also place the INTERLNK.EXE program on the host drive.

3.  Delete the compressed files on the host drive. To do this, the attributes of these files must be

removed. This is done using the command: H:\>ATTRIB DBLSPACE.*-S-H-R. Then give the command DEL DBLSPACE.*. All data are deleted except the system files.

4.  Now restore all data to the uncompressed disk.

    If you are using a second computer as a server, activate the INTERSVR program. The command is as follows where the server drive is referred to as D: on the client, the data are located in the DUPLIC directory and the client drive is called C:

    ```
    D:\>XCOPY \DUPLIC\*.* C:\ /S /E
    ```

### 13.5.1 DoubleGuard

If you are running DoubleSpace in version 6.2, you can also help protect your data by activating the Double-Guard setting. When DoubleGuard is enabled, Double-Space will constantly check its memory for damage by some other program. If any memory damage is detected, DoubleSpace will stop your computer to prevent any damage to your data.

DoubleGuard is normally active when DoubleSpace is in force. You can alter the settings by giving the command:

```
DBLSPACE /DOUBLEGUARD=0|1
```

where the 0 option switches DoubleGuard off and the 1 option switches it on. You will have to restart your computer before any switch takes effect.

# 14    Help functions from MS-DOS 5 onwards

The following functions are available from MS-DOS 5 onwards:

■ You can request both general and specific information about commands.
■ You can display context-oriented help about functions and menu options in the MS-DOS Shell and the editor.
■ Specified commands can be used again and edited.

In addition, there are extra files containing information not included in the manual:

README.TXT          This contains information about MemMaker and memory management, Windows, Microsoft programs, programs made by other manufacturers and DoubleSpace.

NETWORKS.TXT        This contains information concerning the compatibility of networks which run under MS-DOS 6.0 and 6.2.

OS2.TXT             This file contains information about the installation of MS-DOS 6.0 or 6.2 on a computer on which OS/2 has been installed.

## 14.1   Displaying Help information

**Displaying general information.** You can specify the following command behind the DOS prompt to gain an overview of all MS-DOS commands:

```
HELP
```

**Result under MS-DOS 5:** In MS-DOS 5, the overview occupies five screen pages. It shows the names of the commands and provides a concise description of each command. The overview is continued by pressing any key. The information can be printed out by giving the command HELP > PRN.

**Result under MS-DOS 6.0 and 6.2:** In MS-DOS 6.0 or 6.2, a window appears displaying a list of commands between green brackets, occupying two screen pages. By selecting a command using the cursor keys and then activating it by pressing Enter (or click using the mouse), you switch to a separate window containing detailed information about the command in question. You are given information concerning the syntax and applicable parameters. Additional notes and examples can be gained from the *Notes* and *Example* menus in the upper part of the window. The *File* and *Search* menus are located in the menu bar at the top of the screen. The *File* menu contains the *Print* and the *Exit* options. The former enables you to print the help text, the latter terminates the help function. The *Search* menu enables you to look for a certain command. The menus are activated by pressing Alt-F and Alt-S respectively.

It is also possible to directly summon the help function for a certain command by typing the name of the required program file along with the HELP command behind the DOS prompt, for instance, HELP BREAK.

**Displaying a concise description.** If you wish a short explanation containing the most important information about a specific command, type the name of the program file behind the DOS prompt along with the characters /?, for instance BREAK/?. The result is a brief description of the command, the syntax and the key combinations if any. You can also print this text using the > PRN redirection instruction, for instance BREAK/? > PRN.

**The help function in the MS-DOS Shell**

You can display context-oriented information about
commands and menu options in the MS-DOS Shell and
in the editor by selecting the command or option and
pressing F1. Press Esc to quit the help window.

Most help windows contain a menu bar with buttons
which you can activate in order to acquire supplementary information (Keys, Index, Help). You can also
browse backwards (Back) or quit the window (Close).
See also chapters 10 and 11.

# 14.2   Re-using specified commands

Commands which have been entered can be placed behind the DOS prompt once more by means of the Cursor Up and Cursor Down keys. They are then activated
by pressing Enter. Certain key combinations, comparable to those used when working with the editor, enable you to edit the commands first. In order to make
use of this function, you must start up a command which
has the following syntax:

```
DOSKEY [/reinstall] [/bufsize=bytes]
[/h][/insert] [/overstrike][/m]
[macroname=[macrotext]]
```

/reinstall            Removes the contents from the
                      command buffer (Alt-F7 key combi-
                      nation).

/bufsize=bytes        Alters the size of the command buf-
                      fer; this is normally set to 512 bytes.
                      The minimum number of bytes is
                      256.

/h                    Displays the commands which are
                      currently stored in the command
                      buffer. If you give the command
                      along with this parameter you will
                      get a list of commands in the order
                      of sequence in which they were
                      given. Pressing F7 also produces

| | |
|---|---|
| | this list but with a number in front. Typing this number will place the command behind the prompt. |
| /m | Displays a list with all defined macros. Macros are key combinations which activate individual commands or series of commands. |
| /macroname=[macrotekst] | Defines a macro command. If the [macrotext] is not specified, the macro is removed. |
| /insert | The insert mode becomes the default setting when editing commands. Even if you press the Ins key to alter the mode for a particular command, the insert mode is active again when dealing with the following command. |
| /overstrike | The typeover (overstrike) mode becomes the default setting. |

Commands, once they have been specified, can be recalled, edited, deleted etc. by means of the commands listed below. A recalled or edited command is activated by pressing the Enter key.

**Recalling commands:**

| | |
|---|---|
| cursor up | Summons the last command specified. |
| cursor down | Summons the following command in the list. |
| PgUp | Summons the first specified command. |
| PgDn | Summons the last specified commandd. |
| F7 | Displays a list of all specified commands. |
| Alt-F7 | Clears the command buffer. |
| beginning-letter+F8 | Summons a command which begins with a certain letter or letters ('A' for instance). Repeat by pressing F8. |

F9+number              Summons the command with
                       the specified number.

**Editing command text:**
cursor left            Moves the cursor left.
cursor right           Moves the cursor right.
Ctrl-cursor left       Moves the cursor to the beginning
                       of the previous word.
Ctrl-cursor right      Moves the cursor to the beginning
                       of the next word.
Home                   Places the cursor at the beginning
                       of the line.
End                    Places the cursor at the end of the
                       line.
Ins                    Activates either the insert or over-
                       strike mode.
Del                    Deletes the character under the
                       cursor.
Backspace              Deletes the character to the left of
                       the cursor.
Ctrl-End               Deletes the line from the cursor po-
                       sition onwards.

In addition, you can use all the key combinations which
are referred to in chapter 2 as being valid for all MS-
DOS versions.

*Example:* The command buffer is to be activated with a
memory of 1024 bytes. Subsequently, several commands are to be specified. Then a list of all specified
commands is to be displayed and two commands from
the list are to be implemented. Finally, a macro command is to be defined which has the function of displaying the AUTOEXEC.BAT file.

```
DOSKEY /BUFSIZE=1024                                    (1)

C:\>                                                    (2)
1:type autoexec.bat
2:doskey /?
3:cls
```

```
 4:dir
 5:dir \wp
 6:cd wp
 7:cd exmpl
 8:dir
 9:dir /p
10:cd letters
11:dir
12:cd\
C:\>t                                            (3)
C:\>Line number: _                               (4)

doskey auto=type autoexec.bat                    (5)
auto

LH C:\DOS\DOSKEY.COM /BUFSIZE=1024               (6)
```

(1) This command installs the command buffer with a memory of 1024 bytes. If you wish to use this function in each computer session, include the command in the AUTOEXEC.BAT file (see section 12.2, the MIRROR command).

(2) When several commands have been specified, the list is displayed using F7.

(3) The first command is to be recalled. To do this, the letter t is specified, followed by F8. Since no other command begins with a t, this is sufficient. The same result could have been brought about by typing PgUp.

(4) F9 has been pressed. The number of the required command is specified and the command is activated by pressing Enter.

(5) A macro called AUTO is installed to display the AUTOEXEC.BAT file on the screen. The macro is then implemented.

(6) This command, which can be included in AUTOEXEC.BAT, loads the DOSKEY program in the upper memory (see chapter 15).

# 15    Optimizing memory under MS-DOS 5, 6.0 and 6.2

**New memory management.** For reasons of compatibility between the various types of PC, MS-DOS can only use 640 Kb of the available computer memory as working memory. MS-DOS requires a part of this for its own tasks. Thus, applications have less than 640 Kb at their disposal. Up until version 5 of MS-DOS, this could even be as little as 500 Kb with unfavourable settings. This is easily sufficient for some programs, but increasingly more programs demanding more working memory are being brought on to the market. These are mainly programs which process large amounts of data, such as spreadsheets and database programs. From version 5 onwards, MS-DOS has a different type of memory management which enables the available part of working memory to be considerably extended, subject to hardware restrictions. In addition, extended memory and expanded memory can also be used.

*Note:* This chapter is no more than an introduction to MS-DOS memory management. An extensive discussion of various hardware configurations is beyond the scope of this book.

**Hardware requirements.** The MS-DOS memory management can be used as follows in conjunction with the hardware below:

■ With a computer with an 80386 or 80486 processor and memory in excess of 1 Mb, all optimizations of the memory can be carried out. With only 1 Mb, part of the optimization can be implemented, either as HMA or UMB (see below).
■ In the case of an AT computer having an 80286 processor and memory of 1 Mb, partial optimization can be carried out in the HMA. If the computer has less than 1 Mb, it is not possible to optimize the memory.

■ The memory of XT computers (8086/8088) cannot be optimized.

**Optimizing working memory.** Optimization of memory takes place as follows. Parts of the operating system which were stored in the conventional memory up until now, thus in the memory area up to 640 Kb, are relocated to other areas by means of special programs. The conditions described above must be fulfilled.

In order to move parts of the operating system, two memory areas can be used: the HMA *(high memory area)* and the UMBs *(upper memory blocks)*. The HMA has a capacity of 64 Kb and is located in extended memory. The UMBs have a capacity of almost 100 Kb under MS-DOS 5 and roughly 170 Kb under MS-DOS 6.0 and 6.2. They are located in an address area which was not used by MS-DOS prior to version 5.

**Specifying the settings.** The optimization of the working memory is executed by means of specifications in CONFIG.SYS and the installation of operating programs in AUTOEXEC.BAT.

*Example:* A computer with an 80386 processor and available memory of more than 1 Mb is to have its working memory increased to a minimum size of 600 Kb by means of specifications in CONFIG.SYS and operating programs in AUTOEXEC.BAT.

*Procedure:* The files mentioned are displayed by means of the DOS (or other) editor. They are then edited and saved. They should look something like the illustration on the following page.

(1)    Shows the contents of the CONFIG.SYS file on the screen.
(2)    The HIMEM.SYS operating program from the DOS directory on the harddisk is installed for the HMA. This command must be located at the beginning of the file.
(3)    The EMM386.EXE operating program is installed for the UMBs. The NOEMS option dictates that no

expanded memory (EMS) is to be installed. If you require EMS memory as well as the UMBs for certain programs, use the RAM option instead of NOEMS.

```
C:\>type config.sys                               (1)
DEVICE=C:\DOS\HIMEM.SYS                            (2)
DEVICE=C:\DOS\EMM386.EXE NOEMS                     (3)
DOS=HIGH,UMB                                       (4)
SHELL=C:\DOS\COMMAND.COM C:\DOS\  /P               (5)
COUNTRY=031,437,C:\DOS\COUNTRY.SYS                 (6)
BUFFERS=30,0                                       (7)
FILES=30
REM DEVICEHIGH=C:\DOS\RAMDRIVE.SYS 4096 512 1024 /E    (8)
DEVICEHIGH=C:\DOS\SMARTDRV.EXE 2048 1024           (9)
DEVICEHIGH=C:\DOS\MOUSE.SYS                        (10)


C:\>type autoexec.bat                             (11)
@ECHO OFF                                          (12)
PATH C:\DOS;C:\;C:\WINDOWS;C:\WP;C:\DOS\UTILS;     (13)
PROMPT $P$G                                        (14)
SET TEMP=C:\WIN\TEMP                               (15)
LH C:\DOS\MODE LPT1:,,P                            (16)
LH C:\DOS\DOSKEY \BUFSIZE=1024                     (17)
LH C:\DOS\MIRROR.COM C: /TC                        (18)
```

(4)    This is the command for the operating system to use both HMA and UMBs. This command must be placed subsequent to the installation of HIMEM and EMM386.

(5)    This command loads the COMMAND.COM command interpreter. In fact, this command only needs to be placed if the file is not located in the root directory of the startup disk or if another command interpreter is being used. The /P option attaches the command interpreter to the operating system permanently (see section 6.3).

(6)    The British specifications for date, time and currency.

(7)    The number of buffers and maximum number of opened files (see section 6.3).

(8)    This command is made temporarily redundant by means of the REM command, which ensures that the whole line is regarded as being a remark. The DEVICEHIGH command loads the program specified behind the equals sign in the UMBs. The RAMDRIVE.SYS program installs a virtual disk (RAM drive) in the extended memory (the /E option). This virtual drive has a capacity of 4096 Kb

(MS-DOS 5 has a maximum of 4 Mb; MS-DOS 6.0 and 6.2 have a maximum of 16 Mb), a sector of 512 bytes, and a maximum of 1024 directories can be created on this disk. When the RAM drive is active, you can address it using the letter D: as if it were a real drive. But when the computer is switched off, all data on this disk will be lost.

(9)     A cache program with a capacity of 2048 Kb is installed in the UMBs. This considerably speeds up the exchange of data between the harddisk and the processor. SMARTDRV.EXE has replaced the SMARTDRV.SYS program which was supplied with previous versions of MS-DOS.

(10)   The operating program for the mouse is loaded in the UMBs.

(11)   Displays the contents of the AUTOEXEC.BAT file.

(12)   This and the following commands are not to be displayed on the screen when the file is being executed.

(13)   A search path is installed.

(14)   Determines the prompt style (MS-DOS 6 standard).

(15)   A DOS environment variable is set which the Windows program recognizes. The name of the \WINDOWS\TEMP directory is stored in this variable. This directory uses Windows to buffer utility files.

(16), (17), (18)
         The specified programs are loaded in the UMBs by means of the LH command (LOADHIGH).

**Checking the specifications.** The results of the specifications made can be easily checked using the following command:

```
MEM /C¦MORE [/P]
```

/C          Displays the memory allocation along with the installed programs.

¦ MORE   Displays the list page by page. An additional > PRN option enables you to print out the list on the printer.

/P          From MS-DOS 6.0 onwards, this parameter replaces the ¦ MORE redirection parameter.

*Example:* Displaying the memory allocation under MS-DOS 6.0 and 6.2

```
C:\>mem /c/p                                                        (1)
 Modules using memory below 1 MB:                                   (2)

  Name      Total    =   Conventional  +  Upper Memory
 --------  ---------------   ---------------   ---------------

  MSDOS     16061   (16K)     16061   (16K)        0    (0K)
  HIMEM      1168    (1K)      1168    (1K)        0    (0K)
  EMM386     3120    (3K)      3120    (3K)        0    (0K)
  COMMAND    3248    (3K)      3248    (3K)        0    (0K)
  GRAB      23792   (23K)     23792   (23K)        0    (0K)
  SETVER      832    (1K)         0    (0K)      832    (1K)
  FASTBIOS  37504   (37K)         0    (0K)    37504   (37K)
  EANSI      1936    (2K)         0    (0K)     1936    (2K)
  DBLSPACE  44448   (43K)         0    (0K)    44448   (43K)
  POWER      4688    (5K)         0    (0K)     4688    (5K)
  SMARTDRV  27280   (27K)         0    (0K)    27280   (27K)
  MODE        480    (0K)         0    (0K)      480    (0K)
  DOSKEY     4144    (4K)         0    (0K)     4144    (4K)
  MOUSE     17088   (17K)         0    (0K)    17088   (17K)
  Free     660992  (646K)    607808  (594K)    53184   (52K)

 Memory Summary:                                                    (3)

  Type of Memory   Totaal   =    Used    +     Free

 --------------   --------------   --------------   -----------------
  Conventional    655360  (640K)    47552  (46K)    607808   (594K)
  Upper           191584  (187K)   138400 (135K)     53184    (52K)
  Adapter RAM/ROM 131072  (128K)   131072 (128K)         0     (0K)
  Extended (XMS)  3216288 (3141K) 1270688 (1241K)  1945600  (1900K)
 --------------   --------------   --------------   -----------------
  Total memory    4194304 (4096K) 1587712 (1551K)  2606592  (2546K)

  Totaal under 1 Mb 846944 (827K)  185952 (182K)    660992   (646K)

  Largest executable program size   607632  (593K)                 (4)
  Largest free uper memory block     40480  (40K)
  MS-DOS is resident in the high memory area.
```

(1) Displays memory allocation.

(2) The first part provides a survey of the memory allocation under 1 Mb, in both conventional memory and in the UMBs.

(3) Gives a summary of the memory with data concerning the total available memory, the amount in use and the amount free. Of the total 4 Mb memory, a little more than 2 Mb is available, of which 646 Kb under 1 Mb.

(4) Data about the maximum size of an executable program which can be loaded in conventional memory. There is space available in the UMBs for a 40 Kb program. MS-DOS is loaded in HMA.

**Memory management.** These data can be more clearly illustrated by the following diagram:

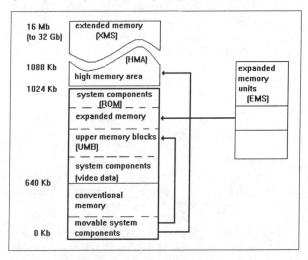

**Addressable area of MS-DOS.** The dark frame contains the area from 0 to 1024 Kb which can be addressed by MS-DOS. 640 Kb of this is actually accessible. The rest, 384 Kb between 640 and 1024 Kb is partially used by the system. This area contains, for instance, the ROM components with the BIOS and the memory with the video electronics. Some areas were not used at all until recently. From version 5 onwards, MS-DOS stores parts of the operating system here.

**Extended memory.** Extended memory can be added to the addressable area between 0 and 1024 Kb. This can reach to 16 Mb in the case of computers with an 80286 processor, and to 32 Gb in the case of computers with an 80386 or 80486 processor (32x1024x1024 Kb). The extended memory cannot be addressed directly by MS-DOS; from version 5 onwards, MS-DOS makes use of the HIMEM.SYS memory manager to do this.

MS-DOS version 6.2 has an important improvement in this area. From this version onwards, HIMEM automatically tests your system's memory when you start up your computer. This test can trace chips which are no longer 100% reliable, which could result in loss of essential data. If you do not wish to make use of the memory test, add the /TESTMEM:OFF switch to the command which activates HIMEM in your CONFIG.SYS file. Thus:

```
device=c:\dos\himem.sys /testmem:off
```

For more information concerning syntax on this topic, consult MS-DOS Help (type HELP HIMEM at the DOS prompt).

Applications can also make use of the extended memory by means of the XMS standard (*extended memory specification*).

**SMARTDrive.** The SMARTDRV command activates or configures SMARTDrive which creates a disk cache in extended memory. This disk cache is an area of memory where data can be temporarily stored. This increases the speed of usage, since data need to be retrieved less often from the harddisk. SMARTDrive will not load after Windows has been started up.

In MS-DOS version 6.0, SMARTDrive was configured as a read-and-write cache for harddisks. In version 6.2,

Setup configures SMARTDrive as a read-only cache unless you change the settings yourself. Even if write-caching is activated, no MS-DOS prompt appears until SMARTDrive has written the contents of the cache to your disk. This prevents you giving the command to close down before data are saved.

In MS-DOS version 6.2, SMARTDrive will also cache CD-ROM drives. In order to enable this, the MSCDEX program must be loaded prior to SMARTDrive. If you wish to find out whether SMARTDrive is caching your CD-ROM drive, type SMARTDRV at the command prompt. If SMARTDrive displays the letter representing your CD-ROM drive, it means that the drive is being cached.

You can change the default settings by altering the SMARTDrive startup command in AUTOEXEC.BAT. Behind **smartdrive** you should specify a plus sign behind the drive letter for which write caching is to be enabled. For those drives which are to have no caching at all, place a minus sign behind the drive letter. If you do not specify either a plus or a minus sign, only a read cache will be installed for the specified drive. Thus, if you want to have write caching for drives C and D, and no caching for A and B, give the following command:

```
c:\dos\smartdrv a- b- c+ d+
```

**Expanded memory.** Available memory can be used as expanded memory (*EMS: expanded memory specification*) instead of, or as a supplement to, extended memory. This is a form of memory in which the extra memory is divided into sections of 64 Kb and adopted into the area addressed by MS-DOS, according to the requirements. The so-called LIM standard has been developed by the Lotus, Intel and Microsoft companies for this function. Programs such as Lotus 1-2-3 and dBASE IV make use of this memory. In order to be able to make use of expanded memory, an operating program is required. The operating system provides the EMM386.EXE program for this, from version 5 of MS-DOS onwards.

**Using MemMaker to optimize memory allocation (from MS-DOS 6.0 onwards)**

In the case of computers with an 80386 or 80486 processor and extended memory, it is possible to optimize the allocation of programs in working memory by means of the MS-DOS 6 program MemMaker. This program moves as many system programs as possible from conventional memory to extended memory so that applications can make use of conventional memory as much as possible.

The program examines the working memory configuration, checks the amount of space required by the system programs and registers their position in memory. Accordingly, an optimal allocation of memory can be calculated. In this, certain commands in AUTOEXEC.BAT and CONFIG.SYS may be altered. The settings only become active when the computer is started up again. Backups are made of the old files, so that you can always restore the previous settings if you wish. You only need to use MemMaker once, after the installation of MS-DOS 6.0 or 6.2, and again when the computer configuration is altered, for instance when you install new operating programs.

It is advisable to allow the optimization to be dependent on the programs to be used. If, for example, you are only working with Windows and Windows applications and you possess relatively little extended memory (a mere 2 Mb for instance), it is better not to optimize the memory because Windows requires a great deal of extended memory. If, on the other hand, you are working mainly with DOS programs (even under Windows), it is advisable to optimize the memory.

**Implementing the optimization.** Prior to implementing the optimization, you must check the AUTOEXEC.BAT and CONFIG.SYS files for unnecessary commands and remove them or convert them to comment lines (see chapter 6). Then activate the MemMaker program by typing the command MEMMAKER and follow the instructions given on the screen. The program provides the choice between an *Express Setup* and a *Custom Setup*. The former option executes a normal optimization, the latter enables you to specify the optimization yourself, for instance if you are not working with SuperVGA, Windows or expanded memory (EMS). The new memory allocation is displayed at the conclusion of the procedure.

**Revoking the optimization.** Problems with the computer may arise in the optimization of certain system programs. If the program freezes or if error messages appear at the system startup, you can undo the optimization (unless you wish to search for the cause of the error messages). To do this, give the command:

```
MEMMAKER /UNDO
```

The program then activates the backups of the AUTO-EXEC.BAT and CONFIG.SYS files, and when the computer has be restarted, the old situation is restored. If the computer will not start up again due to an erroneous optimization, proceed as follows:

Switch on the computer and press F8 as soon as the message *Starting MS-DOS...* appears. This ensures that the commands from CONFIG.SYS will be shown on the screen one by one, and you can determine whether each individual command is to be carried out. When you reach those commands which you think might cause problems, answer the confirmation question with N(o). You can subsequently undo the optimization using the command mentioned above.

*Example:* The computer memory allocation is to be optimized.

The figure on the following page shows the system files prior to optimization:

(1)  Displays the contents of the CONFIG.SYS file. The individual command have been explained previously in this chapter (Specifying the settings).

(2)   Displays the contents of the AUTOEXEC.BAT file.

```
C:\>type config.sys                                   (1)
DEVICE=C:\DOS\HIMEM.SYS
DEVICE=C:\DOS\EMM386.EXE NOEMS
DOS=HIGH,UMB
BUFFERS=10
FILES=90
SHELL=C:\DOS\COMMAND.COM C:\DOS\  /p
COUNTRY=044,, C:\DOS\COUNTRY.SYS
DEVICE=C:\WIN\MOUSE.SYS /Y
DEVICE=C:\DOS\SMARTDRV.EXE DOUBLE_BUFFER
DEVICE=C:\DOS\DBLSPACE.SYS /MOVE
STACKS=9,256

C:\>type autoexec.bat                                 (2)
@ECHO OFF
C:\DOS\SMARTDRV.EXE
SET COMSPEC=C:\DOS\COMMAND.COM
PATH C:\DOS;C:\;C:\WINDOWS;C:\WINWORD;C:\WP
PROMPT $P$G
SET TEMP=C:\WINDOWS\TEMP
CLS
```

Proceed as follows:

1.   Terminate all programs, including Windows.

2.   Give the following command behind the DOS prompt:

     MEMMAKER

An introductory text is shown on the screen, along with a short description of the functions and operating instructions. More information can be gained by pressing F1.

3.   Press Enter in order to continue the program. The program offers the choice between *Express Setup* and *Custom Setup*.

4.   Confirm the default setting, *Express Setup* by pressing Enter. MemMaker then asks whether you are working with programs which use expanded memory (EMS). Only affirm this if you are absolutely sure that this is the case.

5. Confirm the *No* default setting if your programs do not need EMS.

The program then checks to see if Windows is installed on the computer. Subsequently, a message is displayed on the screen and the computer is started up again. If the computer does not start up again as it should, perform a reset using Ctrl-Alt-Del. The program then restores the original settings.

6. Press Enter. The optimization is implemented. The program starts up the computer once more in order to try out the new commands. Pay close attention to any error messages here. If any problems arise, the alterations can be undone by performing a reset.

7. Press Enter. The program asks whether the computer has been correctly started up.

8. Confirm the *Yes* default setting using the Enter key if no problems have arisen.

A message then appears about the optimization and the new memory allocation. This screen will look something like this:

```
Microsoft MemMaker
_____

MemMaker has finished optimizing your system's memory. The following
table summarizes the memory use (in bytes) on your system:

                               Before     After
    Memory Type                MemMaker   MemMaker    Change

    Free conventional memory:  592,624    615,712     23,088

    Upper memory:
        Used by programs       20,256     43,344      23,088
        Reserved for Windows        0          0           0
        Reserved for EMS            0          0           0
        Free                  138,272    115,184

    Expanded memory:          Disabled   Disabled

Your original CONFIG.SYS and AUTOEXEC.BAT files have been saved
as CONFIG.UMB and AUTOEXEC.UMB.  If MemMaker changed your Windows
SYSTEM.INI file, the original file was saved as SYSTEM.UMB.

ENTER=Exit  ESC=Undo changes
```

The optimization program has increased the available conventional memory by 23,088 bytes. Applications can now be executed more effectively.

The figure below illustrates the alterations which the MemMaker program has made to the CONFIG.SYS and AUTOEXEC.BAT files.

```
C:\>type config.sys
DEVICE=C:\DOS\HIMEM.SYS
DEVICE=C:\DOS\EMM386.EXE NOEMS
BUFFERS=10,0                                              (1)
FILES=99
DOS=UMB                                                   (2)
FCBS=4,0                                                  (3)
DOS=HIGH
SHELL=C:\DOS\COMMAND.COM C:\DOS\ /p
COUNTRY=044,, C:\DOS\COUNTRY.SYS
DEVICEHIGH /L:1,55168 =C:\WIN\MOUSE.SYS /Y               (4)
DEVICEHIGH /L:1,42624 =C:\DOS\SMARTDRV.EXE DOUBLE_BUFFER
DEVICEHIGH /L:1,44096 =C:\DOS\DBLSPACE.SYS /MOVE
STACKS=9,256

C:\>type autoexec.bat
@ECHO OFF
LH /L:0;1,42896 /S C:\DOS\SMARTDRV.EXE                   (5)
LH /L:1,6528 C:\DOS\DOSKEY.COM
SET COMSPEC=C:\DOS\COMMAND.COM
PATH C:\DOS;C:\;C:\WINDOWS;C:\WINWORD;C:\WP
PROMPT $P$G
SET TEMP=C:\WINDOWS\TEMP
CLS
```

(1) An extra zero has been specified in order to indicate that no buffer has been installed in the secondary buffer cache.

(2) The command DOS=HIGH,UMB has been split into two commands.

(3) The number of FCBs (file control blocks) which can be simultaneously open has been set to four.

(4) The operating programs have been loaded in the upper memory area using the command DEVICE-HIGH. The number behind the /L: option defines a certain area in this memory. The number behind the comma determines the minimum size which can be used by the program when running.

(5) These two programs are loaded in the upper memory using the LH (Loadhigh) command. The /L option has the same effect as that described under (4). The /S option means that the memory area is restricted to its minimum size and thus better used.

# Appendix

# Alphabetical list of MS-DOS instructions

| Instruction | Result | Examples |
| --- | --- | --- |
| A:, B:, C: | Change current drive | A:\>B: ->B:\><br>B:\>A: ->A:\><br>A:\>C: ->C:\> |
| APPEND (external) | Make path to data files | C:\>APPEND /E /X<br>C:\>APPEND \WP\<br>    LETTERS;\WP\MSDOS |
| ASSIGN (external) | Rename drive | A:\>ASSIGN C=B |
| ATTRIB (external) | Display/allocate file attributes | C:\>ATTRIB +RA<br>          LETTER.TXT<br>C:\>ATTRIB -RA<br>          LETTER.TXT |
| BACKUP (up to MS-DOS 5) (external) | Make backup of data on harddisk | C:\>BACKUP C: A:/S<br>C:\>BACKUP C:*.TXT A: |
| BREAK | Extend influence of Ctrl-C (also via CONFIG.SYS) | BREAK ON(OFF)<br>(C:\>)BREAK |
| BUFFERS | Specify number of disk buffers; via CONFIG.SYS | BUFFERS=20 |

| CALL | Activate batch file (.BAT) from out another batch file | CALL test<br>CALL testfile 1 2 3<br>(Activate TESTFILE.BAT<br>     with three parameters) |
|---|---|---|
| CHCP | Activate character set for specific country | C:\>CHCP 437<br>(standard character set) |
| CHDIR (CD) | Change current (sub)directory | C:\>CD text\letters<br>C:\>CD basic |
| CHKDSK (external) | Check harddisk, diskette or files | A:\>CHKDSK B:<br>A:\>CHKDSK B:*.*/V<br>C:\>CHKDSK /F |
| CHOICE (from MS-DOS 6.0) (external) | Make a choice in a batch program; choose a key; indicate ERRORLEVEL | CHOICE /C IF ERROR-<br>     LEVEL W GOTO word |
| CLS | Clear screen | C:\>CLS |
| COMMAND | Load extra command interpreter | A:\>COMMAND /C DIR C:<br>SHELL=C:\COMMAND.COM<br>     /E:400 /P |
| COMP (up to MS-DOS 5) (external) | Compare (copied) files | A:\>COMP A:tstfile1.txt<br>          B:tstfile2.txt<br>A:\>COMP *.txt B:*.bak |
| COPY | Copy files | A:\>COPY<br>          A:NUMBERS.TAB<br>          B:NUMBERS.TAB<br>A:\>COPY *.txt B:<br>A:\>COPY data.* B:<br>B:\>COPY *.* A:<br>A:\>COPY<br>     A:letter1.txt+A:letter2.txt<br>          B:letters.txt |

| | | |
|---|---|---|
| COPY CON | Make text file from keyboard (CON-SOLE) | A:\>COPY CON part1.txt<br>... text ...<br>^Z |
| COUNTRY | Specify country-oriented settings; via CONFIG.SYS | C:\>COUNTRY=044,437,<br>C:\DOS\COUNTRY.SYS<br>(values for UK) |
| CTTY | Switch to other standard input/output device | A:\>CTTY COM1 (to serial<br>interface)<br>A:\>CTTY CON (back to<br>CONSOLE) |
| DATE | Enter/request date | C:\>DATE<br>C:\>DATE 12-11-93 (new<br>date) |
| DBLSPACE<br>(from<br>MS-DOS 6.0)<br>(external) | Load DBLSPACE.BIN compression program (CON-FIG.SYS) | DEVICEHIGH=<br>C:\DOS\DBLSPACE.SYS/<br>MOVE (loads program in<br>upper memory) |
| DEBUG<br>(external) | Test assembled program | C:\>DEBUG<br>C:\>DEBUG test.com |
| DEFRAG<br>(from<br>MS-DOS 6.0) | Reorganize the disk | C:\>DEFRAG |
| DEL | Delete files | C:\>DEL A:command.001<br>C:\>DEL B:storage.*<br>A:\>DEL *.xyz<br>C:\>DEL *.* (careful!) |
| DELTREE<br>(from<br>MS-DOS 6.0) | Delete directory and all files and subdirectories | C:\>DELTREE c:\basic |

| DEVICE DEVICEHIGH (from MS-DOS 5) | Load driver; via CONFIG.SYS | DEVICE=ANSI.SYS |
|---|---|---|
| DIR | Display list of files in a directory | C:\>DIR<br>C:\>DIR /P<br>C:\>DIR /W<br>C:\>DIR B:*.txt<br>A:\>DIR B:command.* |
| DISKCOMP (external) | Compare copies of diskettes (made using DISKCOPY) | A:\>DISKCOMP A: B:<br>A:\>DISKCOMP |
| DISKCOPY (external) | Copy entire diskette | A:\>DISKCOPY A: B:<br>A:\>DISKCOPY B: A:<br>B:\>DISKCOPY A: B: |
| DOS (from MS-DOS 5) | Activate HMA and UMBs (CON-FIG.SYS) | DOS=HIGH<br>DOS=UMB<br>DOS=HIGH,UMB |
| DOSKEY (from MS-DOS 5) (external) | Re-use commands already specified (also AUTOEX-EC.BAT) | C:\>DOSKEY<br>LOADHIGH=DOSKEY<br>                /BUFSIZE 1024 |
| DOSSHELL (from MS-DOS 5) (external) | Activate graphic user-interface | C:\>DOSSHELL |
| DRIVPARM (DOS 3.20) DRIVER (DOS 3.21) | Specify device pa-rameters for disk or tape drive; via CON-FIG.SYS | DEVICE=DRIVPARM /D:2<br>        /F:2 /H:2 /T:80 /S:18<br>        (diskdrive 720 Kb) |

| ECHO | Switch display of commands on/off (for batch files), display statements (from batch file) | @ECHO ON(OFF) ECHO statement |
|---|---|---|
| EDIT (from MS-DOS 5) (external) | Start the text editor | C:\>EDIT<br>C:\>EDIT autoexec.bat |
| EDLIN (until MS-DOS 5) (external) | Start the line editor | C:\>EDLIN test.txt<br>C:\>EDLIN newfile.abc/B<br>(binary load: ignore end-of-file) |
| EMM386 (from MS-DOS 5) (external) | Operating program for extended memory EMM (LIM standard) and UMBs (CONFIG.SYS) | DEVICE(HIGH)=<br>EMM386.EXE NOEMS |
| ERASE | Delete file | (analogous to DEL) |
| EXE2BIN (until MS-DOS 5) (external) | Convert .EXE file to .COM file | C:\>EXE2BIN command.exe command.com |
| EXIT | Quit Command interpreter (or SHELL) | C:\>EXIT |
| EXPAND (from MS-DOS 5) (external) | Uncompress and copy compressed files | C:\>EXPAND A:*.EXE C:\DOS\*.EXE |
| FASTHELP (from MS-DOS 6.0) (external) | Display concise information about a command | C:\>FASTHELP break (analogous to break/?) |

| | | |
|---|---|---|
| FASTOPEN<br>(external) | Load a number of<br>file directions for<br>fast search | C:\>FASTOPEN C:=50<br>D:=34 |
| FC<br>(external) | Compare contents<br>of two files | (analogous to COMP) |
| FCBS | Specify number of<br>file control blocks;<br>via CONFIG.SYS | FCBS=12,6 (opens a<br>maximum of 12 FCBs<br>simultaneously, the first six<br>protected against automatic<br>closure) |
| FDISK<br>(external) | Partition harddisk | A:\>FDISK (presents a<br>menu) |
| FILES | Specify maximum<br>number of simulta-<br>neously open files;<br>via CONFIG.SYS | FILES=20 |
| FIND<br>(external) | Search for a string<br>in a file (filter) | A:\>FIND "COMPUTER"<br>B:letter.txt |
| FOR | Loop command (for<br>batch files) | FOR %%x IN (t1.txt t2.txt<br>t3.txt) DO TYPE %%x<br>(displays the contents of the<br>three files successively) |
| FORMAT<br>(external) | Prepare disk (be<br>careful with hard-<br>disks! /U is irre-<br>versible from MS-<br>DOS 5)) | C:\>FORMAT B:<br>C:\>FORMAT A:/T:40 /N:9<br>A:\>FORMAT B:/S<br>C:\>FORMAT A:/Q /F:720<br>C:\>FORMAT A:/U |
| GOTO | Move command<br>(for batch files) | GOTO end<br>... other commands ...<br>:end |

| | | |
|---|---|---|
| GRAFTABL (until MS-DOS 5) (external) | Load extended character set (ASCII 128-255) | C:\>GRAFTABL 437 (standard character set) |
| GRAPHICS (external) | Enables display of graphic (colour) screen on printer | C:\>GRAPHICS |
| HELP (from MS-DOS 5) (external) | Display information | C:\>HELP C:\>HELP format |
| HIMEM (from MS-DOS 5) (external) | Operating program for extended memory (CONFIG.SYS) | DE-VICE(HIGH)=HIMEM.SYS |
| IF | Condition for the specified command | IF %==t1.txt GOTO display IF NOT EXIST t1.txt GOTO end |
| INSTALL (from MS-DOS 4.01) | Implement one or more of the resident programs in CONFIG.SYS (specify parameters if necessary) | C:\>INSTALL=C:\DOS\ FASTOPEN.EXE C:75 |
| INTERLNK (from MS-DOS 6.0) (external) | Connect two computers (CONFIG.SYS) | C:\>INTERLNK (activate the client) DEVICEHIGH=C:\DOS\ INTERLNK.EXE (install) |
| INTERSVR (from MS-DOS 6.0) (external) | Connect two computers | C:\>INTERSVR (activate the server) |

| JOIN (from MS-DOS 5) (external) | Address a drive as a directory | A:\>JOIN A: C:\TEST (address A: via C:\TEST) |
|---|---|---|
| KEYBxx (up to MS-DOS 3.2) KEYB (from MS-DOS 3.2 onwards) (external) | Load keyboard adjustment; via AUTO-EXEC.BAT | C:\>KEYBUK C:\>KEYB UK,437, C:\DOS\KEYBOARD.SYS |
| LABEL (external) | Specify/alter name (max. 11 characters) of a disk | C:\>LABEL B:TESTDISK |
| LASTDRIVE | Specify maximum number of drives (only meaningful in networks); via CONFIG.SYS | LASTDRIVE=M |
| LOADHIGH, LH (from MS-DOS 5) | Load resident programs in UMB area (AUTOEXEC.BAT) | LOADHIGH C:\DOS\GRAPHICS |
| MEM (external) | Display memory usage | C:\>MEM [/PROGRAM] [/DEBUG] C:\>MEM /C |
| MIRROR (MS-DOS 5) (external) | Activate safeguard program | C:\>MIRROR C:/TC |
| MKDIR (MD) (external) | Make directory | C:\>MD \text\memo C:\>MD basic |
| MODE x (external) | Screen: number of characters per line | C:\>MODE 40 C:\>MODE 80,R,T |

| MODE LPT#<br>(external) | Printer: specify<br>characters per line,<br>line spacing or<br>printer port | C:\>MODE LPT1:132,8<br>C:\>MODE LPT1=COM1 |
|---|---|---|
| MODE COMn<br>(external) | Regulate serial in-<br>terface | C:\>MODE COM1:12,N,8,P |
| MORE<br>(external) | Display information<br>per screen | C:\>TYPE t1.txt\|MORE<br>C:\>MORE<t1.txt<br>C:\>TREE\|MORE |
| MOVE (from<br>MS-DOS 6.0)<br>(external) | Move files or re-<br>name directories | C:\>MOVE *.DOC \<br>                    DOCUMENT<br>C:\>MOVE WP5 WP51 |
| MSBACKUP<br>(from<br>MS-DOS 6.0)<br>(external) | Start up backup pro-<br>gram | C:\>MSBACKUP |
| MSD (from<br>MS-DOS 6.0)<br>(external) | Activate Microsoft<br>diagnosis program | C:\>MSD |
| NLSFUNC<br>(external) | Load country-spe-<br>cific information for<br>national language<br>support | C:\>NLSFUNC [C:\DOS\<br>COUNTRY.SYS] (or an<br>own file) |
| PATH | Install path for ex-<br>ecutable files<br>(.EXE, .COM, .BAT) | C:\>PATH \basic;\<br>C:\>PATH \text\memo |
| PAUSE | Discontinue display<br>of batch file (unless<br>ECHO is OFF, the<br>prompt 'Press any<br>key..' always ap-<br>pears) | PAUSE<br>PAUSE statement |

| | | |
|---|---|---|
| POWER<br>(from<br>MS-DOS 6.0)<br>(external) | Activate energy-<br>saving program | LH C:\DOS\POWER.EXE |
| PRINT<br>(external) | Print files using the<br>print queue | C:\>PRINT t1.txt/P t2.txt<br>C:\>PRINT command.dat/C<br>C:\>PRINT /T |
| PROMPT | Alter system<br>prompt; redefine<br>key from ASCII<br>code X to Y | PROMPT $P$G<br>PROMPT $e[X,Yp |
| RECOVER<br>(until<br>MS-DOS 5)<br>(external) | Reconstruct dam-<br>aged files | C:\>RECOVER B:letter.txt<br>A:\>RECOVER C: |
| REM | Place commentary<br>in batch files and<br>CONFIG.SYS | REM *** Commentary ***<br>REM Remove diskette |
| RENAME<br>(REN) | Rename file | A:\>REN B:old.123<br>                    B:new.456<br>A:\>REN t1.txt letter.txt |
| REPLACE<br>(external) | Replace/supple-<br>ment files on target<br>disk from a source<br>disk | C:\>REPLACE A:*.txt<br>                    C:\WP\CCC /A |
| RESTORE<br>(external) | Copy back backup<br>copies (made using<br>BACKUP) | A:\>RESTORE A: C:/S<br>A:\>RESTORE A: C:*.txt |
| RMDIR<br>(RD) | Remove directory | C:\>CD \text\memo<br>C:\>DEL *.*<br>C:\>CD \<br>C:\>RD \text\memo |

SELECT
(MS-DOS 3)
(external)

Make new system
diskette containing
country-oriented
data

C:\>SELECT A: B: 044 UK


SET

Display or initialize
variables in the MS-
DOS system envi-
ronment

A:\>SET (display system
environment only)
A:\>SET file=new.123


SETVER
(from
MS-DOS 5)
(external)

Simulate a different
MS-DOS version
for certain programs

DEVICE(HIGH)=
SETVER.EXE
PROGRAM.EXE 3.31
C:\>SETVER C: (overview)


SHARE
(external)

Allow simultaneous
use of same file in
network (AUTOEX-
EC.BAT)

SHARE /F:4096 (reserve
4096 bytes for file
information)


SHELL

Install new com-
mand interpreter;
via CONFIG.SYS

SHELL=C:\DOS\
NEWCOMM.COM


SHIFT

Move batch file vari-
ables leftwards

Before: %4=t1.txt %5=t2.txt
SHIFT
After: %3=t1.txt %4=t2.txt


SMARTDRV
(from
MS-DOS 5)

Activate the cache
program for the
harddisk (also CON-
FIG.SYS)

C:\>SMARTDRV
DEVICE=C:\DOS\
SMARTDRV.EXE
(with DOS 5, this is
SMARTDRV.SYS)


SORT
(external)

Sort text file lines al-
phabetically

C:\>SORT <t1.txt >t2.txt
C:\>SORT /R <a1 >a2
C:\>DIR ¦ SORT >LPT1

| STACKS | Define number and size (in bytes) of the stacks; via CONFIG.SYS | STACKS=0,0 (no stacks) STACKS=16,512 (reserve 16 stacks of 512 bytes) |
|---|---|---|
| SUBST (external) | Replace a directory with a drive letter (/D means Cancel) | C:\>SUBST B: C:\WP C:\>SUBST B:/D |
| SYS (external) | Copy the MS-DOS system files later (until MS-DOS 3, the diskette must be formatted and empty) | C:\>SYS B: |
| TIME | Display/specify time | C:\>TIME C:\>TIME 12:32 |
| TREE (external) | Display list of directories (/F also shows files) | C:\>TREE C: A:\>TREE C:/F |
| TYPE | Display contents of file on screen (on the printer using Ctrl+PrtSc or using the >PRN redirection) | C:\>TYPE table.dat A:\>TYPE C:\text\t1.txt C:\>TYPE a.txt >PRN |
| UNDELETE (from MS-DOS 5) (external) | Restore deleted files | C:\>UNDELETE A:calc1.exe C:\>UNDELETE A:/ALL C:\>UNDELETE A:/DOS |
| UNFORMAT (from MS-DOS 5) (external) | Undo disk formatting | C:\>UNFORMAT A: C:\>UNFORMAT A:/TEST C:\>UNFORMAT /PARTN |

| | | |
|---|---|---|
| VER | Show MS-DOS version number | A:\>VER |
| VERIFY | Activate or request test mode for writing to disk | C:\>VERIFY (ON/OFF)<br>C:\>VERIFY<br>... VERIFY is on/off |
| VOL | Show name of disk | C:\>VOL B:<br>C:\>VOL |
| VSAFE<br>(from<br>MS-DOS 6.0)<br>(external) | Activate anti-virus control program (also AUTOEXEC.BAT) | C:\>VSAFE<br>LH C:\DOS\VSAFE.COM |
| XCOPY<br>(external) | Copy contents of directory, including subdirectories | C:\>XCOPY \text A:\text\<br>/E/S |

| Key combination | Result | Remarks |
|---|---|---|
| Alt+Ctrl+Del | Restart system (warm start) | Wait until harddisk has stopped! |
| Ctrl+PrtSc | Print screen contents; switch off function using same combination | Hardcopy |
| Ctrl+NumLock<br>(Pause) | Stop screen roll | Continue by pressing any key |

# Index

*Aubin Imprimeur*

LIGUGÉ, POITIERS

Achevé d'imprimer en février 1994
Nº d'impression L 44646
Dépôt légal février 1994
Imprimé en France